D0470675

ASSESSMENT:

Timesaving Procedures
· F O R ·
Busy Teachers

FOURTH EDITION

BERTIE KINGORE
AUTHOR

Jeffery Kingore
GRAPHIC DESIGN

**Professional Associates
Publishing**
www.kingore.com

Current Publications by
Bertie Kingore, Ph.D.

VISIT DR. KINGORE ONLINE!
www.BertieKingore.com

Alphabetters: Thinking Adventures with the Alphabet (Task Cards)
Assessment Interactive CD-ROM
Bertie's Book Notes 2008
Centers in Minutes!
Centers CD-ROM Vol. 1: Grades K-8
Centers CD-ROM Vol. 2: Literacy Stations, Grades K-4
Developing Portfolios for Authentic Assessment, PreK-3
Differentiation: Simplified, Realistic, and Effective
Differentiation Interactive CD-ROM
Engaging Creative Thinking: Activities to Integrate Creative Problem Solving
Integrating Thinking: Strategies that Work!, 2nd ed.
Just What I Need! Learning Experiences to Use on Multiple Days in Multiple Ways
Kingore Observation Inventory (KOI), 2nd ed.
Literature Celebrations: Catalysts for High-Level Book Responses, 2nd ed.
Reaching All Learners: Making Differentiation Work!
*Reading Strategies for Advanced Primary Readers: Texas Reading Initiative Task Force for the
        Education of Primary Gifted Children*
Reading Strategies for Advanced Primary Readers: Professional Development Guide
Recognizing Gifted Potential: Planned Experiences with the KOI
Recognizing Gifted Potential: Professional Development Presentation
Teaching Without Nonsense: Translating Research into Effective Practice, 2nd ed.
We Care: A Curriculum for Preschool Through Kindergarten, 2nd ed.

FOR INFORMATION OR ORDERS CONTACT:
PROFESSIONAL ASSOCIATES PUBLISHING
PO Box 28056
Austin, Texas 78755-8056
PHONE/FAX: 866-335-1460
E-MAIL: info@kingore.com

VISIT US ONLINE!
www.kingore.com

ASSESSMENT: Timesaving Procedures for Busy Teachers
FOURTH EDITION

Copyright © 2007 Bertie Kingore

Published by **PROFESSIONAL ASSOCIATES PUBLISHING**

Printed in the United States of America
ISBN: 0-9787042-4-X
ISBN: 978-0-9787042-4-7

Table of Contents

Reproducible Figures

Introduction

All glory comes from daring to begin.

—Eugene F. Ware

This implementation research began as I worked with districts interested in initiating or refining authentic assessment. The challenge in most cases was not to convince educators of the value of authentic assessment but rather to determine how the process could be accomplished in a more realistic and accountable manner that would benefit students, teachers, and schools.

For several years, I have worked with thousands of teachers and administrators to analyze authentic assessment needs, problem solve, increase efficiency and value, as well as celebrate successes. Two factors especially kept driving the work:

1) The observed value to students in terms of self-esteem and motivation to excel, and

2) The change authentic assessment invited in the way teachers teach.

The processes and products described here have been implemented with students in pre-kindergarten through college. The school districts included both rural and urban districts ranging in size from approximately 400 to 600,000 students. European-American, African-American, Asian-American, Native-American and Latin-American students whose socioeconomic status ranged from poverty level through upper-middle class were involved. In many classrooms, forms had to be translated by dedicated teachers into languages other than English so more students could be successful.

Rather than an academic discussion of assessment and evaluation, the focus of this book is classroom tools, processes, and applications. The objective is to make assessment efficient and integrated with instruction.

This fourth edition expands and reorganizes previous editions in significant ways.

• The research base related to assessment and achievement is updated and expanded to guide assessment decisions.

• Chapter 3, Assessing Young Children, expands the authentic assessment procedures in pre-kindergarten through first-grade classrooms. The pictorial rubric generator is expanded in response to requests from

Kingore, B. (2007). *Assessment,* 4th ed. Austin, TX: Professional Associates Publishing.

primary teachers for rubrics appropriate for young learners and ELL students.

- Chapter 7, Open-Ended Techniques, incorporates observation, checklists, interviews, inventories, self-assessment forms, and numerous simple assessment procedures.
- Chapter 8, Products, discusses the relationship between products and assessment as it shares multiple examples that customize product options to different learning profiles.
- Chapter 9, Integrating and Assessing Learning Standards, responds to assessment needs resulting from national, state, and district academic standards.
- New forms are included, and all forms, including the Rubric Generator, are refined, updated, and/or expanded to increase application ease. The Rubric Generator now emphasizes three tiers of complexity to more efficiently construct rubrics that support continuous learning for a wide-range of learners.
- More examples are included to increase clarity.

The goal of this book is to provide teacher-useful and student-friendly procedures for implementing authentic assessment. This book contains many of the best answers worked out in this collaborative effort with teachers across the nation. Three icons appear throughout the book to call attention to tips and applications.

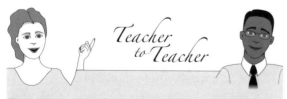

This icon signals observations, suggestions, opinions, and insights teachers have shared regarding assessment concerns. Discussing these ideas promotes decisions about the best assessment practices for classrooms.

This icon alerts the reader to tips that particularly relate to the content being addressed. These tips are simple suggestions to more efficiently and successfully implement assessments.

This icon signals a technique or learning experience valuable for preassessment. Applications are woven throughout the book inasmuch as preassessment requires ongoing applications.

Many of the strategies and procedures in this book use special forms. While I continue to believe that higher-level student responses are often prompted by blank paper, many teachers expressed a need for ready-to-use forms and graphic organizers to make the assessment process more efficient and effective. This edition includes over 140 reproducible forms, templates, posters, and student examples for photocopying. In response to numerous requests, these reproducibles are also available on a CD-ROM that enables teachers and students to more efficiently customize assessment procedures.

Warm regards and thanks to the professors, administrators, teachers, and students in Canada, Hong Kong, Alabama, Arkansas, California, Colorado, Florida, Georgia, Hawaii, Idaho, Illinois, Indiana, Iowa, Kansas, Kentucky, Louisiana, Maryland, Michigan, Minnesota, Missouri, Montana, Nebraska, Nevada, New Jersey, New York, North Dakota, Ohio, Oklahoma, Oregon, South Dakota, Tennessee, Texas, Virginia, Washington, and Wisconsin. Their cooperation, suggestions, questions, feedback, and candor proved invaluable in refining this process.

Kingore, B. (2007). *Assessment,* 4th ed. Austin, TX: Professional Associates Publishing.

CHAPTER 1

Developing an Assessment System

We have a wide range of complex achievement targets to assess. We need all the tools we have at our disposal to do this job. Our challenge is to find ways to use all these tools well and to use them in balance.

—Richard Stiggins

Assessment and instruction work in tandem and are woven together so imperceptibly in successful classrooms that they seem one continuous whole. Assessment is integral to teaching and guides instructional decisions about what and how information is taught and what and how students learn. Scott-Little, Kagan, and Frelow (2003) explain the relationship among learning standards, curriculum, and assessment by noting that standards articulate what students should learn, curriculum dictates how students will learn the required standards, and assessments measure how effectively the standards and curriculum are implemented. Assessment data guides initial instruction that is then continually assessed to determine needed adjustments in the instructional pace and level as well as to substantiate the degree of success in terms of students' achievements. This book focuses upon classroom tools, processes, and applications that make assessment efficient and integrated with instruction. The intent is to help teachers implement assessments that are practical and result in useful, high-quality information.

TERMINOLOGY AND RELATIONSHIPS

The terms *test*, *assessment*, and *evaluation* are frequently used interchangeably. Analyzing similarities and differences in their attributes and intents, however, clarifies their applications and promotes balanced assessment decisions (see Figure 1.1).

Test is the narrowest of the terms and refers to using a set of questions or tasks to measure a sample of learning behavior at one point in time. A test can provide quick, reliable data on student performance. It is structured so it can be consistently administered and scored to gather data, form comparisons, and record achievement. A test is an application of both assessment and evaluation because it involves the gathering and grading of data. Testing benefits students when results are used to diagnosis strengths and guide instructional changes that increase learning. A related term, *high-stakes test,* is frequently used with standards-based programs and means

Kingore, B. (2007). *Assessment,* 4th ed. Austin, TX: Professional Associates Publishing.

Figure 1.1: BALANCED ASSESSMENT

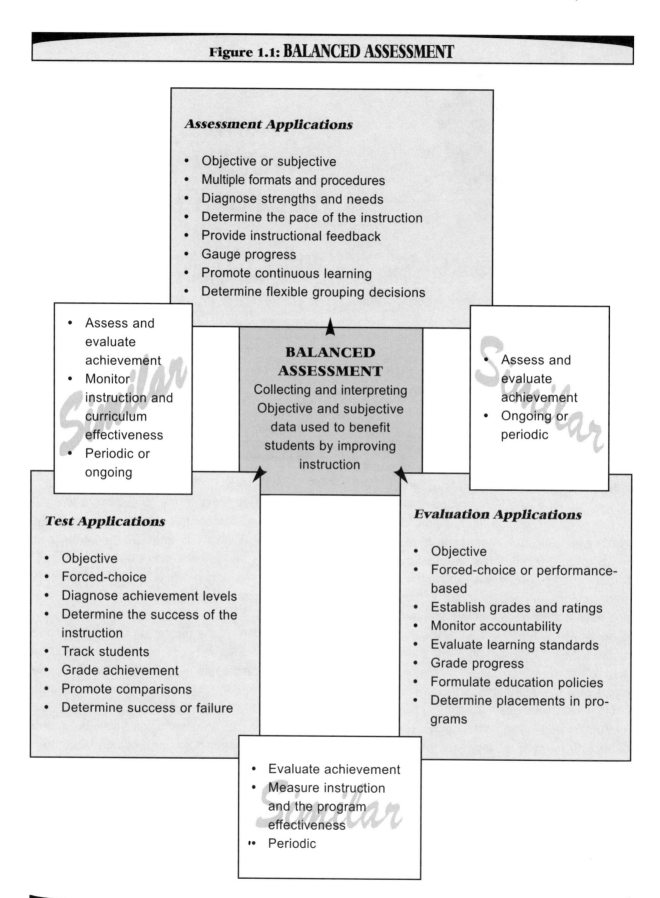

Assessment Applications

- Objective or subjective
- Multiple formats and procedures
- Diagnose strengths and needs
- Determine the pace of the instruction
- Provide instructional feedback
- Gauge progress
- Promote continuous learning
- Determine flexible grouping decisions

BALANCED ASSESSMENT
Collecting and interpreting Objective and subjective data used to benefit students by improving instruction

- Assess and evaluate achievement
- Monitor instruction and curriculum effectiveness
- Periodic or ongoing

Similar

- Assess and evaluate achievement
- Ongoing or periodic

Similar

Test Applications

- Objective
- Forced-choice
- Diagnose achievement levels
- Determine the success of the instruction
- Track students
- Grade achievement
- Promote comparisons
- Determine success or failure

Evaluation Applications

- Objective
- Forced-choice or performance-based
- Establish grades and ratings
- Monitor accountability
- Evaluate learning standards
- Grade progress
- Formulate education policies
- Determine placements in pro-grams

- Evaluate achievement
- Measure instruction and the program effectiveness
- Periodic

Similar

Kingore, B. (2007). *Assessment,* 4th ed. Austin, TX: Professional Associates Publishing.

that the consequences for performance on that test are substantial. It signals that the test results significantly impact students in terms of promotion and graduation as well as the school and teachers in terms of school accreditation and public recognition.

Assessment is more encompassing, incorporating multiple formats and sources. It is the systematic, continuous, and purposeful gathering of data to inform instructional actions by determining students' capacities and accomplishments. It is intended to inform administrators, teachers, students, and families; it is used to drive instruction, analyze curricula, and enable students to continue progressing in their learning. Assessment includes varied procedures, such as observations, checklists, focused interviews, analysis of portfolios, and conferences. A related term, *authentic assessment,* is used to distinguish that the assessment procedure represents real work in classrooms rather than the proxy of learning sampled on a test or commercial assessment. Authentic assessment occurs in learning environments as instruction and learning intersect. It is continuous and diagnostic as it enables teachers to respond to students' capabilities and promotes learners' self-assessment to develop and refine their skills.

Evaluation is the interpretation and judgment of assessments, testing information, and students' accomplishments. Its function is to interpret data and reach decisions of quality; it is used to grade the degree of students' learning and their level of performance. Typical examples of evaluative procedures include grading products, rubrics, and tests. When used to judge the level of school-wide performance, related terms emerge, such as *adequate yearly progress* and *school improvement.* While both classroom and school-wide evaluation are related, this book addresses classroom rather than school-wide performance.

In summary, testing provides a photograph of learning achievement. It may be clear or out of focus inasmuch as it samples specific knowledge and skills at one specific time and in one context. Assessment provides a videotape, or portfolio, of learning. It encompasses a developmental view over time with more comprehensive data from multiple perspectives and procedures. Evaluation produces a judgment of assessment results. The three are decidedly interdependent: the efficacy of one affects the efficacy of all.

Quality Assessments and Evaluations

Well-designed assessments are:

- *Clear, complete, and compelling.*[1]
  Assessments must clearly define the levels of quality and include the key facets of performance that are considered the best thinking by experts in the field.

- *Practical.*
  The process must efficiently balance the time and effort expended by students and teachers with the quality of the procured information. The data must be used to benefit students. An assessment is practical for student use when the language is student-friendly.

- *Diagnostic and aligned with the standards.*
  The information must be meaningful and guide instruction. Assessments must be aligned with learning standards to direct students toward important learning targets and include a range from low baseline to high ceiling in order to measure the diverse range of students' learning.

- *Valid and reliable.*
  The assessments must measure what they purport to measure. They must provide a consistent measurement of the quality of knowledge and skills from one occasion to the next and from one evaluator to the next.

---

[1] Stiggins, R., 2005.

Kingore, B. (2007). *Assessment,* 4th ed. Austin, TX: Professional Associates Publishing.

Developing a System

- *Equitable.*
  Quality assessments must provide a more objective standard in scoring and feedback so they are less subject to rater bias and inconsistent expectations.
- *Varied.*
  Variety is important to maintain interest in the assessment process, but more importantly, to access the different ways students learn.

Preassessment, Continuing Assessment, and Summative Assessment

In the classroom, use a variety of assessment procedures to provide tangible evidence of students' understanding and achievement throughout the learning process–before instruction begins (preassessment or diagnostic assessment), as instruction progresses (continuing or formative assessment), and at the end of a segment of instruction (summative or culminating evaluation).[2] Educators' assessments and students' self-assessments are applicable at each of these learning junctures. Involving students in self-assessment for any of these assessment occasions increases students' responsibility for learning and motivation to work toward a higher level of quality.

Preassessment clarifies students' prior knowledge, interests, and levels of readiness; it signals at which level and pace to initiate instruction for different students' needs. McTighe and O'Connor (2005) pose an apropos analogy when they note that preassessment

"...is as important to teaching as a physical exam is to prescribing an appropriate medical regimen" (p.11). For any segment of learning, some students may have already mastered much of the material,[3] others are likely to understand a number of the concepts, some are precisely ready for that instruction, and still others may not have had the opportunity to experience prerequisite skills.[4] Furthermore, students harbor misconceptions, such as thinking that an equal sign (=) means *answer* instead of representing relational *equivalence*.[5] To uncover misconceptions and initiate the appropriate pace and level of instruction, teachers can use a variety of short and simple preassessment techniques, such as sketches, Venn diagrams, concept maps, true or false response cards, and K-W-L charts.[6] There is also a growing technology application of student-response systems that empowers teachers to collect and collate data instantaneously.[7]

Continuing assessment supports instruction. Recent research documents that the regular use of continuing assessment promotes learning by substantiating the learning in progress, providing feedback for students, and guiding teaching.[8] These assessments occur throughout an instructional segment to guide instructional decisions regarding students who would benefit from reteaching, additional practice, or acceleration of pace or skill levels. Continuing assessment techniques include non-graded quizzes, exit tickets.[9] learning logs, think-alouds, drafts, and oral questioning. To effectively influence learning, feedback from continuing assessment must be *specific* and inform students what is done well and what to do to improve. It must also be *timely,* shared

---

[2] Stiggins, 2005; Tomlinson et.al., 2002.

[3] Ross, 1993.

[4] Castellano, & Diaz, 2002; Payne, 2003.

[5] McNeil, 2006.

[6] Ogle, 1986. K-W-L stands for *What I Know, What I Want to Learn,* and *What I Learned.*

[7] Cook, 2005.

[8] Black, Harrison, Lee, Marshall, & Wiliam, 2004.

[9] Kingore, 2007b. Exit tickets are short answer responses teachers request at the end of a lesson to assess students' level of understanding and guide grouping decisions for instruction the next day.

Kingore, B. (2007). *Assessment,* 4th ed. Austin, TX: Professional Associates Publishing.

with students promptly following the assessment, so students can initiate change before the segment of learning concludes.[10]

Summative assessment is evaluative and results in a score or grade to document students' levels of achievement following instruction. In addition to determining grades, summative evaluation guides flexible grouping decisions for reteaching or advancing to the next instructional segment. Students and their families particularly attend to summative assessments because those results appear on report cards and transcripts. However, as McTighe and O'Connor (2005) admonish: "Waiting until the end of a teaching period to find out how well students have learned is simply too late" (p.10).

USING AN ASSESSMENT SEQUENCE TO MOTIVATE ACHIEVEMENT

Rather than label students, assessment results should motivate future learning by providing baseline data to measure growth. *This is your beginning or current level. Let's see how far we can help you progress.* Both preassessment and continuing assessment can particularly motivate students' aspirations for higher levels of achievement when used as an indicator by which to compare future learning and concretely show learning growth.

Assessment techniques that are used for preassessment, continuing assessment, and summative assessment are not mutually exclusive; indeed, many of the same techniques or learning experiences can be used as assessments at any or all of these junctures in learning. The two examples shared here use a concept map with a younger student and an analysis grid with a secondary student to illustrate this process. In these examples, three separate samples are used to simulate each assessment juncture over time. In reality, students produce only one product on which they use different colors to show the changes in their knowledge and understanding at each assessment occasion. The following sequence delineates the achievement process that a combined application of preassessment, continued assessment, and summative assessment allows.

1. PREASSESSMENT

Each student completes a preassessment. Students document their work by writing on the assessment their name, date, and a score–the number of correct answers or the degree of mastery according to a rubric. Typically, this score is for comparative purposes rather than a recorded grade. Students should set goals regarding the changes in their achievement that they intend to accomplish by the next assessment. The teacher or students store the preassessment for comparison at a later date.

2. CONTINUING ASSESSMENT

At teacher-designated times during instruction, students retrieve their preassessments and use a different colored pen to embellish, delete, or correct items on the originals. The use of a different color helps students concretely validate their increased accuracy, understanding, and quantity of information. Students add a legend to the top of the assessment with the beginning date written in the first color and the review dates written in other colors to clarify changes in their knowledge and understanding over time. Based upon this continuing assessment information, students revisit their goals and make adjustments for continuous learning.

3. SUMMATIVE ASSESSMENT

After instruction is complete, students retrieve their previous assessments and use a

---

[10] Wiggins, 1998.

Kingore, B. (2007). *Assessment,* 4th ed. Austin, TX: Professional Associates Publishing.

different colored pen to embellish, delete, or correct items on those assessments. This final application is then graded using a shared rubric. Summative assessment results are typically recorded as grades. The teacher, often with a student, reviews the summative assessment to determine any reteaching needs before advancing to the next instructional segment.

When aligned with learning standards and accompanied with clear quality targets shared with students prior to the task, this assessment process is clear, diagnostic, valid, equitable, and easily varied. This procedure is practical as the class time invested produces learning changes. It is useful as it results in products that document growth and serve as discussion prompts among teachers, students, and families. It also demystifies the assessment process and elevates it to shared information for reaching learning targets. Students and parents benefit from these concrete demonstrations of changes in students' levels of knowledge and understanding.

From the perspective of educators, the primary purpose of testing or assessment is to benefit students by providing information regarding how to improve instruction

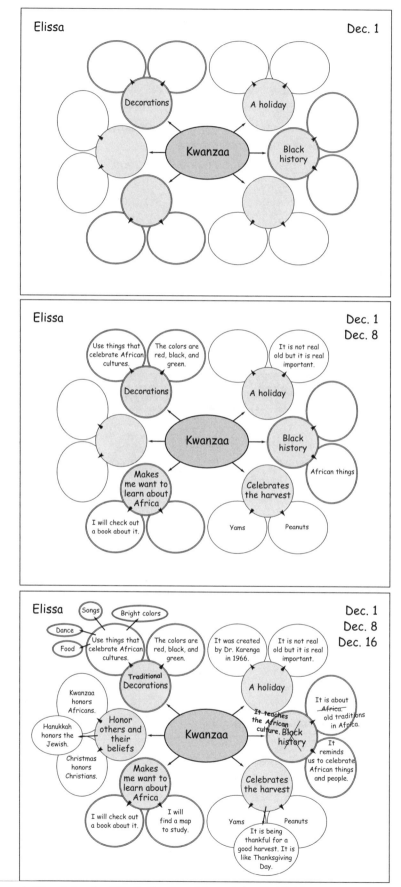

Kingore, B. (2007). *Assessment,* 4th ed. Austin, TX: Professional Associates Publishing.

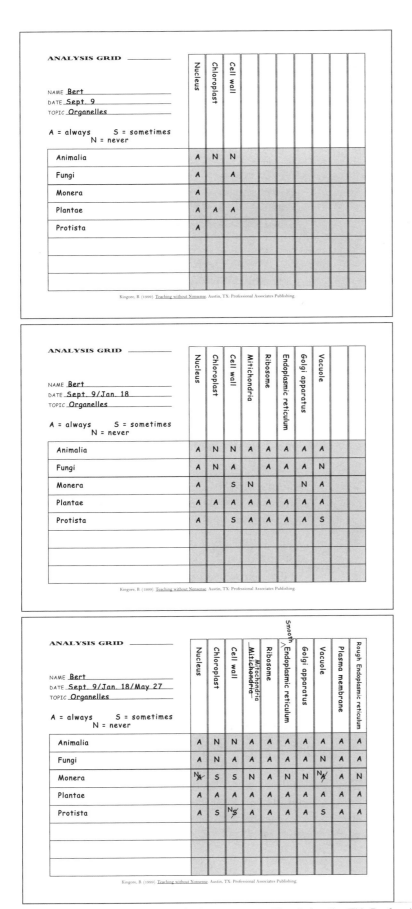

ANALYSIS GRID

NAME Bert
DATE Sept. 9
TOPIC Organelles

A = always   S = sometimes
          N = never

	Nucleus	Chloroplast	Cell wall
Animalia	A	N	N
Fungi	A		A
Monera	A		
Plantae	A	A	A
Protista	A		

Kingore, B. (1999). Teaching without Nonsense. Austin, TX: Professional Associates Publishing.

ANALYSIS GRID

NAME Bert
DATE Sept. 9/Jan. 18
TOPIC Organelles

A = always   S = sometimes
          N = never

	Nucleus	Chloroplast	Cell wall	Mitichondria	Ribosome	Endoplasmic reticulum	Golgi apparatus	Vacuole
Animalia	A	N	N	A	A	A	A	A
Fungi	A	N	A		A	A	A	N
Monera	A		S	N			N	A
Plantae	A	A	A	A	A	A	A	A
Protista	A		S	A	A	A	A	S

Kingore, B. (1999). Teaching without Nonsense. Austin, TX: Professional Associates Publishing.

ANALYSIS GRID

NAME Bert
DATE Sept. 9/Jan. 18/May 27
TOPIC Organelles

A = always   S = sometimes
          N = never

	Nucleus	Chloroplast	Cell wall	Smooth Mitichondria	Ribosome	Endoplasmic reticulum	Golgi apparatus	Vacuole	Plasma membrane	Rough Endoplasmic reticulum
Animalia	A	N	N	A	A	A	A	A	A	A
Fungi	A	N	A	A	A	A	A	N	A	A
Monera	N/A	S	S	N	A	N	N	N/A	A	N
Plantae	A	A	A	A	A	A	A	A	A	A
Protista	A	S	N/S	A	A	A	A	S	A	A

Kingore, B. (1999). Teaching without Nonsense. Austin, TX: Professional Associates Publishing.

rather than to compare and pigeonhole students. The National Council of Teachers of Mathematics (2006) warns that placing too much emphasis on testing can undermine the quality of education and jeopardize the quality of opportunity. Thus, assessment must rely on multiple measures that seek a balance of data from authentic assessments and standardized tools to promote a broader sampling of students' performances. National education organizations staunchly recommend a balanced application of multiple means of assessment and evaluation.[11] A combination of tests, assessments, and evaluations ensures a more accurate consideration of the multiple facets of students' learning capacities and potential.

Educators' continuing concerns about high-stakes testing should not be interpreted as a disregard for professional accountability. Teachers have practical options they can pursue in order to address various accountability issues. For example, the International Reading Association (1999) purposed several different

[11] Association for Supervision and Curriculum Development, 2006a; International Reading Association, 1999; National Association for the Education of Young Children & National Association of Early Childhood Specialists in State Departments of Education, 2003; National Council of Teachers of Mathematics, 2006.

Developing a System

Kingore, B. (2007). *Assessment,* 4th ed. Austin, TX: Professional Associates Publishing.

accountability recommendations to teachers, including the following.

- Construct more rigorous and reliable assessments for classrooms and communicate the inherent value of those procedures in instructional decision making so external audiences increase their confidence in those measures.

- Communicate to parents, community members, and policy makers the multiple forms of assessment and testing that are in use and how the combined data improves instruction and benefits students.

- Inform parents, students, and vested others about tests and their results.

- Demonstrate ethical practices when familiarizing students with the format of the test.

- Educate external audiences that it is not ethical to spend substantial time *teaching to the test* nor focus on students most likely to raise test scores while ignoring groups less likely to improve.

- Resist the temptation to improve scores through investments in time and actions not based on benefiting long-term learning.

CHANGING ROLES

As Figure 1.2 delineates, authentic assessment changes the traditional roles of the people with vested interests in assessment information. Balanced assessment invites more collaboration among teachers, students, and parents. Teachers experience a shift away from what Betts (1999) refers to as a *DOK* (*Dispenser of Knowledge*) toward being a *guide on the side.* Students increase their active participation and ownership in assessment processes. A collaborative communication forum between schools and families replaces the traditional approach in which professionals know what is best and parents need to be educated.[12] Instead, parents and students are viewed as both a valued source of assessment information and an audience for assessment results.[13] Family members, students, and educators benefit from a collaborative attitude of mutual respect, cooperation, and shared responsibility as they engage in an ongoing information exchange.[14]

ASSESSMENT AND EVALUATION FORMATS

Descriptions of a variety of assessment and evaluation formats, including what each tool is and what is its application, provide a menu of options to assess students' learning (Figure 1.3). Review the formats to guide decisions regarding the desired balance of assessment and evaluation options. Select formats that match instructional goals with students' capabilities and potential. Balance the selection of test data and forced-choice responses with assessment tools and techniques that are ongoing, occur in authentic learning situations, match students' learning profiles, and require students to generate responses. Students learn differently and benefit from assessment techniques that elicit their strengths while demonstrating learning. As McTigue and O'Connor (2005) remind us: "Responsiveness in assessment is as important as it is in teaching"–some assessment formats may be efficient, but favor some students and penalize others (p. 13). Consider expanding traditional applications so many formats become useful for preassessment, continuing assessment, summative evaluation, and/or students' self-assessment.

Balanced assessment requires collaboration. Both administrators and teachers are inherently involved in determining or adapting assessment formats because an assessment system cannot survive without administrative

[12] NAEYC, 1997.

[13] Shepard, Kagan, & Wurtz, 1998.

[14] NAEYC & NAECS/SDE, 2003.

Figure 1.2: AUTHENTIC ASSESSMENT ROLES

Teacher	Student	Parent
Collaboration	Cooperation and collaboration	Collaboration
Integrate learning standards	Master and transfer learning standards	Understand and support learning standards
Leader/co-learner	Co-learner; provides personal perspective	Co-learner; provides information and family perspective
Coach and facilitator	Organizer and manager	Encourager
Customize instruction to student's needs	Goal set; achiever	Support students' goals and achievement
Individual and class assessment	Self and peer assessment	Interpret assessment
Assesses to guide instruction	Review assessments to adjust goals and continue learning	Support continuous learning
Interpreter	Idiosyncratic learner	Supporter; inform the participant
Attitude: What you think and feel is important to me and to your ability to learn.	Attitude: I have the responsibility to learn all I can.	Attitude: I want to understand and support learning goals.
Uses time differently—time for facilitating, reflecting, and conferences	Uses time differently—moves from consumer to producer	Participates in student-led conferences and parent-teacher conferences

guidance and support.[15] To create a balanced assessment system, teachers and administrators determine which combination of tools best accommodates accountability and student learning. Their selections must produce an effective and efficient means of both collecting and recording the desired data. The system must efficiently balance the time and effort expended by students and teachers with the quality and usefulness of the procured information.[16] Teachers implement a few techniques and meet with colleagues to discuss their experiences and problem solve needed changes. As teachers develop a shared language and become comfortable with certain kinds of assessments, colleagues help them incorporate additional or different methods to ensure a more complete sampling of student performance.

An assessment system also requires an ongoing commitment to staff development. Teachers require scheduled opportunities to discuss assessment experiences and learn from other colleagues.[17] This staff development is coached by an informed person or group within the school with a deep knowledge of how children learn and how to align assessments to learning goals.

[15] Jones, 2003.
[16] NAEYC & NAECS/SDE, 2003; Stiggins, 2005.
[17] Black, Harrison, Lee, Marshall, & Wiliam, 2004.

Kingore, B. (2007). *Assessment,* 4th ed. Austin, TX: Professional Associates Publishing.

Developing a System

Figure 1.3: ASSESSMENT AND EVALUATION FORMATS

FORMAT	EXPLANATION–*This assessment tool is:*
Anecdotal record	An informal record of an observed event or behavior
Assessment accompanying curricula materials	A district or commercial device to assess specific content, topic, or skills
Audition	An assessment of a student's performance of an authentic task
Checklist	A list of standards, skills, or behaviors applicable to achievement
Conference–informal or formal	An informal or formal achievement conversation involving at different times interactions among the teacher, student, peer,and/ or family
Demonstration	An assessment of a student performing authentic tasks associated with standards
Discussion	An informal interactive, inquiry-based conversation among teachers and students or peers
Graphic organizer	A spatial device assessing the relationships among content and concepts
Interest inventory	An informal assessment of interests and experiences
Lab report	A record of content, process, learning responses, and reflections
Learning Log	A record of learning responses and reflections
Math problem solving	An assessment of a student's application of concepts and skills in math
Observations	A teacher formally or informally watching students during a class-room learning situation
Peer collaboration	An assessment guiding students' understanding of learning expec-tations among peers
Performance or performance task	An assessment of a student performing authentic tasks associated with standards
Portfolio and products	A collection over time of significant and representative samples of a student's learning achievements
Project	A learning task associated with standards and/or individual inter-ests; completed by a student or small group
Question/Inquiry	An informal, interactive, inquiry-based assessment–usually oral
Reading record–independent reading of fiction and nonfiction	A record to assess the level and pace of a student's literacy activities
Rubric	An evaluative device specifying criteria and levels of quality for a learning task
Standardized test	A commercially prepared norm-referenced or criterion-referenced test of specific content
Student self-assessment	An assessment format used by students to assess their skills and achievement
Test accompanying adopted materials	A commercial, prepared test of specific content and skills
Unit test–teacher developed	A teacher-prepared test of a segment of instruction
Writing sample	An assessment of a student's application of concepts and skills in written work

Kingore, B. (2007). *Assessment,* 4th ed. Austin, TX: Professional Associates Publishing.

APPLICATION–*This assessment tool is used to:*	ASSESSMENT OCCASION			
	PREASSESSMENT	CONTINUING ASSESSMENT	SUMMATIVE EVALUATION	SELF-ASSESSMENT
Document teachers' insights and observations during classroom activities	•	•	•	•
Diagnose and compare summary information regarding achievement	•	•	•	•
Assess processes and achievement level in an authentic learning situation; document with recordings, checklists, or rubrics	•		•	
Guide and record observations of standards and skills applications	•	•	•	•
Facilitate one-on-one exchanges, elicit a student's perception of achievement, and goal set	•	•	•	•
Assessment of processes and skill applications in an authentic learning situation; document with a checklist, rubric, or recording	•	•	•	•
Assess content integration and a student's perception of content information; document with a rubric or checklist	•	•	•	•
Assess concept complexity, depth, and relationships	•	•	•	•
Provide information to customize a student's learning opportunities and motivate achievement	•	•	•	•
Provide information about a student's knowledge, understanding, and responses to the learning process and content	•	•	•	•
Provide information about a student's perceptions and responses to learning	•	•	•	•
Provide an authentic measure of a student's problem solving skills and conceptual depth; recognize the individuality of product or process	•	•	•	•
Analyze productive or nonproductive learning behaviors and the integration of skills	•	•	•	•
Access group tasks; motivate students to recognize and aim for high standards of quality through cooperative efforts	•	•	•	•
Assess processes and products in an authentic learning situation	•	•	•	•
Analyze complexity, depth, achievement, and growth over time; clarify a student's strengths and modalities	•	•	•	•
Assess content integration through product, process, communication, and cooperative group efforts	•	•	•	•
Assess comprehension, content integration, and a student's perception of content information; document with a rubric or checklist	•	•	•	•
Identify a student's reading levels, use of reading strategies, and instructional capabilities	•	•	•	•
Provide a standard of quality for achievement and grading; provide a quality target for students	•	•	•	•
Allow for district-wide or nationwide comparisons of achievement	•	•	•	•
Help a student recognize levels of expectations and standards of quality; increase learning responsibility and ownership	•	•	•	•
Diagnose and compare summary information regarding achievement; guide instructional planning	•		•	
Diagnose and compare summary information regarding achievement; guide instructional planning	•		•	
Provide an authentic measure of a student's composition skill, vocabulary, and content	•	•	•	•

Kingore, B. (2007). *Assessment,* 4th ed. Austin, TX: Professional Associates Publishing.

Developing a System

An effective assessment system incorporates time for data analysis. Ratcliff (2001) cautions that teachers must take time to think about what students demonstrate and what skills need to be further developed. Teachers need time to review and reflect upon the collected information and discuss insights with colleagues. Regularly scheduling this time enables teachers to develop an understanding of students' progress, capabilities, and potential, and then plan appropriate continuous learning experiences to respond to that understanding.

YEARLONG ASSESSMENT PLAN

After reviewing assessment formats, outline which ongoing assessment and evaluation options will provide comprehensive information throughout the year for classroom needs, such as Figure 1.4. At the beginning of the year, the emphasis is preassessing to diagnose students' readiness and needs. During the year, preassessment, continuing assessment, and summative evaluation are each emphasized to monitor progress and

achievement. At the end of the year, summative evaluation provides documentation of the placement decisions and learning plans for each learner. District-wide or statewide testing is summative evaluation, often scheduled at the end of the year. When scheduled during the school year, if the results are available in a timely fashion, it potentially has diagnostic value. The results are sometimes useful as continuing data that guides and redirects instruction.

Determine which records will best organize and document the results of the assessment process. Then, analyze who needs to know this information, such as current and future teachers (T), students (S), family members (F), and administrators or specialists (A). Strive to keep students and their families very involved in the process as the more information sources and the more everyone understands achievement, the more children can benefit. Use the following example of one grade level's assessment plan to prompt the yearlong decisions that integrate assessment and instruction.

Figure 1.4: YEARLONG ASSESSMENT PLAN

SCHEDULE	ASSESSMENT FORMATS	DOCUMENTATION RECORDS	AUDIENCE
Beginning of the Year	Content-area preassessments Interest inventory Parent information	Pre-tests; standards checklists Completed inventories/interviews From Family to School forms	T S F A T S F T S
During the Year	Each unit: • Preassess, • Continuing, and • Summative evaluation Testing Conference and goal setting	Portfolios, students' self-assessments, learning logs, anecdotal records, rubrics, unit tests, and report cards Learning standards state test Conference notes; goal setting plans	T S F T S F A T S F
End of the Year	Tests Student products Conferences	District achievement test School Career Portfolio Conference notes	T S F A T S F A T S F

Kingore, B. (2007). *Assessment,* 4th ed. Austin, TX: Professional Associates Publishing.

· CHAPTER 2 ·
Student-Managed Portfolios

Never do for students what they should do for themselves.
—Anonymous

A portfolio is a compass for authentic assessment. It guides instructional decisions by providing educators and students with an excellent means of collecting varied evidence of a student's learning achievements and assembling that documentation into a coherent whole.[18] This collection, then, becomes a means of comparing and communicating a student's effort, growth, or achievement status over a period of time. Assessment experts and national organizations recommend portfolios as a foundational component in a balanced assessment system.[19]

Portfolios encourage the capabilities of all children. Regardless of their current levels of development, portfolio products validate that students are learning and making progress. These work samples substantiate the concepts and skill levels attained by students with fewer skills, students on grade level, students with learning differences or special needs, and students who would benefit more from extended learning opportunities. Determine the portfolio definition and guidelines that are most applicable to instructional objectives, and then, develop organization and management procedures that promote a student-managed portfolio system.

DEFINITION, OBJECTIVES, GUIDELINES, AND IMPLEMENTATION TOOLS

DEFINITION
A portfolio is a systematic collection of work that is typical for a student. The student and teacher assemble products to document readiness, achievement levels, and learning growth over time.

Systematic is a significant word in this definition. A systematic collection ensures that portfolios develop purposefully and continually

Student-Managed Portfolios

---

[18] Stiggins, 2005.

[19] ASCD, 2006a; Cooper & Kiger, 2005; Farr & Tone, 1998; Herman, Baker, & Linn, 2004; International Baccalaureate Organization, 2007; NAEYC & NAECS/SDE, 2003; NCTM, 2002; Stenmark, Bush, & Allen, 2001. Stiggins, 2005.

Kingore, B. (2007). *Assessment,* 4th ed. Austin, TX: Professional Associates Publishing.

by establishing when and which products are assembled, the management details, and the assessment applications. The products must be representative of the work that is typical of that child and not just the student's best work. Representative products reflect learning patterns and trends over a period of time and avoid isolated examples. Multiple procedures for developing a systematic collection are described in this chapter. Appendix A presents an outline to guide a successful implementation of a portfolio system.

In this definition, the selection of products by both teachers and students is essential. To document readiness, learning standards, and achievement status, teachers determine a menu of significant items that are required portfolio pieces for all students. Then, the remainder of the products must be student-selected to individualize the portfolio, confirm interests, recognize students' ownership in the process, and motivate students to review contents to goal set and extend their learning accomplishments. This chapter shares specific recommendations for determining the kind and number of products in a portfolio, which items students select, and the menu of pieces teachers select.

Documenting learning growth over time is a unique feature of a portfolio. Students and other vested individuals should review the portfolio to determine how each student is developing as a learner. Indeed, many students are more motivated to excel when they see for themselves that their efforts result in achievement. Later in this chapter, techniques, such as repeated tasks and triplets, illustrate specific means to document students' growth.

Educational resources use a variety of names for portfolios. In this publication, the primary portfolio is referred to as a yearly portfolio. In actuality, different kinds of portfolios become components in classroom portfolio systems. Consider the four kinds of portfolios in Figure

2.1 to determine the portfolio or combination of portfolios germane to an effective system.

Objectives

Ultimately, portfolios must be educationally useful for teachers as well as beneficial and personally satisfying to students and their families. Teachers use portfolios for feedback as they monitor and improve instruction in the classroom and evaluate curricula effectiveness. These work samples provide authentic support for judgments about students' achievement and for communication with students and families. Portfolio Objectives for Students (Figure 2.2) detail the potential benefits for elementary and secondary students and families. Since the portfolio process is simplified in prekindergarten, kindergarten, and first grade classrooms, Chapter 3 delineates the objectives and procedures for those young children.

Guidelines

Effective portfolios emphasize product and process, effort and achievement, student ownership, and self-assessment. Figure 2.3 offers comparative guidelines for effective versus ineffective portfolios.

Implementation Tools

Tools, such as outlines and checklists, assist portfolio implementation by guiding preparations and decisions. Figure 2.4 outlines a plan for analyzing and reaching decisions regarding the potential components in a portfolio system. Figure 2.5 is a checklist to guide the preparation of needed materials. Use both tools during professional development opportunities to promote discussion and guide collaborative decisions.

Figure 2.1: KINDS OF STUDENT PORTFOLIOS

YEARLY PORTFOLIO

The yearly portfolio is an ongoing and varied collection of the products and reflections assembled throughout the year by the student and teachers to document learning achievements. This portfolio is actively used during the school year. At the end of the year, the majority of the portfolio is bound and taken home as a keepsake.

SCHOOL CAREER PORTFOLIO: A SHOWCASE PORTFOLIO

This portfolio solves the dilemma of how to share work with next year's teacher while avoiding massive storage problems. At the end of each year, a limited number of items from the yearly portfolio, typically less than eight products, are collaboratively selected by the student and teacher to demonstrate the student's significant accomplishments and levels of achievement. These products are placed in the School Career Portfolio and forwarded to the next teacher. The School Career Portfolio is added to each year and then bound and presented to the student after several years or at graduation.

PROFESSIONAL PORTFOLIO

A professional portfolio is typically developed during the high school years. A small number of items are carefully selected to present the details of the individual's experience and talents related to specific employability or interviews for college admission. Students are encouraged to focus on the skills required in the field in which they intend to work or the college they wish to attend rather than attempt to develop a generic or global view of talents. This portfolio should reflect the individual.

CLASS PORTFOLIO

Particularly in elementary and middle school classrooms, a class portfolio is an appealing component to incorporate into the portfolio process to reflect the achievements and projects of the class as a whole. Typically, it is a photo album in which weekly entries are made to herald the content and experiences of the class. Students take turns serving as the class historian who makes choices about what to record and which examples to include as a representative sample of the learning topics, skills, and events of that week in class. Eventually, every student should have the opportunity to serve as class historian. The class portfolio becomes a collective scrapbook or data base in which all of the students have an opportunity to evaluate class work and gain ownership in the learning process as they celebrate completed tasks and occasions. It is a unique opportunity for students to select work and reflect upon learning accomplishments as a community of learners rather than only as individuals. Over time, it promotes teacher and student assessment and reflection as it represents the curriculum and class experiences for the entire year.

Kingore, B. (2007). *Assessment,* 4th ed. Austin, TX: Professional Associates Publishing.

Student-Managed
Portfolios

Figure 2.2: PORTFOLIO OBJECTIVES FOR STUDENTS

1. Enhance self-concept
Students enhance their self-concept as they review their portfolios over time and observe concrete connections between prior knowledge and current learning. They substantiate to themselves that their efforts result in achievement.

2. Increase responsibility for learning
Students' responsibility for learning increases as they analyze examples of their work to select portfolio products supported by their reflection upon their learning and achievements.

3. Refine organization and management
Organization and management are valued life skills at home and school. A clearly structured portfolio system models for students how to organize and manage their work over time.

4. Implement self-assessment and collaborative evaluation
As students review portfolio products, they self-assess and reflect on what they have earned by their effort. Well-developed criteria, often shared in the form of rubrics, foster students' self assessments and lead to collaborative evaluations between teachers and students.

5. Document learning readiness and determine learning goals
Portfolio contents confirm student readiness, incorporate preferred modes of learning, augment understanding of information from standardized evaluations, and form a foundation for collaborative goal setting.

6. Document district and state learning standards
Students substantiate their application of the concepts and skills targeted by learning standards by the products produced over a period of time. Students' reflections can specifically address the standards inherent in the product.[20]

7. Document abilities for present and future placements
The portfolio documents achievements that relate to placement in classes, interviews for college admission, and employability. It supports teachers, students, and parents as they advocate for appropriate intervention, initiated in a timely fashion.

8. Celebrate learning and share information with others
Students review their portfolios to acknowledge learning accomplishments. Portfolios promote students' celebrations of learning and provide a communication tool to share evidence of progress with family, teachers, and peers informally or through student-involved conferences.

[20] Chapter 9 includes examples of procedures that directly relate student reflections to learning standards.

Kingore, B. (2007). *Assessment,* 4th ed. Austin, TX: Professional Associates Publishing.

Figure 2.3: GUIDELINES FOR EFFECTIVE PORTFOLIOS

EFFECTIVE PORTFOLIOS:	INEFFECTIVE PORTFOLIOS:
• Authentically develop through the daily classroom activities and are thoroughly integrated into the instructional program. *This is one of the ways we demonstrate learning.*	• Are contrived, containing a few products stuck in during the last week of school. *We do this because we are told we have to do portfolios.*
• Benefit students and guide instructional decisions by documenting students' capacities and potential.	• Represent a random set of products.
• Seamlessly weave the instruction and assessment together.	• Are viewed as a separate entity.
• Require students to be responsible and accountable for their learning.	• Increase teachers' workload with filing and paper management.
• Support the work students do by allowing them to polish and refine over time what they are learning.	• Accent the deficiencies and weaknesses of students' work.
• Encourage students' metacognition and increase their capacity for monitoring and self-evaluation.	• Largely exclude students from the assessment and evaluation process. Evaluation continues to be something done to students.
• Promote challenge, originality, and complexity in students' thinking and in the works they produce.	• Are dominated by products with single correct answers and simplistic, fill-in-the-blank tasks.
• Support opportunities for dialogue and invite students to share portfolio items and their learning perceptions with others.	• Are only used for accountability issues or for conferences between parents and teachers.
• Are student-centered and motivate students to maintain high expectations for themselves.	• Are controlled by teachers but maintained by students because they are required to do so.
• Enable students to set learning goals and celebrate learning accomplishments.	• Fail to integrate the cognitive and affective domains in learning.

Kingore, B. (2007). *Assessment,* 4th ed. Austin, TX: Professional Associates Publishing.

Figure 2.4: PLANNING A PORTFOLIO SYSTEM

Plan a system so the portfolio process develops purposefully and continuously. Use the following guided outline to create or refine the system by addressing the questions, reaching decisions, and implementing the plan.

Purposes and audiences

- How will portfolios benefit students, families, and teachers?
- How will the portfolio help a student review past learning experiences to guide future learning goals?
- How does this correlate to school, district, or state learning standards and assessment requirements?
- Who will want or need to view the portfolio?
- How can portfolios provide instructional feedback and increase instructional effectiveness?

DECISIONS: _____

_____

_____

Potential products

- On which curriculum areas should portfolios focus?
- What kinds of products will best document learning?
- How can very large or three-dimensional items be managed without excessive storage space?
- How can portfolio products support all the different ways students learn best?

DECISIONS: _____

_____

_____

Selection

- How can students realistically and actively be involved in the selection process?
- Which selection criteria are appropriate and most significant?
- What menu of items should teachers require?
- How many products should be included?
- When and how often should pieces be selected?

DECISIONS: _____

_____

_____

Kingore, B. (2007). *Assessment,* 4th ed. Austin, TX: Professional Associates Publishing.

Organization and management

- How can the organization remain simple enough to enable students to manage portfolios?
- Which containers are most appropriate?
- Which filing system works best to keep the products organized?
- Where should portfolios be stored?

DECISIONS:

Assessment and evaluation

- How can portfolios document what students have learned and provide assessment information to vested adults?
- How can a portfolio be used to document state learning standards?
- How do teachers involve students in interpreting the information in their portfolios and making judgments about their own learning instead of just collecting products?
- How can a portfolio help students gauge growth and achievements as they goal set?
- Which self-assessment techniques promote student ownership in achievement?
- How can students and teachers use a portfolio to assist conferencing or sharing instructional information with students, parents, and colleagues?
- How does a portfolio support the grades on a grade card?

DECISIONS:

Additional questions

Student-Managed Portfolios

Figure 2.5: MATERIALS CHECKLIST

Use this checklist to record a list of needed materials and forms to copy. Keep the list short and inexpensive so cost does not prevent a successful portfolio experience.

❑   **Audiotapes and tape recorder**

❑   **Camera–digital or with film**

❑   **Collection folders**

❑   **Computers**

❑   **Crate, box, or file drawer to store class portfolios**

❑   **Date stamp**

❑   **Disks or CDRs for digital portfolios**

❑   **Filing system**

❑   **Forms:**   PAGE/FIGURE:

    ❑   _____   _____

    ❑   _____   _____

    ❑   _____   _____

    ❑   _____   _____

    ❑   _____   _____

    ❑   _____

❑   **Hanging Files**

❑   **Paper of various colors and sizes**

❑   **Portfolio containers:**

    ❑   **Envelopes**

    ❑   **Folders**

    ❑   **Binders**

❑   **Post-it™ notes**

❑   **School supplies:**

    ❑   **Pens, pencils, crayons, and markers**

    ❑   **Scissors**

    ❑   **Stapler**

    ❑   _____

❑   **Timer**

❑   **Videotapes and access to a video camera**

❑   _____

❑   _____

Kingore, B. (2007). *Assessment,* 4th ed. Austin, TX: Professional Associates Publishing.

Determine which areas of the curriculum are the intended focuses of your portfolios. Single subject portfolios are possible but may end up accenting the weakest skill area for some students. An integrated curriculum portfolio has the advantage of increasing the opportunity for each student to excel in one or more areas. In self-contained classrooms, educators determine three or four content areas to include. In departmentalized classrooms, form a team approach with a core of three or four teachers so students produce an integrated portfolio instead of developing separate portfolios in each subject.

ORGANIZATION AND MANAGEMENT

> *I used to collect work from my students, but the piles just got higher and higher. **I never had time to file them.** It didn't work as well as I had hoped.*
>
> *I can't keep portfolios for all of my students. **My classes are too big!***
>
> *I know portfolios are important, but I **just don't want the mess.***

These comments from teachers are typical of the concerns associated with the portfolio process. Most teachers appreciate the idea of portfolios but feel overwhelmed by the organization and management. One aspect of the problem is teachers using the pronoun *I* when they discuss together the management of

portfolios. Portfolios are too much to manage when teachers attempt to do most of the work for the students. The key is to organize the process in such a way that the students manage their own portfolios. With student-managed portfolios, students make many decisions about what goes in the portfolio and analyze the results over time to assess how they change as learners. Students are responsible for managing and filing their own work, and the emphasis is on self-reflection.

In thousands of classrooms, students, age four through adults, are successfully managing their own portfolios by using the procedures discussed in this chapter. Student-managed portfolios evolve from teachers' artful planning. Teachers determine a filing system, appropriate containers, collection files, and an organization method for the portfolio contents that enables students to proceed toward independence.

Filing System

A filing system keeps the containers organized. When portfolio containers are just stored in a box, the containers tend to get mixed-up every time one is in use. For example, students take their portfolio containers to their desks to share with peers; when finished, they are not likely to be returned to the same location within the box. A filing system is needed to solve this potential disarray.

An effective yet simple filing system uses hanging files in a box, crate, or file drawer. The hanging file is the place-holder; it is not the portfolio container. The portfolio container goes in and out of that file while the hanging file always stays in place and keeps the system organized. Each student has a hanging file; each hanging file has a tab with a student's name or photo on it. The files may be arranged alphabetically by students' names or numbered and filed in sequence.

Kingore, B. (2007). *Assessment,* 4th ed. Austin, TX: Professional Associates Publishing.

Some teachers use several different colors of hanging files in groupings in the same crate. The colored sections help students find their own portfolios quickly. However, ensure the sections do not unintentionally group and categorize the students.

Containers

The significance of portfolios is determined by the contents of the portfolio rather than the style of the container. However, most teachers are apprehensive about the containers and how much classroom space this process will consume. Address this concern directly and early when planning to avoid confusion and disarray later in the school year.

A wide variety of containers are successfully used in classrooms across the nation. The secret to the perfect container is not to worry about what others are using and select the container that best fits classroom

needs and teaching style. With a large number of students, for example, containers that require little space are important assets. If three-dimensional products are used frequently, the containers need to accommodate those products or allow for the use of photographs and videotapes of those large items.

Consider the following factors when determining the best choice of container for the class.

1. **Sturdy**. The containers must be strong enough to withstand frequent use throughout a whole year.
2. **Product appropriate.** The container needs to be appropriate to the type of products that will be collected.
3. **Storage appropriate.** Choose containers that will not occupy more classroom space than is comfortably available in your room.
4. **Economical.** Limiting the cost of supplies makes the project more feasible.
5. **Accessible.** Plan containers that are readily accessible to students. Then, they can manage their own paperwork, and the process is more naturally incorporated into daily learning activities.

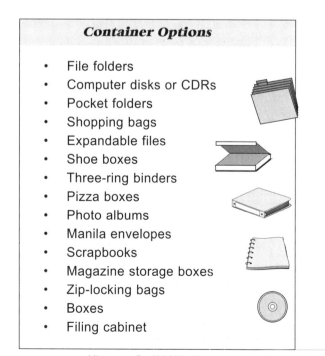

Container Options

- File folders
- Computer disks or CDRs
- Pocket folders
- Shopping bags
- Expandable files
- Shoe boxes
- Three-ring binders
- Pizza boxes
- Photo albums
- Manila envelopes
- Scrapbooks
- Magazine storage boxes
- Zip-locking bags
- Boxes
- Filing cabinet

Teacher to Teacher

A computer disk is the smallest and simplest solution to use as a portfolio container. However, if interested in using computer disks for more than typed products, ensure that students have ready access to a scanner and digital camera. Plan simple procedures that allow students to complete most or all of the process so adults are not left with such time-intensive tasks.

Kingore, B. (2007). *Assessment,* 4th ed. Austin, TX: Professional Associates Publishing.

After determining which containers to use, make them available to the students to design or decorate. Personalizing the containers adds individuality as it sets the tone that each student and each portfolio is unique.

Formats for students to use to customize their portfolio container

- Portrait of self or family
- Drawing of home
- Collage of favorites, including words, animals, represented ideas, or symbols
- A picture or collage of interests, places, or books
- A map to a favorite place that is real or symbolic
- *Things I Like to Do*
- *Things I Want to Learn*
- *Things that Are Important About Me*
- Patterns or designs
- Tangram illustrations
- Tessellations
- A bio poem for self
- An I Am reflection
- Quarterly images–Divide the cover into quadrants; students illustrate a different idea each quarter of the school year.

In addition to photographing oversized items, encourage students to be creative and fold large paper items to fit in smaller containers. Then, small containers don't totally dictate product size. The portfolios resemble pop-up books as students unfold pages to show their work.

Collection Files

The collection file is the storage place holding work for later consideration or before work is taken home. Students need to analyze several products in order to evaluate which ones to include in their portfolios. Have them save completed work in the subject areas represented in the portfolio until the next regularly scheduled portfolio selection session. Then, students review this collection file to select a portfolio piece. The remaining work that is not selected for the portfolio is taken home by the student so parents continue to see school work on a regular basis.

Many classes already use work folders to store completed papers so they have a collection file process in place. Another simple solution that works well is a plain manila folder stored in front of the portfolio container in each hanging file. Use this plain folder to hold all completed work until portfolio selections occur. While other options are possible, this method takes little additional space, is easy to maintain, and requires no additional materials except manila folders.

Work that is to be graded is first completed by the student, then graded by the teacher, and finally placed in the collection folder by the student when it is returned with a grade. Work that is not to be graded is placed directly in the collection file as the student completes that assignment.

Kingore, B. (2007). *Assessment,* 4th ed. Austin, TX: Professional Associates Publishing.

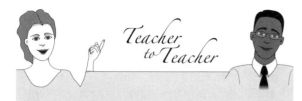

Create a small picture symbol for your portfolios, such the ones below. Tape that symbol on your class calendar on the day that portfolio selection is scheduled so students are more concretely aware of the schedule. Then, move the symbol ahead to the next selection date each time you complete portfolio selection.

Organizing Portfolio Contents

Several options help students organize their products within their portfolio. Choose from the following options or develop one more suited to the specific learning environment class.

⇨ *Chronological order*
Sequence the portfolio from the beginning to the end of the school year. This arrangement is easily managed by requiring students to consistently file new products in the back of the other work in their portfolios.

⇨ *Subject area*
Organize the portfolio with separate colored files, dividers, or pockets for each curriculum area, such as writing, math, or science. The students then organize their completed products into each designated subject area of the portfolio.

⇨ *Themes*
Organize the students' portfolios around the themes of the campus or class for the school year, such as challenges or patterns.

⇨ *Topics*
Divide the portfolio for specific topics of the class and/or interests of each student, such as dinosaurs, medicine, or oceanography.

⇨ *Genres*
Divide the portfolio into types of products or genres of particular curriculum subjects, such as reading genres.

⇨ *Talents*
Particularly when completing professional portfolios, high school students can organize their portfolio products according to the talents they wish to accent to prospective employers, such as communication skills, technology, systems comprehension, or interpersonal skills.

⇨ *Combinations of the above*
The organization types may be combined to better accommodate students needs. As an example, the products can be chronologically arranged within separate subject areas.

Young students and students inexperienced in portfolio management are more successful when their portfolios are initially organized chronologically. It is the simplest organizational method to initiate and maintain. Even four-year-olds students can successfully file their work when portfolios are organized chronologically.

Actively involve older students in selecting an organizational format. After a class discussion of options, students determine the portfolio organizational format they think will work best for them and then exchange ideas among themselves. This process has the advantage of customizing organizational choice to the students and reinforcing that the portfolio is student-centered and managed.

Kingore, B. (2007). *Assessment,* 4th ed. Austin, TX: Professional Associates Publishing.

A self-esteem boost often results when students file each new entry in the back of their portfolio. The added benefit is that students see their earlier work each time they add to their portfolios. This concretely reminds them of their own growth. Young students, struggling students, and students with special learning needs particularly benefit from clearly viewing their progress over time.

Potential Portfolio Products

Teachers often wonder what kinds of products are effective choices for portfolios. There are certainly no absolutes, as the portfolio should reflect the instructional climate of the classroom. However, the list on Figure 2.6 is a compilation of products teachers reported as most helpful in providing assessment and evaluation information about their students. The list is not intended to dictate what products to include but rather to suggest options to consider. Skim the list and check any products that match instructional priorities. At the bottom of the form, write additional products that would result in significant information.

Make portfolio products an integral reflection of the curriculum and what students learn rather than a random collection of activities and isolated skills. Effective portfolios have a preponderance of open-ended products based upon researched strategies. Products that develop from research-based strategies better document the different thinking levels and learning achievements of students. Open-ended tasks encourage students to produce various levels of complexity and depth that reflect their abilities rather than recall a more simple, single-correct answer. Incorporate the following guidelines from current research and the best practices when reaching product decisions.

- The quality of the learning opportunities offered students determines the level of their responses. If we fail to ask high-level questions and provide opportunities for students to engage in challenging tasks, we reduce students to basic product responses instead of high accomplishments (Kingore, 2001; Payne, 2003).
- Products that require high-level thinking are vital. Knowledge and skills are certainly necessary but are not sufficient elements of understanding for long-term retention and achievement (Anderson & Krathwohl, 2001; Shepard, 1997; Wiggins and McTighe, 2005; Willis, 2006).
- Research documents that vocabulary is directly related to comprehension and learning achievement (ASCD, 2006b; Marzano, 2004; NRP, 2000). Elicit subject-specific vocabulary in portfolio products and reflections.
- Similarities-differences and summarization are strategies with the highest potential for achievement gains (Marzano, Pickering & Pollock. 2001). Products resulting from these strategies are priorities when documenting achievement.
- The brain seeks meaning by connecting the unknown to what is known and when there is an emotional response integrated into a learning experience (Caine, Caine, Klimek, & McClintic, 2004; Sousa, 2001; Sylwester, 2003). Worthwhile products result from learning experiences that build upon prior experiences, interests, and emotional engagement
- Ensure that product assignments respond to multiple modes of learning the diverse ways that students learn best (Gardner, 1996; Grigorenko and Sternberg, 1997).
- Strive to design product tasks with an appropriate balance between just enough versus too much challenge. Drawing upon the work of Vygotsky (1962), product assignments should be challenging but attainable.

Kingore, B. (2007). *Assessment,* 4th ed. Austin, TX: Professional Associates Publishing.

Student-Managed Portfolios

Figure 2.6: POTENTIAL PORTFOLIO PRODUCTS

- ❏ Products and captions documenting the achievement of learning standards.
- ❏ Art, symbols, graphic connections to content
- ❏ Attitude, surveys, interest inventories, or investigative surveys
- ❏ Photographs, sketches, or videotapes of three-dimensional products, demonstrations, presentations, or competition entries; a written explanation is attached
- ❏ Photocopies of products, awards, or honors
- ❏ Dictations or originally written reports, literature extensions, or stories
- ❏ First drafts and revisions–a biography of a product
- ❏ Math products that provide evidence of problem solving and higher-level thinking
- ❏ Goals set by students (and parents or teachers)–academic, behavioral, social, study skill, or research goals
- ❏ Lab reports and observations
- ❏ Learning logs and/or journal responses
- ❏ Integration or transfer of skills across subject areas
- ❏ Maps, charts, graphs, and other graphic organizations of content (especially those designed by the individual student)
- ❏ Personal response to a current event, issue, or problem
- ❏ Self-evaluations and reflections
- ❏ Audiotapes of oral reading, math process explanations, reports, or story retellings
- ❏ Computer-generated student products
- ❏ Tests or quizzes
- ❏ Research and individual investigations
- ❏ Cooperative investigations; group reports or projects
- ❏ Repeated tasks
- ❏ Triplets
- ❏ _____
- ❏ _____
- ❏ _____
- ❏ _____
- ❏ _____
- ❏ _____
- ❏ _____
- ❏ _____

Kingore, B. (2007). *Assessment,* 4th ed. Austin, TX: Professional Associates Publishing.

Group products are often created in classrooms using cooperative learning techniques. Teachers conclude that group products may be included in individual portfolios if the name of every group member is listed on the product to ensure that reviewers understand that it was a group project. Furthermore, the product should be one that can be photocopied so more than one group member can select that product for their portfolios.

Use a camera to photograph items too large to store in portfolio containers. A photograph helps solve the problem of how to represent large projects in small containers. Students attach a narrative to the photograph describing the main points of the process and product.

Portfolios should be as individual as the teachers and students involved. It is not always necessary for all students to select the same type of product. Determine a menu of items that should be included in every portfolio for documentation of achievement; and then, let the students select products according to their unique talents, interests, needs, and feelings of accomplishment.

PRODUCT SELECTION

A Portfolio Is a File, Not a Pile.

Avoid the scrapbook syndrome: *I'll just put this stuff in it.* Effective portfolios require

students to discuss and analyze their work. Students must make decisions about what items are the most significant representations of their learning. Thus, the procedure involves more than just saving papers. Effective portfolios require a three-fold process: collection, selection, and reflection.

There is a difference between collection (merely saving items) and selection (the decision-making process of prioritizing which items to include). After students collect their work over a short period of time, they review those products and use the specific criteria discussed later in this chapter to select one for their portfolio. Selection requires students to analyze the multiple aspects of their work. The high-level thinking required of students in this process results in portfolios with greater assessment and evaluation validity. Before they file work in the portfolio, students reflect on their decision and write a reflection statement or caption to attach to the product. This metacognitive process significantly benefits students.[21] Much of students' success in learning and work environments depends upon the strength of their ability to analyze alternatives and problem solve. Thus, the class time devoted to this selection and reflection process models life-skills related to students' future achievements. Additionally, an important benefit of engaging students in selection and reflection is the opportunity it provides adults to learn from students' perspectives and value their active participation in learning.

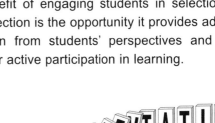

To make portfolio selection a regular part of the class schedule, establish a specific day and time when selection always occurs. (Refer to the bulletin board illustration later in this chapter that features students' selections for their portfolios.)

[21] Chapter 4 has several examples of metacognitive forms and responses for students to use.

Kingore, B. (2007). *Assessment,* 4th ed. Austin, TX: Professional Associates Publishing.

Student-Managed Portfolios

Number of Products

Control the size of a portfolio by reasoning in reverse. Determine the total number of products preferred in the portfolio at the end of the year. The number of items should be small enough to manage and store, but it should be large enough to concretely demonstrate students' growth, document levels of achievement, and reflect individuality. Also, plan the ratio of student-to-teacher selections so the individual student determines the majority of the portfolio contents.

When the teacher chooses most of the products, the portfolio becomes something students do because they are required to rather than the portfolio being personally important and satisfying to the student.

In self-contained classes, control the total size of each portfolio by thinking in terms of approximately an inch or an inch-and-a-half thickness. To attain this size, have students select one product each week, resulting in approximately thirty-six products selected by the student. The teacher might select ten to twelve additional pieces making the yearly portfolio total almost fifty products. Depending upon the size of the products, that quantity usually results in a portfolio that is one to two inches thick. Teachers find that amount to be an excellent sample of students' learning experiences while maintaining a manageable size.

In departmentalized classes, think approximately one-fourth to one-half inch thickness per portfolio. Departmentalized classes have less time per day in each class. Thus, one product selected every three weeks is suggested for a total of twelve products. These teachers typically choose an additional six to eight pieces so the total number of products in the portfolio is approximately twenty. If three or four departmentalized teachers work as a team, the products selected from each

class are combined into an integrated portfolio about one inch to two inches thick.

In classes with younger children, think one-fourth to one-half inch thickness for each portfolio. Young children produce fewer paper products;[22] much of the learning completed with this age group is process-oriented. Therefore, one product selected every two or three weeks is sufficient for these classes. Most of the portfolio selections are determined by the teacher to validate the growth the children demonstrate in their learning.

Include Three Things on Every Portfolio Product

For most elementary and secondary students, each portfolio product needs to have a **name, date,** and **reflective statement or caption** on it. The name obviously is needed to identify whose work it is. The date allows students to be aware of the changes in their own learning and their growth over time. The reflective statement or caption defines why that product was selected, what it means in relation to previous learning benchmarks, or what specific value it has to the learner.

Teachers sometimes wonder if it would be simpler to omit the reflective statements when the portfolio process is initiated. It seems easier to have one less thing to manage as you begin. If possible, however, incorporate the reflective statements from the very start. Products without captions have less significance over time. When parents, teachers, or even students look back on portfolio products without a caption, it is more difficult to understand and value the importance of each piece. The reward for incorporating reflective statements is that students, families, and teachers gain an increased awareness of the student's patterns of learning strengths and attitudes toward their learning.

[22] See Chapter 3 for further discussion.

Kingore, B. (2007). *Assessment,* 4th ed. Austin, TX: Professional Associates Publishing.

Young students and students with special learning needs may require different considerations to successfully complete the selection and reflection process. Chapter 3 presents several helpful alternatives for these students.

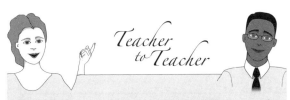

Ask students to use a pencil to lightly number the products in their portfolio in sequential order. Then, if items drop out, they are more easily returned to the correct place.

Portfolios substantiate a concrete record of the development of students' talents and achievements during a year or more. In classrooms where all students develop portfolios, the process enables each student to be noticed for the level of products completed. In this manner, portfolios increase inclusion by providing multiple opportunities for children from every population to demonstrate talents and potential. Portfolios allow schools to honor the diversity of students and discover the strengths of each learner.

Teacher Product Selection

Who completes the reflection when teachers require a specific product to be included in every student's portfolio? It is not authentic for students to write the caption because they did not make the choice. An option most teachers find helpful is to use a teacher product caption form, such as Figure 2.7. A teacher fills in the date, product, and a statement explaining the significance of the portfolio item choice. The teacher's reflection is then photocopied so each student can staple a copy to the product. On the bottom of the form, the student then adds a response about the product or the selection. The teacher selection form clarifies the reason for

the product being selected and clearly signals to parents and others who view the portfolio which items are teacher-selected.

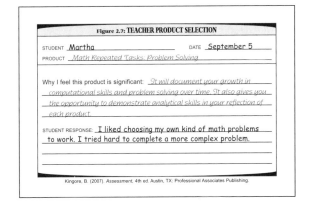

Selection Criteria Charts

A criteria chart lists criteria for portfolio product selection. Post it in the classroom for students and visitors to reference. As students review several pieces of their work and ponder which product to select for entry into their portfolio, the criteria chart helps them focus on specific criteria. This process encourages students to analyze and develop their ability to monitor and evaluate their own achievements.

Older students can develop a criteria chart as a cooperative group task (Figure 2.8). Each small group writes five questions to consider when selecting a portfolio item and then graphs the significance of each question on a scale of one (low) to ten (high). In a class discussion, the groups merge their results into a class criteria chart.

To develop a criteria chart with younger students, post a large sheet of chart paper or poster board on the wall. Write a title and a leading sentence on the chart. Then, while discussing selection criteria with students, record ideas on the chart in the vocabulary expressed by the students.

Do not attempt to complete the chart at one time. Higher levels of responses emerge

Student-Managed Portfolios

Figure 2.7: TEACHER PRODUCT SELECTION

STUDENT _____   DATE _____

PRODUCT _____

Why I feel this product is significant: _____

_____

_____

_____

STUDENT RESPONSE: _____

_____

_____

_____

Kingore, B. (2007). *Assessment,* 4th ed. Austin, TX: Professional Associates Publishing.

Figure 2.8: PORTFOLIO CRITERIA CHART

STUDENTS _____   DATE _____

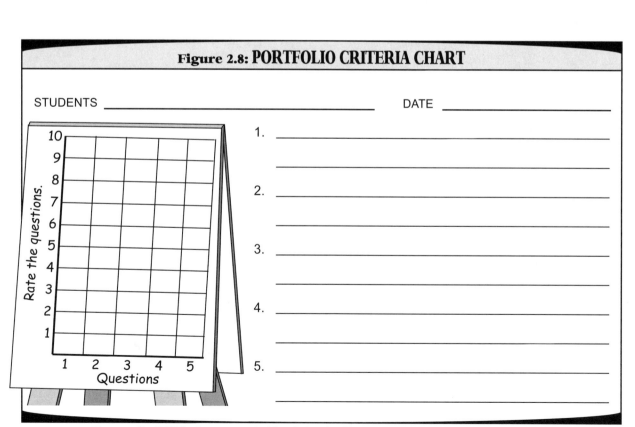

1. _____

_____

2. _____

_____

3. _____

_____

4. _____

_____

5. _____

_____

Kingore, B. (2007). *Assessment,* 4th ed. Austin, TX: Professional Associates Publishing.

as students become aware of many ways to think about and evaluate their work. Within a few weeks, the class produces a criteria chart which has great value because of their ownership in the process.

The following criteria charts are examples that model the process in a kindergarten and a middle school class. Every criteria chart should be unique to the specific classroom and reflect the vocabulary and priorities of the class.

Criteria charts are one way to guide students toward writing more thoughtful captions. When students too frequently use simple response traps such as *I like it* or *I got a 100 on it,* ask them to look over the criteria chart, choose another criterion, and add that idea to their caption.

As you record a criteria statement on the chart, add the initials of the student who suggested that idea. Those initials serve to recognize the student for a strong idea and increase the motivation for others to add thoughtful responses.

Portfolio Selection Bulletin Boards

A bulletin board is a useful component in the portfolio selection process. It can help organize the process as it provides a showcase for the products students select. By using the bulletin board, teachers do not have to wonder if everyone appropriately completed the selection process. One glance at the bulletin board confirms that everyone is finished or indicates who may need assistance. In self-contained classes, this bulletin board changes

Criteria Chart: *Kindergarten Class*

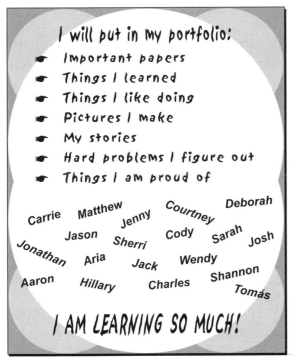

Criteria Chart: *Middle School*

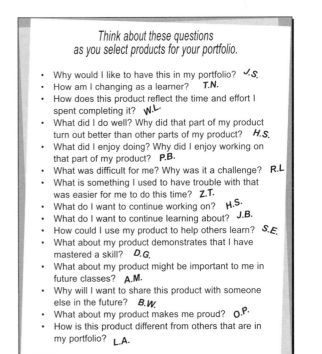

Kingore, B. (2007). *Assessment,* 4th ed. Austin, TX: Professional Associates Publishing.

every week and celebrates students' work. In departmentalized classes, alternately use the board to highlight different class sections. Students enjoy seeing what peers in other class sections have done.

PREPARATION

Use a bulletin board that is available all year for portfolio products. Put a light colored backing on the board and add a border if you prefer. Then, use different colors of construction paper or yarn and a stapler to divide the board into boxes, enough for the number of students in one class or in one section. Put one student's name in each box. Add a caption, such as *Portfolio Parade* or *Learning in Progress.*

APPLICATION

After students have selected and captioned a product for their portfolio, they post it in their box on the board. Students use self-adhering plastic clips, push pins, clothespins, or staples to post their work. When it is time to select new products, students take down and file the posted product in their portfolio before choosing the next product to display. In this manner, the bulletin board remains up all year yet changes every week. It is student-centered instead of teacher-decorated.

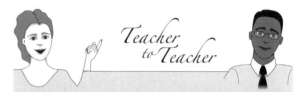

Organization is an issue with very young and special needs students. If it is too troublesome for these students to take down and file their work, just staple the newly selected product on top of last week's selection. Each reporting period, take down the products for students to file as a packet in their portfolio.

Learning in Progress

Christopher	Julian			Joshua	Brian
Ramita	Emily	Abigail	Thomas	Maria	Hannah
Timothy	Ethan	Michael	Caitlyn	Jacob	Isabella
Samantha	CJ	Bianca	Olivia	Matthew	Don

Kingore, B. (2007). *Assessment,* 4th ed. Austin, TX: Professional Associates Publishing.

ASSESSMENT TECHNIQUES THAT DOCUMENT STUDENT GROWTH

One value of portfolios is their potential to concretely demonstrate learning changes over time. Many students are more motivated to excel or try harder when they see that their efforts result in improvements. Repeated tasks and triplets are assessment techniques that specifically substantiate student growth.

Repeated Tasks

Repeated tasks simply make systematic a technique that effective teachers have always used. Repeated tasks are learning experiences that students complete at one point in time and then later complete again to note gains in skills or achievement. Pre-tests and post-tests are traditional examples of repeated tasks. In the portfolio process, incorporate several repeated tasks that enable students, parents, and teachers to clearly evaluate growth.

Initially, survey learning standards to determine the skills students must demonstrate by the end of the year. Then, plan and implement learning tasks for students to complete that incorporate those skills. Students complete these tasks early in the year and then two or more additional times to document growth and achievement gains over time. Any learning experience germane to the curriculum is a potential repeated task. Consider the several examples of effective repeated tasks relating to a variety of grade levels and diverse learning profiles that follow in this section.

> *One value of portfolios is their potential to concretely demonstrate learning changes over a period of time.*

Repeated tasks are an excellent preassessment tool when the tasks directly relate to the skills and concepts students are to know by the end of the year. Students complete the task the first time to provide information regarding their levels of readiness and learning needs. Prior knowledge and skill levels are particularly evident from these assessments. That beginning repeated task is filed in the portfolio. Later, the task is repeated one or more times and the results compared to document growth and continued learning needs.

Three-Minute Celebrations

After completing a repeated task for a second time, students compare and contrast both tasks. In approximately a three-minute celebration of learning, students are encouraged to talk with one or two classmates about what they notice and how they feel they are changing as learners.

KINDERGARTEN-GRADE ONE

Each child:
- Draws a picture of self, family, or where the child lives (not limited to a house) with dictation or the child's written explanation.
- Retells a folk tale or story on an audio or videotape.
- Produces a fine-motor sample by tracing one hand and cutting it out.
- Completes a *Look What I Can Do* book–half-page books in which students demonstrate their levels of skills applications relating to learning standards. Each half page prompts an application of a

Kingore, B. (2007). *Assessment,* 4th ed. Austin, TX: Professional Associates Publishing.

required learning standard, such as writing an original math story problem, the letters of the alphabet, or all of the geometric shapes they can draw.[23]

ELEMENTARY GRADES

Each student:
* Draws a picture of family with sentences written by the child about the family.
* Produces a handwriting sample by writing content that includes every letter of the alphabet. For example, Figure 2.9 shares a brief response spaced for primary handwriting, and Figure 2.10 provides a longer response spaced for intermediate handwriting. Jo Hackenbracht and Linda Coffman, teachers in Urbana, Ohio, shared a third example sentence: *If you just mix apples, berries, and grapes with poppy seeds, you can have a quick, zippy salad.*
* Writes and completes the hardest math story problem the student knows how to solve that applies math operations and concepts currently being studied.
* Completes a literacy and vocabulary task by writing in five minutes the most important words the student knows.
* Assesses spelling mastery based upon a list of 100 to 500 high-frequency words.
* Composes writing samples, possibly focusing on different types of writing, such as narrative, persuasive, or expository. The writing prompt or writing topic does not need to be the same each time.
* Sketches or illustrates specific content-related vocabulary.
* Draws a map of where the student lives. The student is encouraged to include as many details and as much specific information as possible.
* Writes the five most significant facts or concepts the student knows about a science, math, or social studies topic.
* Duplicates reading samples of fiction and

nonfiction showing the student's independent reading level.
* Records a reading sample documenting fluency and independent reading skills.

Older students initially date and complete a repeated task using one color of ink. Later, the second task is dated and completed on the same paper using a second color ink as the student embellishes, deletes, and corrects any items on the initial work. The change in color accents growth. Additional colors can be used over time to expand upon the original response.

At the beginning of the year, have students design the front of their portfolio container and date their work. At the end of the year, they design the back of their container and date it. The portfolio design thus becomes one more repeated task without extra materials.

MIDDLE SCHOOL AND HIGH SCHOOL

Each student:
* Draws a map for geography or social studies or fills in details on an appropriate blank map before and after studying that location.
* Completes a literacy and vocabulary task by writing for five minutes the most important words the student knows related to the course or topic.
* Assesses spelling based upon a list of 100 to 500 high-frequency words or the vocabulary specific to this course or topic.

---

[23] See Chapter 3 for a sample *Look What I Can Do* book and additional repeated tasks for young children.

Kingore, B. (2007). *Assessment,* 4th ed. Austin, TX: Professional Associates Publishing.

Figure 2.9: HANDWRITING

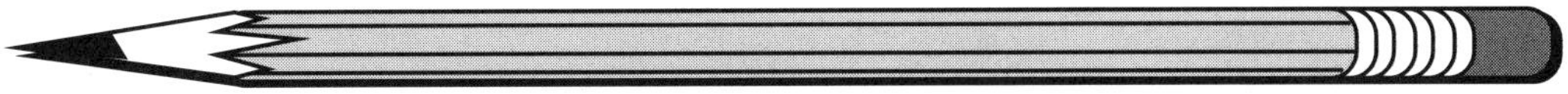

The quick, brown fox jumps over the lazy dog.

NAME _____   DATE _____

NAME _____   DATE _____

Kingore, B. (2007). *Assessment,* 4th ed. Austin, TX: Professional Associates Publishing.

Figure 2.10: HANDWRITING

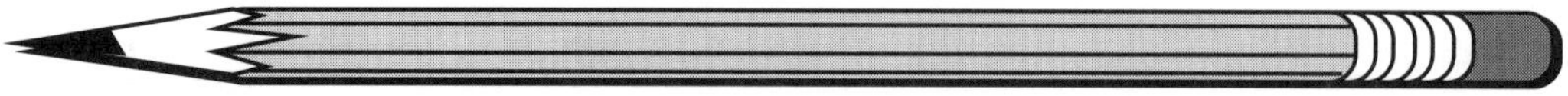

This is just one example of how my writing is very neat and legible. I am quickly developing into an amazing writer!

NAME _____ DATE _____

_____
_____
_____
_____
_____
_____
_____

NAME _____ DATE _____

_____
_____
_____
_____
_____
_____

- Creates a concept map organizing the concepts and relationships known and understood at the beginning and the end of a topic or a reporting period.
- Writes and completes the hardest math story problem the student knows that applies current math concepts and processes.
- Composes writing samples, possibly focusing on different types of writing, such as narrative, persuasive, or expository. Periodically, each student rereads writing samples and composes a comparative essay reflecting upon the changes in the student's writing and which class experiences or personal efforts have been the greatest influence on the student's writing.
- Poses context applications or illustrates key terms related to a specific topic.
- Develops written explanations of how to complete a process, such as a science experiment or math problem.
- Incorporates learning logs in math, science, and history.
- Draws a flow chart of a process or sequence.
- Records a videotape showing and explaining a history fair or science fair entry.

These two suggestions simplify the use of repeated tasks.

1. Put repeated tasks in a plain manila folder. Store it in front of the portfolio container so these tasks are easier to find for repeated completions.
2. Use colored paper to highlight the location of repeated tasks. Have the second completion of that task done on the back of the same paper to make the comparisons of growth more obvious.

AUDIO AND VIDEO TAPING

Oral Reading

Audio or videotapes are useful as repeated tasks with fiction or nonfiction text to concretely demonstrate students' oral reading progress over time. Reading samples are periodically recorded by students and then compared to determine students' progress. Each student uses the Book Taping Log on Figure 2.11 to keep a record of the recordings. This process enables the teacher and student to analyze the patterns of the student's response to text in decoding, construction of meaning, fluency, vocabulary, and the complexity of the reading material.

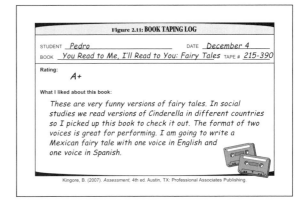

Figure 2.11: BOOK TAPING LOG

STUDENT _Pedro_   DATE _December 4_
BOOK _You Read to Me, I'll Read to You: Fairy Tales_ TAPE # _215-390_

Rating: _A+_

What I liked about this book:

These are very funny versions of fairy tales. In social studies we read versions of Cinderella in different countries so I picked up this book to check it out. The format of two voices is great for performing. I am going to write a Mexican fairy tale with one voice in English and one voice in Spanish.

Kingore, B. (2007). *Assessment*, 4th ed. Austin, TX: Professional Associates Publishing.

Prompts

FICTION TEXT
- *Read the whole book if it can be read in three minutes.*
- *Choose a significant event or key part of the story to read and share with a classmate.*
- *Read the turning point of the book.*

NONFICTION
- *Prepare and record excerpts which reveal the most significant concepts.*
- *Read excerpts that denote the main ideas of this material.*
- *Focus on reading excerpts from the beginning, middle, and end of the text to organize a summary.*

Kingore, B. (2007). *Assessment,* 4th ed. Austin, TX: Professional Associates Publishing.

Time

- Allow approximately three minutes for each recording.
- A timer works well as simple time management tool.

Math Story Problems

TAPE RECORDED STORY PROBLEM

To keep students actively engaged in understanding and computing story problems, periodically ask students to create and record story problems related to the concepts or operations currently being studied. The student uses Figure 2.12 to keep a record of this repeated task.

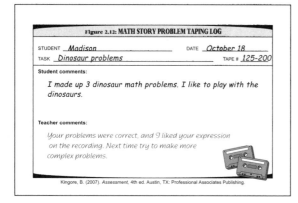

Figure 2.12: MATH STORY PROBLEM TAPING LOG

STUDENT _Madison_   DATE _October 18_
TASK _Dinosaur problems_   TAPE # _125-200_

Student comments:

I made up 3 dinosaur math problems. I like to play with the dinosaurs.

Teacher comments:

Your problems were correct, and I liked your expression on the recording. Next time try to make more complex problems.

Kingore, B. (2007). *Assessment*, 4th ed. Austin, TX: Professional Associates Publishing.

Prompts

- *Using these plastic dinosaurs, create different story problems that equal nine.*
- *Use these circle fraction tiles to create different story problems about groups of people trying to share one pizza.*
- *Use this button collection to create different story problems comparing the ratio of one kind of button to others.*

Time

- Encourage more extensive thinking by not timing students' planning.
- Using a timer, allow approximately three minutes to record each story problem.

WRITTEN STORY PROBLEM

Students can also write original math story problems. Figure 2.13 outlines a format for students to create and solve a story problem that includes the student, family, or friends. After completion, peers read, solve, and evaluate each other's problems. This interactive feedback guides students' development of strategies and concepts.

A videotape is an excellent way to record large displays. After the science fair or history fair, for example, allow students to videotape their display as they briefly explain their main ideas. Use a timer to limit students' performance time and encourage students to carefully plan what they want to include on the recording.

Ask students to bring a videotape from home for school recordings. The same tape becomes a school-life video and can be used for several years if recorded segments are kept to a brief recording time. Parents are very excited when they later receive the school-life videos.

Kingore, B. (2007). *Assessment,* 4th ed. Austin, TX: Professional Associates Publishing.

Figure 2.11: BOOK TAPING LOG

STUDENT _____   DATE _____

BOOK _____   TAPE # _____

Rating:

What I liked about this book:

Kingore, B. (2007). *Assessment,* 4th ed. Austin, TX: Professional Associates Publishing.

Figure 2.12: MATH STORY PROBLEM TAPING LOG

STUDENT _____   DATE _____

TASK _____   TAPE # _____

Student comments:

Teacher comments:

Kingore, B. (2007). *Assessment,* 4th ed. Austin, TX: Professional Associates Publishing.

Figure 2.13: MATH STORY PROBLEM

STUDENT _____   DATE _____

MATH CONCEPT OR SKILL _____

1. Write the most complex math story problem you can that uses this math concept or skill and includes you, your family, or at least one of your friends.

2. On the back of this form, solve the problem and draw a graphic or illustration.

3. Check each item below when you complete it. The problem:
    - ❏ Uses the math concept or skill listed at the top.
    - ❏ Includes you, your family, or your friends.
    - ❏ Lists the equation.
    - ❏ Is written in complete sentences.
    - ❏ Includes a solution.
    - ❏ Includes an illustration or graphic.

4. Have another student read your story problem, solve it without looking on the back, and then write an evaluation of your story problem.

    STUDENT _____   DATE _____

    Circle a Rating: *(LOW)* **1 • 2 • 3 • 4 • 5** *(HIGH)*

    EVALUATION:

Kingore, B. (2007). *Assessment,* 4th ed. Austin, TX: Professional Associates Publishing.

TRIPLETS

The triplet technique developed in response to a problem experienced by many teachers and students when using the portfolio to conference with parents. Often, the parents became so interested in the portfolio that they wanted to discuss every product. That process took more time than typically planned for parent conferences or student-involved conferences. Thus, the teacher and/or student need to pre-plan which products to emphasize in a parent conference rather than attempt to review the entire portfolio.

A triplet is a set of three products that the student or teacher selects from the student's portfolio in advance of the conference. The purpose of the triplet is to demonstrate the main instructional point that the parent needs to understand. For example, a product from the beginning, middle, and end of the year is selected to substantiate the student's growth throughout the year. Or, three products typical of the special needs or behaviors that the student is demonstrating are selected. During the conference, the teacher or student uses the triplet as concrete documentation to focus the interactive discussion. Inform the parent about other scheduled times when students can share their portfolios with their families so the portfolio can be reviewed more often than just during a conference

TRIPLET EXAMPLES

Primary and Elementary
Three products are selected by the teacher to focus on a significant instructional point about a student's achievements.

Upper Elementary, Middle School, and High School
Each student chooses three products to respond to the questions: *What should your portfolio tell me about your achievements?*

What products can you use to show an employer your special talents and skills?

When products are taken out of the portfolio, someone has to refile them, and it takes time to get them back in exactly the same place. When conferencing with a particular item, avoid the refiling problem by using a sticky note as a flag on the edge of that selected product. Now the teacher or student can quickly turn to each product when ready to discuss it and never take it out of the storage sequence.

Portfolios are not collections of best works. They are documentations of learning.

FROM TEACHER TO TEACHER: WORDS OF EXPERIENCE

Teachers across the nation shared advice, support, and ideas for simplicity. This section presents a composite of some of the most frequent suggestions from teachers in elementary through high school who implemented portfolios and authentic assessment.

One surprise for me is how few discipline problems I have encountered. In each of the three years I have used portfolios, I believe my

Kingore, B. (2007). *Assessment,* 4th ed. Austin, TX: Professional Associates Publishing.

Student-Managed Portfolios

students felt more successful because they were able to see the changes in their own learning. That truly motivates them to try harder, and they spend less time off-task in class.

Portfolios are a self-esteem boost for the special-needs students in my inclusion class. They see they are doing better each time we review the portfolio products.

I assess portfolio products to assure that a level of depth and complexity is reached that is appropriate for my advanced-level students. Their products can demonstrate and document all their areas of giftedness.

We began by collecting work for seven weeks before we stopped to have students select items for their portfolios. We were avoiding the selection process because we were not sure what we were doing. But waiting that long produced a gigantic mess! Our message to teachers is to plan your portfolio system and put your whole organization system to work from the start.

Rather than feel as if you have to do it all, plan for the year and set realistic goals for yourself according to your level of experience with portfolios (beginner, intermediate, or advanced).

I've learned that students inevitably achieve at higher levels when they are aware of the assessment criteria before they begin the assignment.

Conferences are more successful when students are prepared for the questions to be discussed during the conference. Give students a sample of questions to think about prior to conference time so they have time to reflect.

Our team found out that the students or teachers did not do goal setting, product selection, and reflection if we did not schedule it. We had to set aside specific times to address those issues.

Use rolling files for students' accessibility to portfolios in your classroom. They can be moved easily about the room as needed.

Authentic assessment has significantly influenced the way I teach. I find myself watching more intently and informally questioning students more about their process.

When students survey their collection of work to select a piece for their portfolio, you get a clear view of your teaching priorities and the kinds of learning tasks you've been providing. I'm a better teacher because I am using the portfolio for my assessment, too.

Authentic assessment has taught me to trust students more. They really do care about succeeding when the learning experiences are relevant and when they understand how to be successful.

Keep all of the supplies most often needed for portfolios, such as a stapler, date stamp, scissors, and forms, in a central area or with your portfolio filing system.

I think one of the most amazing things to me was how supportive the parents have been. They seem really impressed with what their kids know about their own learning.

Most of our first year, we just kept worrying if we were doing it all right. Our advice is to relax and learn along with the students what parts work best in your classes.

One of the most significant changes in my middle school students since using portfolios is the increased value they place on their own learning. They definitely express more ownership in projects and assessment criteria.

Kingore, B. (2007). *Assessment,* 4th ed. Austin, TX: Professional Associates Publishing.

• CHAPTER 3 •
Assessing Young Children

The major purpose of early childhood assessment is to guide and improve instructional practice while providing a means of understanding how young children are developing competence.

—Lorrie Shepard, Sharon Kagan, & Emily Wurtz

Assessment of young children is most valid when it works in concert with high-quality learning experiences that support children's active engagement, elicit their perspectives on learning, and teach standards of quality.[24] The assessment priority in early childhood classrooms, then, is for teachers Is to assess what is happening in the classroom and how to change things to better support children's learning. To ensure a more complete picture of the developing child, educators seek ways to balance any standardized test data with authentic assessment procedures reflecting the whole child—emotionally, socially, and physically as well as academically.[25] Hence, it is paramount to collect multifaceted, evidence-based data that increases understanding and guides decision-making regarding the many aspects of young children's readiness and modes of learning.[26] Effective and efficient methods of assessment and evaluation of young learners include analytical observation, student-managed portfolios incorporating repeated learning tasks, and rubrics that simplify the required level of reading and writing. These authentic assessments produce classroom-based evidence of learning that is tied to experiences in which children play, engage in conversations, and construct meaning.[27]

ANALYTICAL OBSERVATION

Early childhood teachers understand the importance of classroom observation. Since young children are more limited in their verbal ability to explain their learning and in their written ability to express themselves, teachers continually analyze children's behaviors to interpret what they see occurring in learning situations. Observations and interpretations of the nuances of children's behaviors

---

[24] High/Scope Educational Research Foundation, 2005; NAEYC & NAECS/SDE, 2003; Potter, 1999.
[25] Noddings, 2005.
[26] NAEYC & NAECS/SDE, 2003; NCTM & NAEYC, 2002.
[27] Jones, 2003.

Kingore, B. (2007). *Assessment,* 4th ed. Austin, TX: Professional Associates Publishing.

during authentic learning experiences enable teachers to substantiate students' capabilities and potential. Analytical observation helps define children's prior knowledge, levels of development, acquired proficiencies, learning needs, and the multiple facets of their talents and potential.

Observation is a valued preassessment tool. It helps guide teachers' decisions regarding the most appropriate instructional pace for specific children and at which levels to initiate instruction.

Analytical observation enables teachers to assess the *process* of children's learning as well as the products they produce. Particularly with young children, the process of learning reveals much about their level of understanding. In fact, there are times when the process is as important as the product in assessing children's achievements and learning needs.

As teachers observe, they verbally interact with their children to elicit the children's perceptions of learning. Numerous inquiry probes, such as *Tell me about your picture*, enable teachers to gain information as children are engaged in learning situations. Examples of inquiry probes effective with young children are included in Chapter 7. The values of analytical observation, what teachers attempt to observe, and how to document observations to share with others are additional aspects of observation explored in Chapter 7.

STUDENT-MANAGED PORTFOLIOS

A productive perspective of portfolios with young children views the child as an active participant and the teacher as a facilitator establishing an effective, child-involved portfolio system. Keep the organization and management process simple enough that children can maintain most of the portfolio themselves, thereby freeing teachers from additional paper management. Children significantly involved in the management of their portfolios are more likely to experience pride and ownership in their work.

Objectives

The portfolio process and the student-management of portfolios expand as the maturity of children develops. The intent of portfolios with prekindergarten, kindergarten, and first-grade children is to initiate the process by involving students in collecting and organizing significant samples of work so they can concretely view evidence of their learning growth and celebrate their learning achievements. As children mature, their involvement and responsibilities in the portfolio process increase. The portfolio objectives for young children and their families are explained in Figure 3.1.

Beginning the Process

Portfolios for young children can be relatively small and yet provide a tremendous source of pride for children and families. Plan about a one-fourth to one-half inch thickness as the total size per portfolio for the year. Young children produce fewer paper products since much of the learning completed by this age group is process oriented. Thus, the teacher, and later the child and the teacher, simply plans to select one product every two or three weeks that children file in their portfolios as documentation of their learning and changes.

Introduce the process by making portfolios as concrete as possible to enable the children to understand what portfolios are and

Figure 3.1:
PORTFOLIO OBJECTIVES FOR EARLY CHILDHOOD

1. Enhance self-concept

As young children review their portfolios and see products to compare over time, they realize that their skills are increasing. They feel important and successful.

2. Organize and manage

A simple but clearly structured portfolio system helps children learn how to organize, manage, and maintain their work.

3. Document learning standards, growth, and achievement

Portfolios document learning standards and growth by substantiating children's increased integration of concepts and skills.[28]

4. Guide instruction

The work children produce substantiates their levels of readiness and potential. Teachers interpret this information to support children's learning and to guide and improve instructional practice.

5. Celebrate learning and share information with others

Children review their portfolios to acknowledge their learning accomplishments. These products promote children's celebrations of learning and provide a communication tool to share evidence of progress with family, teachers, and peers informally or through student-involved conferences.

become excited about creating their own. Show them a portfolio book from last year's class or put together a collection of children's work to create a mock-up of how their portfolios may look. Explain to them that they will take many papers home to show their family but keep a few papers at school to combine into a wonderful book to amaze their family at the end of the year.

Have an adult visitor such as a parent or the principal talk with the class about how wonderful it will be to have this portfolio book at the end of the year. Discuss together how the children can look back through their portfolios when they are older and remember this year of school and the important things they learned.

Some teachers successfully involve young children in the entire process from the start. Other teachers reported that prekindergarten and kindergarten children had difficulty making selections and dictating captions early in the year. They also noted that it takes extensive time to complete the selection and reflection process. Thus, when the difficulties outweigh the benefits, the teacher initially determines which products go in the portfolios. As soon as appropriate, increase children's role in the process so they reap the benefits of self-esteem and ownership while adults benefit from understanding the child's perspective.

Parent support is vital for young children. Teachers report that parents do not always understand the instructional objectives inherent in the products young students complete. To compensate for this communication problem, teachers complete a teacher product selection caption, such as Figure 3.2, and duplicate it for children to staple on their

[28] Chapter 9 includes examples of procedures that directly relate learning standards to student reflections.

Kingore, B. (2007). *Assessment,* 4th ed. Austin, TX: Professional Associates Publishing.

product. This information enables parents to understand the learning task and skills represented within that product.

Figure 3.2: TEACHER PRODUCT SELECTION

NAME: Joan   DATE: Sept. 3

The task was *to draw a picture of your family and tell me about the picture.*

The skills demonstrated by this task were:
- *Fine motor coordination* · *Awareness of features*
- *Vocabulary*
- *Sentence structure.*

Kingore, B. (2007). *Assessment,* 4th ed. Austin, TX: Professional Associates Publishing.

After the teacher or child has selected a product to save in the portfolio, the children write their names on the caption strips. Any stage of scribbling or creative spelling can communicate that child's name as long as it is recognizable to the child! The children's ability to write their names on the teacher selection caption serves as another repeated task since their writing growth will be obvious as the year progresses. If not already on the product, children also need to write the date to record when the product was completed. A date stamp is easily used, or most children can copy the number for the date if it is provided for them on the chalkboard.

Which Products Best Document Young Students' Abilities?

As stated in Chapter 2, a portfolio is an integral reflection of the curriculum and what children learn rather than a random collection of activities and isolated skills. Attention to authentic and meaningful learning tasks is a crucial consideration in selecting products.

Figure 3.2: TEACHER PRODUCT SELECTION

NAME: _____   DATE: _____

The task was _____

_____

_____

_____

_____

The skills demonstrated by this task were:

- _____   · _____

- _____   · _____

- _____   · _____

Kingore, B. (2007). *Assessment,* 4th ed. Austin, TX: Professional Associates Publishing.

Figure 3.3: POTENTIAL PORTFOLIO PRODUCTS FOR YOUNG CHILDREN

PRODUCT	EXPLANATION	PURPOSE
Art	Art pieces should include the child's natural, creative explorations and interpretations (rather than crafts).	Art reflects developmental levels, interests, graphic talents, abstract thinking, perspective, and creativity.
Audiotapes	A child tapes retellings, explanations of concepts, musical creations, problem solutions, ideas, oral reading, and reports.	Audio tapes verify vocabulary, fluency, creativity, high-order thinking, information, and concept depth.
Computer products	A student uses a computer to document computer skills, apply software, and create word processing products.	Computer-generated products indicate computer literacy, content-related academic skills, analysis, and applied concepts.
Dictations	An adult or older child writes a child's dictated explanation of a product or process. Prompt these dictations with statements such as: *Tell me about your work,* or *Tell me how you did that.*	Dictations increase adults' understanding of the why and how of what children do. It elicits perspective, vocabulary, sentence complexity, high-level thinking, fluency, and content depth.
Graphs or charts	Some children produce graphs or charts to represent relationships, formulate problems, illustrate math solutions, and demonstrate the results of independent investigations.	Graphs or charts demonstrate specific skills or concepts applied in the task, high-level thinking, data recording strategies, and organizational skills.
Photographs	A photograph is a record of a child's math patterns, creative projects, dioramas, sculptures, constructions, experiments, models, or organizational systems.	Photographs represent three-dimensional products and processes. They provide a record when no paper product is feasible.
Reading level	An adult duplicates text that a child reads independently. Include the child's reflection of the text to demonstrate analysis skills.	Text samples authentically document reading level and a child's sophistication when interpreting written material.
Research and individual investigation	Research investigations are student-initiated and respond to individual interests to find information.	Research products reveal specific interests, synthesis, content depth, and the complexity of a learner's thinking.
Videotapes	Video tapes document performing arts, learning process, and oversized products.	A video is a significant visual record of the integration of skills and behaviors. It can demonstrate interpersonal and leadership skills during group work.
Written products	Original works written by a student document learning progress and levels. Include stories, reports, scientific observations, poems, letters, and reflections.	Written products demonstrate language skills, thinking, organization, meaning construction, concept depth, complexity, and handwriting development.

Adapted from: Kingore, B., Ed. (2002). *Reading Strategies for Advanced Primary Readers.* Austin: Texas Education Agency.

Assessing Young Children

Kingore, B. (2007). *Assessment,* 4th ed. Austin, TX: Professional Associates Publishing.

Many preschool and primary teachers voice concern about what to put in portfolios because so much of their children's learning does not result in a paper and pencil product. Figure 3.3 describes potential products that are effective in the portfolios of young children. The list is meant to prompt ideas of the wide range of appropriate products and is not inclusive of all of the kinds of work that could be selected.

Repeated Tasks that Accent Learning

The learning demonstrated by young children is often subtle and may evolve slowly. Preschool and primary teachers need specific products in portfolios that concretely validate students' growth or change in skills and achievements. Several repeated tasks are discussed in this chapter as elaborations of tasks listed in Chapter 2. To maximize the value of a repeated task, the task must first be completed early in the year and then repeated later. The contrast of the two or three repetitions documents the students' growth to the children, families, and educators.

Repeated tasks are an excellent preassessment tool. Students complete tasks the first time to provide information to the teacher regarding levels of readiness and at what level to initiate instruction. Background knowledge, beginning literacy, and fine motor coordination are particularly evident from these assessments. These beginning repeated tasks are filed in the portfolio. Later, each task is repeated one or more times and the results compared to document growth and continued learning needs.

THREE-MINUTE CELEBRATIONS

After completing a repeated task, children compare both tasks. During an approximately three-minute celebration, children are encouraged to tell one other person what they notice and how they feel about the two task results.

CHILD'S SELF PORTRAIT

Each child illustrates a picture of self. These portraits reveal a wide range of readiness levels from scribbles to fairly refined human figures. Children complete these drawings at the beginning and the end of the year, or more frequently, to illustrate the child's development of fine motor skills, perspective, and self-image. To increase assessment potential, have children write or dictate a sentence or more about the picture. This addition indicates syntactic complexity, fluency, vocabulary, thinking levels, and feelings.

FAMILY PORTRAIT

Each child draws a picture portraying family members. These pictures can indicate children's awareness of their surrounding environment, size perspectives, and understanding of the individual identity of family members. It provides information to teachers about each child's home environment and whom they consider as members of their family, even when it includes an extended family member or favorite pet! To indicate syntactic complexity, fluency, vocabulary, thinking levels, and feelings, ask children to write or dictate a sentence or more about the picture.

PICTURE INTEREST INVENTORY

A picture interest inventory collects data about young children's preferences and learning interests by incorporating illustrations

Kingore, B. (2007). *Assessment,* 4th ed. Austin, TX: Professional Associates Publishing.

and words. Assessing interests is important because children's motivation to achieve may increase when interests are incorporated in learning experiences. Create two drawing areas by folding large pieces of paper in half. Ask students to draw pictures of their favorite things on one half and illustrate what they are interested in learning at school on the second half. Encourage children to write words and sentences about their pictures while an adult writes dictations as needed. Incorporate this information about children's interests in instructional planning. For example, expand the changes theme to include camouflage in nature because several children are highly interested in animals. For very young children or those with shorter attention spans, each half may be completed at a different time. Simply fold the paper so only the half they are to draw on is exposed. With older children or those with more mature skills, vary the task by folding the paper into four or even six boxes. Children then have an opportunity to illustrate and write words or sentences about multiple things that are favorites and that they want to learn more about at school.

AUDIO TAPE THE RETELLING OF A FOLK TALE

Individually, using each student's personal audiotape, record the child retelling a well-known folk tale such as "Little Red Riding Hood". This process takes two or three minutes for each child, and results in an authentic measurement of oral language development, comprehension, fluency, and sequence for both native language speakers and English language learners when the same folk tale is recorded at the beginning and then again at the end of the year. Begin each entry on the tape by stating the date and the task: *Today is September 27, and Jasmine is going to tell the story of Little Red Riding Hood.* Young readers also use the tape to record reading samples of both fiction and nonfiction once a month or so to document independent reading level.

DRAWING GEOMETRIC SHAPES

Drawing geometric shapes incorporates the same fine motor skills and directionality that is needed to print letters and numerals Provide large paper folded into fourths. Using a progress of shapes from simple to more complex, such as X, circle, triangle, and diamond, dictate a different shape for each child to draw in each of the four boxes to measure fine motor skills, awareness of shapes, and readiness for writing between lines.

LOOK WHAT I CAN DO BOOKS OR ACHIEVEMENT LOGS

Look What I Can Do Books or Achievement Logs are appealing books that children produce to demonstrate mastery of grade-level learning standards. When completed at the beginning, middle, and end of the year, these books document the progress toward acquisition of required learning standards and become a concrete communication device for children to share with families, peers, and educators. Use copies of the blank half of Figure 3.4 or Figure 3.5 to form the pages of the book. On each page, list a different skill for children to demonstrate. The skills should be the most significant skills relative to yearlong grade-level learning objectives. Review your learning standards and focus on the skills students are to master by the end of the year, such as alphabet letters, words, numerals, math story problems, and geometric shapes. The top half of Figure 3.4 or 3.5 becomes the title page when the book is stapled together. Children enjoy making these books and look forward to repeating the task. Plan for children to complete the book at the beginning, middle, and end of the year to document skills and achievements.

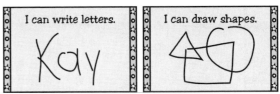

Kingore, B. (2007). *Assessment,* 4th ed. Austin, TX: Professional Associates Publishing.

Assessing Young Children

Figure 3.4: LOOK WHAT I CAN DO

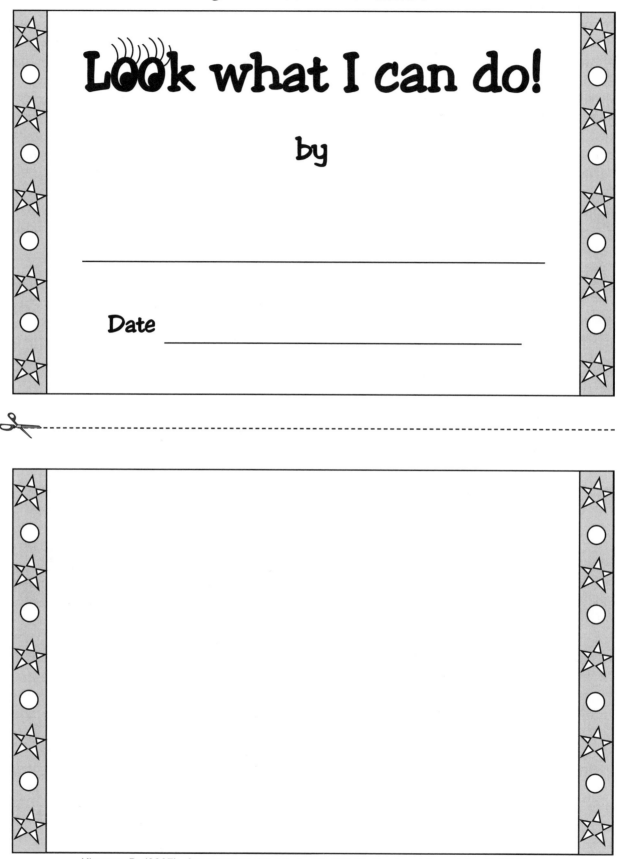

Figure 3.5: ACHIEVEMENT LOG

Achievement Log

NAME _____

DATES _____ TO _____

✂- -

DATE _____

Kingore, B. (2007). *Assessment,* 4th ed. Austin, TX: Professional Associates Publishing.

Teaching Young Students to Manage Portfolios

Most teachers affirm that young children can successfully complete much of the management of their own products when teachers organize the portfolio process in a developmentally appropriate manner. A plastic crate with hanging files is an appropriate choice for portfolios that young children manage. On each hanging file, write a child's name and staple that child's photograph to the portfolio so it extends above the top of the file and is easily seen. Using photographs on each file allows young children to file their own work in their portfolio even if they cannot recognize their written names. Many children enjoy completing their own filing; apparently it makes them feel competent and important.

If student photographs are needed, a digital camera is the easiest means of developing these photos. However, if one is not available, limit the expense of the photographs by using a panoramic camera with film that allows you to include three to five children in one close-up photograph. After the film is developed, create a template pattern so the cutout size of each child's head will be the same on each portfolio.

Make small photographs sturdier by stapling each photo to a popsicle stick and then stapling the stick to a hanging file so the photo extends above the top of the file.

Chronological organization is simplest for young students. Teach children to slide the products forward in their portfolio file and place their newest selections in the back of their portfolio so products remain in chronological order. As students file a product, they see their earlier work and experience a concrete reminder of their learning accomplishments.

As a more concrete process, role-play filing papers into a portfolio container. Exaggerate the action of sliding the products forward in the file to make room to place the newest work in the back of the folder. Share with the children that they will be filing papers just as older students and adults file work.

Create an atmosphere of celebration as children file their first products for the portfolios. Prepare simple notes such as Figure 3.6 to send home and communicate this important beginning to families. Provide a copy of the note for each child; students draw their faces to show how they feel and then write their names at the bottom of the note.

Increasing Young Students' Role in Portfolio Management

Significant benefits result for children when they increase their role in selection and reflection. They assume more ownership in their work, engage in high-level thinking as they analyze choices, and begin developing self-assessment skills. They are also initiating more individual responsibility and the organization and management skills that all students need to develop to be successful.

When appropriate for the children, involve them in product selection. To introduce them to the process, collect two products for each child. Provide a simple caption card, such as one of the samples in Figure 3.7 that states the criterion for children to think about for the two products. Meet with the children, usually in small groups but individually if pre-ferred, and ask each child to choose one of the products. Then, children write their names, plus additional words and illustrations as they wish, on the caption card and staple it to their product while they wait turns to file the product in their portfolio.

This procedure is continued until children are ready to increase their role by selecting from three or more products at a time. For this step, narrow the choices to related products, such as three math papers, to prevent children from feeling overwhelmed by choice. State a positive criterion to structure their thinking: *Select a product and tell something new you learned.* After several successful experiences, increase the frequency and responsibility of children's selection and reflection. Young writers can begin to write more on their captions cards and teachers can add elaborations dictated by those children not ready to write more. Big Buddies are also

useful as scribes to assist children in record-ing or embellishing their reflections.

Set the goal that by the second half of first grade, portfolio selection and reflection are thoroughly incorporated as an authentic high-level thinking and writing task each week. At this point, children select a product for their portfolios every week, have opportunities to share and discuss it with peers during the process, and then complete their reflection as an authentic writing task incorporating rich vocabulary and more than one sentence.

Duplicate the four sample caption cards on Figure 3.7. Then, cut them apart and use one at a time. The cards allow a comfort-able space for children to write their names or sentence reflections without worrying about exact letter formation between handwriting lines. The picture prompts on each card help children understand what the criterion states and how to respond.

Figure 3.6: PORTFOLIO FILING NOTE

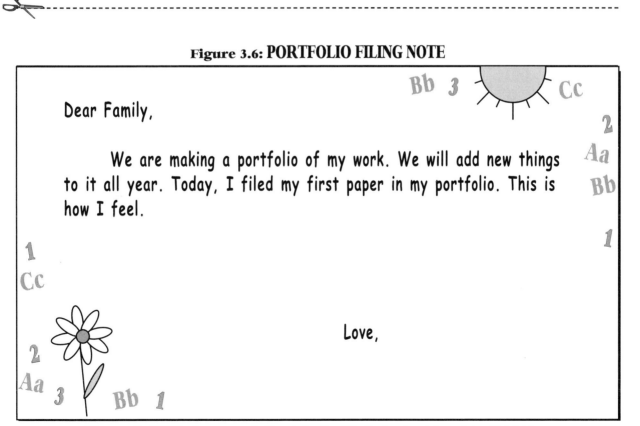

Kingore, B. (2007). *Assessment,* 4th ed. Austin, TX: Professional Associates Publishing.

Figure 3.7: CAPTIONS: FOUR CAPTION CARDS

NAME _____

DATE _____

I am proud of this!

NAME _____

DATE _____

Aha!

I learned something new!

NAME _____

DATE _____

I used my brain!

NAME _____

DATE _____

I liked doing this!

A second version of caption cards combines cutting and pasting skills with students' reflections (Figure 3.8). Students are given one strip of faces and asked to cut out the face that shows how they feel about their work. Students then paste that face on a caption card.

Avoid using *best work* as a criterion for prekindergarten through first grade students. It is very judgmental, and young children are generally not ready to compare or contrast to determine what is best. The words *best work* lead children to rely upon adults and ask what *they* think is best or to only select products with high grades. Children react more comfortably to criteria such as those on the captions shared in this chapter.

In kindergarten and first-grade, teachers use selection and reflection as a small-group language arts activity during the week when selection occurs. The teacher works with one group each day to record those children's dictations. The teacher encourages discussion and productive interaction by prompting children's thinking with inquiry probes and statements.[29]

> *Tell me about your work.*
> *Tell me more so I understand your thinking.*
> *How did you figure this out?*
> *What did you learn by doing this?*
> *What do you like about this product?*
> *What was hard to do?*

As the teacher takes dictations from one student, the others can talk with each other about their work and complete caption cards. This procedure enables the teacher to individualize instruction and complete a few reflections each day instead of working with a whole class at one time.

Some children are certainly capable of using temporary or inventive spelling to write their own captions. Use the caption cards and encourage those children to write their reason for selecting a product or what they think is important about their product. Figures 3.9A and 3.9B are designed flexibly so students can check a response and/or write a response using the handwriting lines or without the handwriting lines. The choice is important because teachers report better success for some children when they use caption cards without lines.

Young children get excited about their portfolios and frequently ask if it is time to file their work! Create a small picture that represents the portfolios, such as the ones shared in the Containers and the Collection Files section of Chapter 2. Taping that picture on the appropriate date on your class calendar shows children when it is time for product selection and filing.

A Portfolio Management Center

Some teachers find it useful to incorporate a portfolio center into the room. The center is a small desk, table, or countertop that stores the portfolios and supplies needed to complete additions to portfolios, including copies of caption cards, pencils, and a stapler. A portfolio poster, such as Figure 3.10, guides children as they work at the center to independently complete reflections and filing.

[29] Additional inquiry prompts for young children are included in Chapter 7.

Kingore, B. (2007). *Assessment,* 4th ed. Austin, TX: Professional Associates Publishing.

Figure 3.8: CAPTIONS: THIS IS HOW I FEEL ABOUT MY WORK

Figure 3.9A: CAPTIONS: CHECK BOXES

NAME _____ DATE _____

I wanted to put this in my portfolio because:
- ❑ I am proud of my work.
- ❑ I took time and thought hard.

Kingore, B. (2007). *Assessment,* 4th ed. Austin, TX: Professional Associates Publishing.

Figure 3.9B: CAPTIONS: CHECK BOXES

NAME _____ DATE _____

I wanted to put this in my portfolio because:
- ❑ I am proud of my work.
- ❑ I took time and thought hard.

Kingore, B. (2007). *Assessment,* 4th ed. Austin, TX: Professional Associates Publishing.

Assessing Young Children

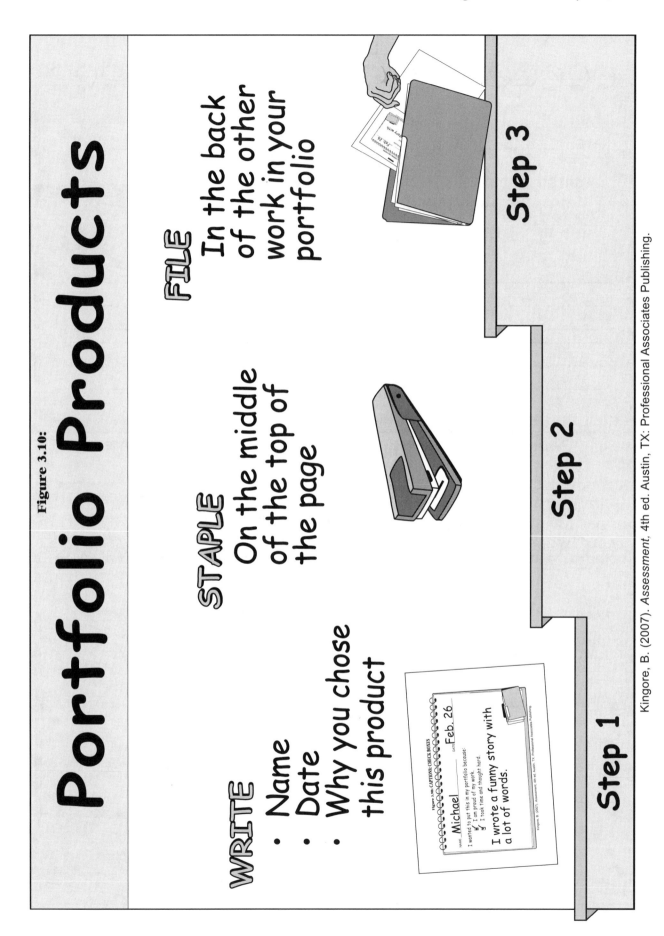

Portfolio Products

WRITE
- Name
- Date
- Why you chose this product

Step 1

STAPLE
On the middle of the top of the page

Step 2

FILE
In the back of the other work in your portfolio

Step 3

Kingore, B. (2007). *Assessment*, 4th ed. Austin, TX: Professional Associates Publishing.

BIG BUDDIES: OLDER STUDENTS AS FACILITATORS

Big Buddies is the name for a project involving older students interacting in learning situations with younger children to provide the individual attention teachers so desire for their students. Big Buddies can involve a whole classroom of older students or only a few older students at a time working in a classroom of younger students. This project affords useful assessment applications in early childhood classrooms.

Observation

As Big Buddies facilitate young students' learning experiences, the teacher is free to oversee the interactions and observe students' skill levels, skill integrations, advanced behaviors, and any special needs.

Documentation

As Big Buddies interact with the young students, the teacher writes notes or completes checklists to document children's achievements and capabilities.

Portfolio Applications

MODELING
* Big Buddies can show their portfolios to the younger children to make the portfolio process more concrete and excite those children about what a final portfolio can become.
* The Big Buddies, working one-on-one or with a small group of younger children, model how to select a product for a portfolio.

REFLECTION
* Particularly with four and five year olds, Big Buddies write the children's dictations for product captions so the younger children see their ideas expressed in print.

RUBRICS FOR YOUNG CHILDREN

Rubrics are guidelines to quality. They enable teachers to clarify to children what is expected in a learning experience and guide children to understand what to do to reach higher levels of achievement. Rubrics are also grading guides that describe the requirements for different levels of proficiency as children respond to a learning task.

Many preschool, kindergarten, and primary teachers are not using rubrics. These teachers may believe that young children cannot comprehend assessment and evaluation. However, young children obviously understand grading systems and quickly comprehend that a happy face, *A*, ✓+, or *Excellent* is what they want on their papers. Even for young children, rubrics remove the guesswork: *I guess she likes my paper,* or *I guess I didn't do very well.*

Young children benefit when they view the more specific information a rubric offers. With time and modeling, they learn to use rubrics and increase their ownership in achievement.

Effective rubrics are shared with children before they begin a task so they know the expectations and the characteristics of quality work. Well-constructed rubrics provide a clear target for which to aim. Additionally, share rubrics with parents and other adults to more clearly communicate achievement standards and students' accomplishments.

At our school, we found that using simple rubrics in kindergarten increased students' high expectations. Teachers in older grades report that children enter their classes expecting to use rubrics and self-assess their work.

Kingore, B. (2007). *Assessment,* 4th ed. Austin, TX: Professional Associates Publishing.

Characteristics of Rubrics for Young Children

Effective rubrics for young children:

- Are short; typically three or four criteria with three levels of proficiency are on one page.
- Reflect the main ideas or most significant elements related to success in a learning task.
- Provide children with information about quality rather than just a list of skills or requirements.
- Provide information more concretely through pictures and simple language.
- Are modeled with both higher and lower product examples so children can understand quality differences.
- Encourage students to set goals and self-evaluate. *To write well, I need to...*
- Enable children, parents, and teachers to accurately and consistently identify the level of competency or stage of development.
- Empower teachers with a standard by which to grade students' work more accurately, fairly, and efficiently.

A rubric increases student ownership in achievement as it increases teacher efficiency.

A Rubric for Group Assessment

Figure 3.11 is an example of a simple rubric for children to use to score their effectiveness when completing a group task. The simple words and accompanying illustrations clearly communicate the expectations of group work and are easily used by children to self-evaluate the merits of their accomplishments. The teacher fills in the clock face to concretely show children at what time they are to finish. The criteria on the left signal students what is important as they work. After modeling and guided applications as a class, small groups of children are able to use this rubric independently.

When the task is completed, children check the level they earned–cloudy for a lower level, partly cloudy, and full sun for a high degree of accomplishment. Letter or number grades can be substituted for the weather scores on the example. Then, teachers can use a different color to evaluate on the same form if a grade in the grade book is desired.

The Pictorial Rubric Generator: Tier I[30]

The Pictorial Rubric Generator is a response to teachers' requests for a concrete and simple way to communicate quality to young children and limited English students. While my original pictorial rubrics used four levels of proficiency, teachers determined during field-testing that three levels are more effective when teaching young children to reach assessment decisions. These teachers confirm that young children can ably interpret and accurately use rubrics constructed with fewer words and simple pictures.

Skim the Pictorial Rubric Generator and other collected rubrics to determine the criteria crucial to the contents, processes, and products typical for a grade level. Photocopy the applicable criteria and levels of proficiencies. Organize those criteria and degrees of success on the blank rubric page, Figure 3.12, for ease in duplication. Then, rewrite and adapt the levels as needed before pasting them in place. In this manner, adults readily construct developmentally appropriate rubrics for learning tasks without starting from scratch each time.

Endeavor to develop rubrics that are as generalizable as possible so each rubric has multiple applications. Different point values can be added to designate the importance of each criterion and the total number of points that are possible for the task. Specifically, the example pictorial rubric shared here has more points listed for information so children understand that

---

[30] See Chapter 6 for the Rubric Generator: Tier II and Tier III.

Kingore, B. (2007). *Assessment,* 4th ed. Austin, TX: Professional Associates Publishing.

Figure 3.11: GROUP ASSESSMENT

NAMES _____

_____

_____

_____

DATE _____

TASK:

Did your group?

1. Listen well?

2. Share?

3. Work together?

4. Think of your own ideas?

5. Finish on time?

Kingore, B. (2007). *Assessment,* 4th ed. Austin, TX: Professional Associates Publishing.

Developing a
Background

it is the most important criterion for this task. Teachers, and children when self-assessing, circle the points earned on each criterion and then record the total score at the bottom.[31]

Figure 3.12: PICTORIAL RUBRIC GENERATOR

NAME _____ DATE _____
TASK _____

Information	Picture	Picture and words	Picture and sentences
POINTS:	4	8	12
Detailed			
POINTS:	2	4	6
Punctuation and Capitalization	do you hear the dog he is very loud	Do you hear the dog he is very loud.	Do you hear the dog? He is very loud!
POINTS:	2	4	6
Summary	Beginning	Beginning and middle	Beginning, middle, and end
POINTS:	2	4	6
TOTAL POINTS: _____			

Kingore, B. & J. (2007). *Assessment Interactive CD-ROM*. Austin, TX: Professional Associates Publishing.

Children and/or teachers can also use a rubric before beginning a segment of instruction to assess their initial level. The same rubric is then used following instruction to evaluate growth and changes in achievements.

FROM TEACHER TO TEACHER: WORDS OF EXPERIENCE

Teachers across the nation share advice, support, and ideas to simplify the process. This section presents a composite of the most frequent suggestions from teachers in prekindergarten through first grade who implemente portfolios and authentic assessment.

I never thought kindergartners could do this.

I found that my enthusiasm for rubrics and the process was infectious to students and parents!

When conferencing with young children, put on a hat, shawl, dangally necklace or crown to signal the other children that you are not to be disturbed.

Rubrics got me lots of recognition from my administrators! They were impressed with how I had woven our districts' standards into rubrics that my students used.[32] I know that the most important value is to the children, but I did love the positive feedback I got about this!

My special education students in my mixed-ability class got a boost from their portfolios. It helped kids get over that idea that everything had only one way to be right.

Attaching students' photographs to their portfolios was a huge success with my class! It increased their independence and simplified management.

Let young students have a small number of sticky notes in their collection folder. They use a sticker to tag a paper they want in their portfolio. Then, they are ready to dictate their reflective caption to a Big Buddy or adult scribe.

Product selection for portfolios worked best with my little ones when we did it in small groups. They enjoyed the more individual attention.

Organization worked best when we used legal sized folders with kindergarten children so their larger projects fit. Legal-sized hanging files fit sideways in most plastic-crate file boxes.

---

[31] Further procedures for using rubric generators are discussed in Chapter 6.

[32] See Chapter 9 for examples of rubrics that integrate learning standards and are appropriate for young learners.

Kingore, B. (2007). *Assessment*, 4th ed. Austin, TX: Professional Associates Publishing.

Figure 3.12: PICTORIAL RUBRIC GENERATOR

NAME _____ DATE _____

TASK _____

POINTS:			
POINTS:			
POINTS:			
POINTS:			

TOTAL POINTS: _____

Kingore, B. (2007). *Assessment,* 4th ed. Austin, TX: Professional Associates Publishing.

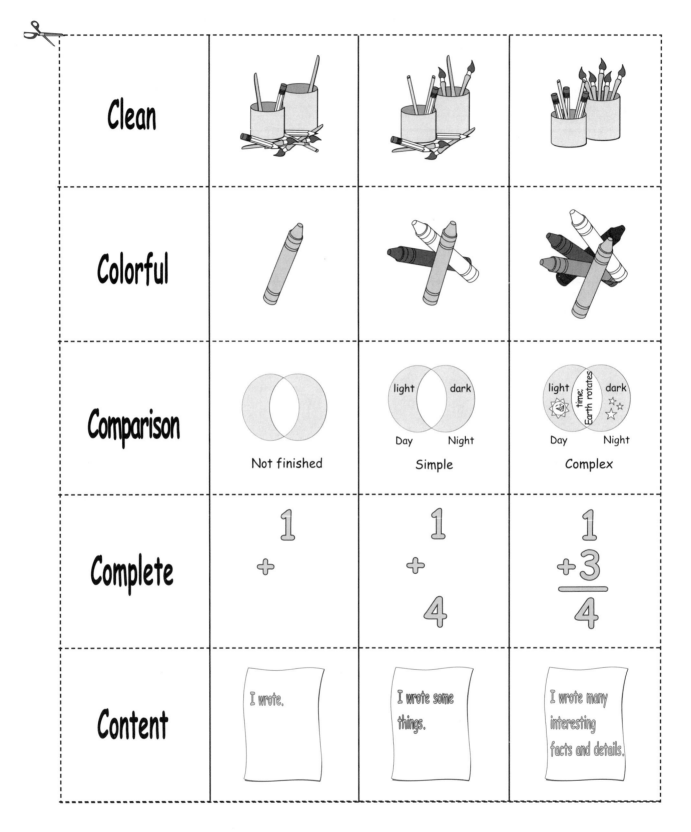

Clean			
Colorful			
Comparison	Not finished	Simple	Complex
Complete	$1 +$	$1 + 4$	$\dfrac{1 + 3}{4}$
Content	I wrote.	I wrote some things.	I wrote many interesting facts and details.

This Pictorial Rubric Generator is intended to serve as a model for developing customized rubrics. If some parts of the Pictorial Rubric Generator are appropriate, add them and rewrite any descriptors that can be better adapted to specific needs.

Kingore, B. (2007). *Assessment,* 4th ed. Austin, TX: Professional Associates Publishing.

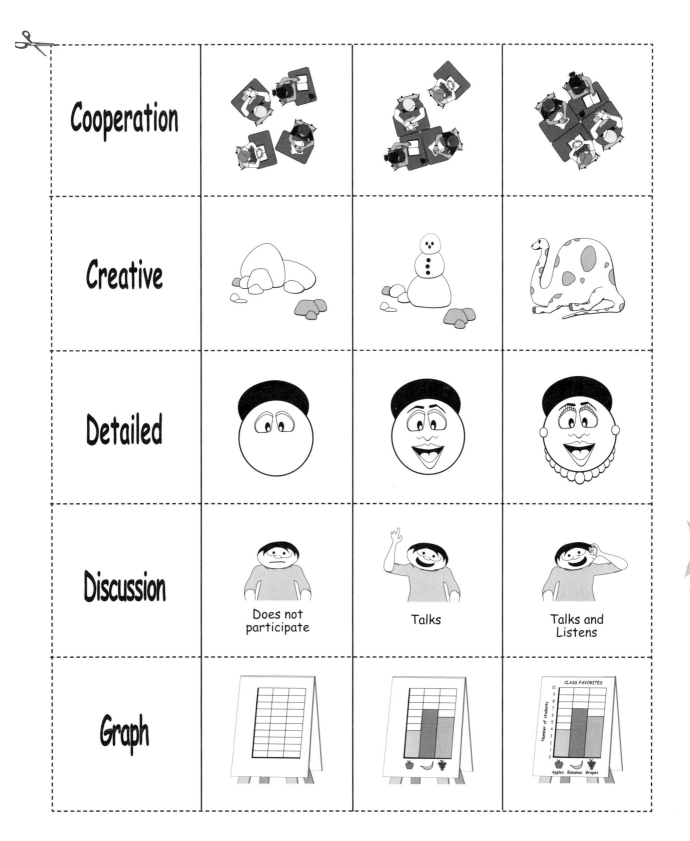

Cooperation			
Creative			
Detailed			
Discussion	Does not participate	Talks	Talks and Listens
Graph			CLASS FAVORITES Apples Bananas Grapes

Enlarge the pictures of the Pictorial Rubric Generator and create a class rubric poster for the wall instead of providing a paper copy for each child. The directions and suggestions for adapting this tool into a poster are shared in Appendix B.

Kingore, B. (2007). *Assessment,* 4th ed. Austin, TX: Professional Associates Publishing.

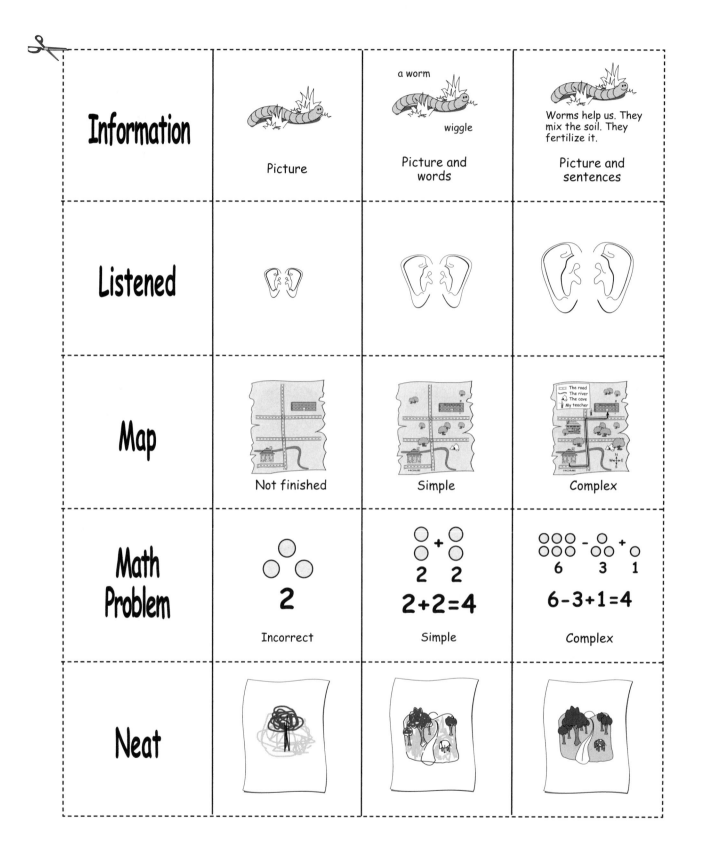

Information	Picture	Picture and words	Picture and sentences
Listened			
Map	Not finished	Simple	Complex
Math Problem	Incorrect	Simple	Complex
Neat			

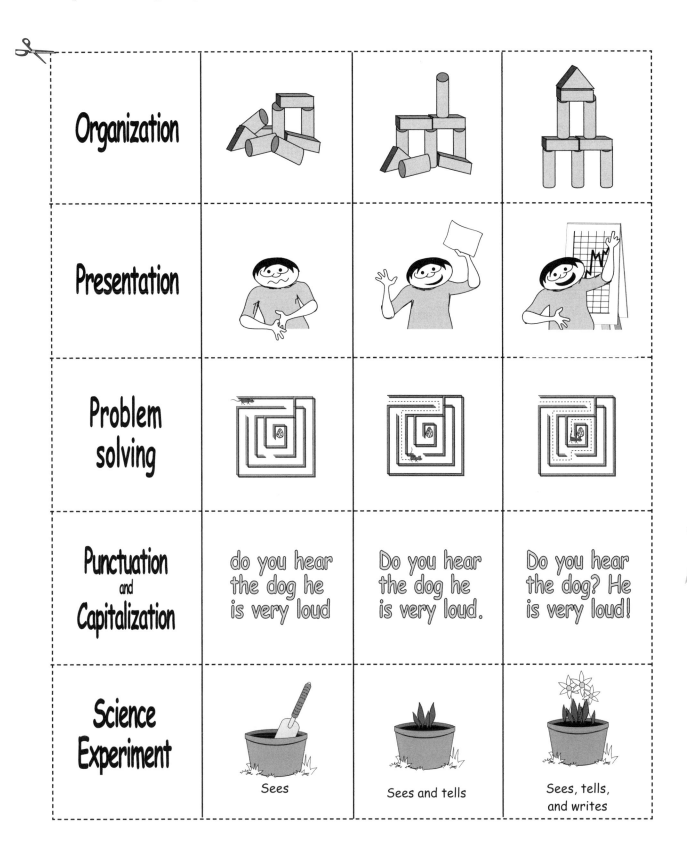

Organization			
Presentation			
Problem solving			
Punctuation and Capitalization	do you hear the dog he is very loud	Do you hear the dog he is very loud.	Do you hear the dog? He is very loud!
Science Experiment	Sees	Sees and tells	Sees, tells, and writes

Assessing Young Children

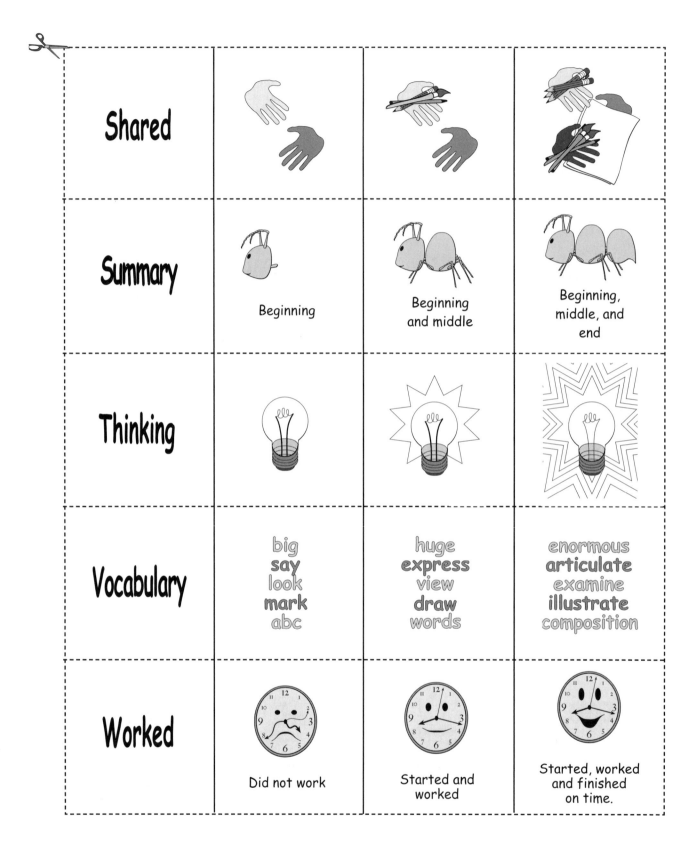

Shared			
Summary	Beginning	Beginning and middle	Beginning, middle, and end
Thinking			
Vocabulary	big say look mark abc	huge express view draw words	enormous articulate examine illustrate composition
Worked	Did not work	Started and worked	Started, worked and finished on time.

CHAPTER 4

Metacognitive Responses:
Goal Setting and Reflection

When the mind is thinking, it is talking to itself.

—Plato

METACOGNITION

Metacognition is the gear that keeps the assessment process moving meaningfully. It requires students to consciously analyze their thinking processes. Jean Kerr Stenmark (2001) noted that the capability and willingness to assess their own progress and learning is one of the greatest gifts students can develop. Those who are able to review their performance, explain the reasons for choosing processes, and identify their next step have a life-long head start.

Metacognition is related to students' ability to transfer knowledge from one situation to another. It involves two basic components.[33]

1. Students' awareness of the processes they need to successfully complete a task, and

2. Students' cognitive monitoring–the ability to determine if the task is being completed correctly and make the corrections as appropriate.

[33] Baker & Brown, 1984.
[34] Cooper & Kiger, 2005.

Use the word *think* or *thinking* often. Words reflect what is important to us, and we surely want students to value the role of thinking. Model thinking processes with students. At times, engage in *think alouds* so students understand how an adult figures something out or arrives at a decision. In this approach, teachers orally share with students their thinking process, and then encourage students to practice the cognitive technique in small groups. Think alouds must occur in a specific context to avoid the activity becoming nothing more than modeling an isolated skill.[34] Consider the following partial think-aloud as a teacher models inference skills.

As I read this paragraph, I am not sure of the subject. It is too ambiguous. After reading more, however, I realize the content is symbolic. The author is using baiting worms as a metaphor for doing something that may seem unpleasant but has an important end result. I like the idea now that I get it. In the next paragraph, the author uses comparison to...

Kingore, B. (2007). *Assessment,* 4th ed. Austin, TX: Professional Associates Publishing.

Students' metacognitive responses take the form of reflections and goal setting. These are explored throughout this chapter.

Reflective Techniques

Students' reflections express their perceptions of their learning process and achievements. Reflective thinking is the foundation of each of the techniques that follow.

> 1. *Ongoing investigative conversations and questioning*
> 2. *Captions or reflective statements*
> 3. *Metacognitive questions*
> 4. *Learning reflections*
> 5. *Reflective learning summaries*
> 6. *End-of-year reflection*
> 7. *Multiple-year reflection*

1. *Ongoing investigative conversations and questioning*

These dialogues are informal, verbal, and often spontaneous interactions between teachers and students or between small groups of students. The intent of these conversations is clarification or elaboration of the students' thinking. Teachers guide students' development of metacognitive strategies by asking questions that highlight the most important ideas, such as the inquiry probes in Chapter 7. These interactions provide a window into students' reasoning.

2. *Captions or reflective statements*

These statements are written responses students add to each product selected for the portfolio. A caption is a main idea statement. The term *caption* is used to signal students that the response can be short and should be the main idea of their analysis. Another commonly used term for this reflection is *entry slip* since it is an entry into the portfolio.

A caption is usually a separate strip of paper that is written and then stapled onto a product before it is filed in the portfolio. These reflective statements can be completed on blank paper or simple duplicated forms containing open-ended prompts. The duplicated forms simplify the captioning process because students have less to write to complete each response. Having less to write is particularly helpful with students for whom handwriting is slow and laborious or for students who view handwriting as punitive.

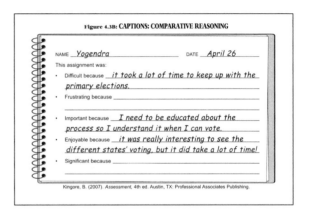

Figure 4.3B: CAPTIONS: COMPARATIVE REASONING

NAME *Yogendra*   DATE *April 26*
This assignment was:
- Difficult because *it took a lot of time to keep up with the primary elections.*
- Frustrating because _____
- Important because *I need to be educated about the process so I understand it when I can vote.*
- Enjoyable because *it was really interesting to see the different states' voting, but it did take a lot of time!*
- Significant because _____

Kingore, B. (2007). *Assessment*, 4th ed. Austin, TX: Professional Associates Publishing.

Many teachers request copies of caption forms to duplicate, so four pages of examples are included in this chapter. These caption forms progress from simple to more expansive. Figure 4.1 provides four copies of the same prompt. This form is a sound choice for beginning the captioning process as it requires only brief responses. After students gain experience writing captions, use Figure 4.2 with four different prompts so students begin making choices about which sentence stem best fits their selected product. Later, consider using the last three caption forms that invite more elaboration. Figures 4.3A and 4.3B prompt comparative reasoning by asking students to respond to two or more of the prompts as they complete their captions. Figures 4.4 and 4.5 highlight students' reflection of learning successes and goals.

Figure 4.1: CAPTIONS: PENCIL STRIPS

NAME _____ DATE _____

I am proud of this because _____

_____

_____

✂ -

NAME _____ DATE _____

I am proud of this because _____

_____

_____

- -

NAME _____ DATE _____

I am proud of this because _____

_____

_____

- -

NAME _____ DATE _____

I am proud of this because _____

_____

_____

Metacognitive Responses

Kingore, B. (2007). *Assessment,* 4th ed. Austin, TX: Professional Associates Publishing.

Figure 4.2: CAPTIONS: FOUR CHOICES

NAME   DATE

I did better on this by

NAME _____   DATE _____

This shows that I know how to _____

_____

_____

_____

NAME _____   DATE _____

I could improve this by _____

_____

_____

_____

NAME _____   DATE _____

This work is important because _____

_____

_____

_____

Kingore, B. (2007). *Assessment,* 4th ed. Austin, TX: Professional Associates Publishing.

Figure 4.3A: CAPTIONS: COMPARATIVE REASONING

NAME _____   DATE _____

This assignment was:

• Hard because _____

_____

• Easy because _____

_____

• Interesting because _____

_____

• Fun because _____

_____

Kingore, B. (2005). *Assessment,* 3rd ed. Austin: Professional Associates Publishing.

✂ -

Figure 4.3B: CAPTIONS: COMPARATIVE REASONING

NAME _____   DATE _____

This assignment was:

• Difficult because _____

_____

• Frustrating because _____

_____

• Important because _____

_____

• Enjoyable because _____

_____

• Significant because _____

_____

Kingore, B. (2007). *Assessment,* 4th ed. Austin, TX: Professional Associates Publishing.

Metacognitive Responses

Figure 4.4: CAPTION: CAN DO!

Can do!

NAME _____   DATE _____

This work demonstrates that I _____

_____

_____

_____

I feel _____

_____

_____

Next time, I want to _____

_____

_____

Kingore, B. (2007). *Assessment,* 4th ed. Austin, TX: Professional Associates Publishing.

- -

Figure 4.5: CAPTION: WRITE ON!

NAME _____   DATE _____

This work demonstrates _____

_____

_____

_____

I have improved _____

_____

_____

_____

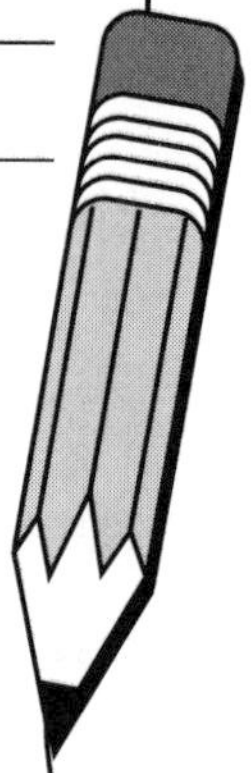

Kingore, B. (2007). *Assessment,* 4th ed. Austin, TX: Professional Associates Publishing.

If intending to bind the yearly portfolio books at the end of the school year, avoid stapling the captions to the product in the usual upper left-hand corner of the paper. Staples located in that corner obstruct the cutting process when binding with plastic comb binders. Instead, staple the captions to the product in the middle at the top of the page. For younger children, place a mark on the caption strip before it is duplicated to guide students where to staple the strip to their paper.

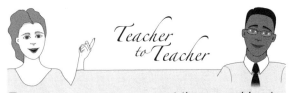

Teacher to Teacher

To save paper-management time, provide students with a page of miscellaneous caption strips to keep in their work or collection file. When they have an item for their portfolio, they simply select, cut off, and complete a caption strip.

3. *Metacognitive questions*

These questions focus students' thinking and reactions to learning. Figure 4.6 provides upper elementary and secondary students with a set of questions applicable to multiple learning situations. Have students store a copy of these questions in their work folder. Then, without the teacher having to develop new metacognitive devices each time, students select and respond to one or more questions as they complete different learning experiences. The intent is to guide students' reflections, prompt choice and variety, and save teachers' time in planning assessments. Encourage students to add questions to their list as quality suggestions are made during a class discussion.

> *The brain is like a muscle.*
> *When we think well, we feel good.*
> *Understanding is a kind of ecstasy.*
>
> —Carl Segan

4. *Learning reflections*

A learning reflection template prompts students' reflection about a specific learning task (Figure 4.7). Asking students to relate the information to another context is a productive strategy for developing transfer and increasing in-depth understanding. *This is like... How this relates to other subjects... How this applies to my life...*

Figure 4.7: LEARNING REFLECTIONS

NAME *Trent*   DATE *May 3*

TOPIC *Honeybees*

INFORMATION SOURCE:
☒ Book   ☐ Magazine   ☐ Newspaper
☒ Discussion   ☐ Internet   ☐ Graph
☐ Interview   ☐ Lecture   ☐ Video

How this relates to other subjects:

SUBJECT	CONNECTION
Health	*Humans also go through different stages.*
Social studies	*Bees live in a colony and have jobs like workers.*
Language arts	*Bees dance to tell each other things.*

1. Three major ideas:
   · *A honeybee dies after it stings something.*
   · *A hexagon makes the hive strong with no space wasted.*
   · *Pollen and nectar feed the hive.*

2. How this applies to me:
On the way to school, I found 11 different flowers bees like. They were yellow, blue, or purple with a sweet smell and a good landing spot to fit a bee.

3. One insight or thought:
Bees have to work so hard and don't live very long. Why? I don't want to be a bee.

4. Questions:
Why are there 25,000 different kinds of bees? Why did they need to specialize so much?

Kingore, B. (2007). *Assessment*, 4th ed. Austin, TX: Professional Associates Publishing.

5. *Reflective learning summaries*

Research documents summarization as a strategy that significantly increases achievement gains.[35] In summaries, students

---

[35] Marzano, Pickering, & Polluck, 2001.

Figure 4.6: METACOGNITIVE QUESTIONS

❏   1.   Why is this important?

❏   2.   What are two strengths of my work?

❏   3.   What would I do differently?

❏   4.   What part caused me the most trouble?

❏   5.   How does this relate to what I already know?

❏   6.   What is something similar to this?

❏   7.   What is the most important thing I learned while completing this work?

❏   8.   How can I use this information in my life?

❏   9.   What are two questions I have about this?

❏ 10.   What have I done to help me understand or learn about this?

❏ 11.   What can I do to substantiate my conclusion?

❏ 12.   How effective have I been in working and completing this process?

❏ 13.   What do I need to do next?

❏ 14.   What is one thing I will remember?

❏ 15.   What analogy can I create to explain this?

❏ 16.   What new goal can I set because of my work on this?

❏ 17. _____

❏ 18. _____

❏ 19. _____

❏ 20. _____

❏ 21. _____

❏ 22. _____

Kingore, B. (2007). *Assessment,* 4th ed. Austin, TX: Professional Associates Publishing.

Figure 4.7: LEARNING REFLECTIONS

NAME _____ DATE _____

TOPIC _____

INFORMATION
SOURCE:

❏ Book	❏ Magazine	❏ Newspaper
❏ Discussion	❏ Internet	❏ Graph
❏ Interview	❏ Lecture	❏ Video

How this relates to other subjects:

SUBJECT   CONNECTION

_____   _____

_____   _____

_____   _____

1. Three major ideas:

    • _____

    • _____

    • _____

2. How this applies to me:

3. One insight or thought:

4. Questions:

Kingore, B. (2007). *Assessment,* 4th ed. Austin, TX: Professional Associates Publishing.

Metacognitive
Responses

reflect upon learning experiences or products and interpret their learning outcomes over several weeks. Summaries allow for periodic review of the current status of learning. They are typically completed before conferences or at the conclusion of reporting periods such as at six-week or nine-week intervals. When completing summaries, students consider what they have accomplished thus far in their learning, what is characteristic of their learning, what needs to be done, and how they feel about their learning processes and achievements.

A summary can be expressed on blank paper or using a variety of forms. Figure 4.8 presents a template for product analysis. When the blank form is photocopied on the front and back of a paper, it provides four different areas to reflect the student's progress and goals over time.

Figure 4.8: LEARNING SUMMARY

NAME *William*

Looking through my portfolio, these are my conclusions about what I have learned, how I feel, and how I have changed as a learner.

DATE *November 2*

I am pleased with my work in science. My lab reports are good. I think I need more pieces of writing in my portfolio. I will finish a major report and include it next time.

I am changing as a learner because I care more now.

DATE *January 11*

My research report on George Orwell is one of my best pieces. I was pleased that Mr. Foster rated it so high.

My algebra is not strong enough. Getting better at algebra is my next goal. Jessica is working with me on Tuesday to practice applications.

I am changing as a learner because I monitor my own work more.

Kingore, B. (2007). *Assessment*, 4th ed. Austin, TX: Professional Associates Publishing.

An appealing variation to a learning summary is to having students write a letter to their parents from the perspective of their teacher. Of course, the parents understand that their child is the author of the letter, but it is interesting to see the student's interpretations of the teacher's point of view. An example letter follows to illustrate the effectiveness of this writing task.

October 23

Dear Mrs. Randall,

Charlene has worked hard in school this six weeks. She is writing longer stories and checking to see that she is spelling everything correctly. She has progressed a lot.

She really likes the new newspaper software in the computer lab. She has written several articles for the school newspaper using it. She does not like the computer tests over the books she reads. I think she would rather enjoy reading the stories than taking a test.

In math, she has mastered her division facts and is working on ratio. It is hard, but she is learning it. Debra is her math partner and they help each other.

Charlene is keeping a portfolio. She will share it with you soon.

Sincerely,
Ms. J. Dowell

6. End-of-year reflection

At the end of the school year, a summative view of learning is effective as a closure task. Ask students to put their achievements in perspective by writing about what they have accomplished, what has changed with time, how their learning satisfies them, and what needs to be done. This reflection is an authentic closure at the end of the year as students review the entire portfolio and select products for their School Career Portfolio.

Figure 4.8: LEARNING SUMMARY

NAME _____

Looking through my portfolio, these are my conclusions about what I have learned, how I feel, and how I have changed as a learner.

DATE

DATE

Kingore, B. (2007). *Assessment,* 4th ed. Austin, TX: Professional Associates Publishing.

Metacognitive Responses

7. Multiple-year reflection

One final opportunity for students' metacognitive reflections is typically completed as the School Career Portfolio is finalized and bound after several years of selection. Students review their selections and respond to their total learning experiences over those years of school.

GOAL SETTING

Goal setting is a result of students' metacognition. To empower them as active participants in their learning, students are encouraged to review their work, assess its strengths, and determine potential areas or skills for growth and development. Students then set goals to accomplish those changes.

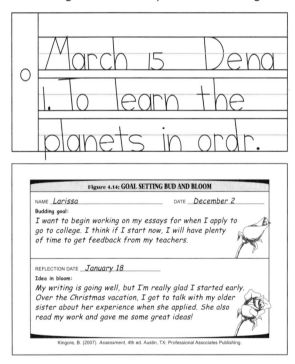

Figure 4.14: GOAL SETTING BUD AND BLOOM

NAME _Larissa_   DATE _December 2_

Budding goal:
I want to begin working on my essays for when I apply to go to college. I think if I start now, I will have plenty of time to get feedback from my teachers.

REFLECTION DATE _January 18_

Idea in bloom:
My writing is going well, but I'm really glad I started early. Over the Christmas vacation, I got to talk with my older sister about her experience when she applied. She also read my work and gave me some great ideas!

Kingore, B. (2007). *Assessment*, 4th ed. Austin, TX: Professional Associates Publishing.

Specific goal setting is a complex task for many students and parents as they typically have had little experience establishing learning goals for themselves. Expect students to progress slowly in their ability to set realistic and appropriate goals, and plan steps to teach this process.

Model the goal setting process by providing examples of goals that are appropriate for specific grade levels and learning tasks. Teachers suggest that educators provide students and parents with a sample bank of goals so parents understand the development of their child's individual goal plan, such as Figure 4.9. These goal examples are not listed hierarchically or developmentally. Rather, they are intended as a sample of goals to help generate more individual ideas when working with students to establish their specific goals. When working together with students and parents, keep in mind the unique strengths and needs of each student and avoid a one-goal-fits-all mentality. The psychology of goal setting suggests that students are more likely to work toward achieving goals in which they feel ownership.

Graphic organizers for goal setting simplify this metacognitive process. Multiple examples of goal-setting formats are provided in this chapter.

Collaborative Goal Setting

Parents, students, and teachers can collaborate on goal setting. Since multiple goal setting applications are possible, Figure 4.10 encourages collaborators to consider the goals for a student's learning in academic, social/behavior, or study skill areas. Dividing goal setting into different categories helps focus the task and makes it less overwhelming. Rather than attempting to establish goals in all three areas, the objective is to respond to those areas that are most appropriate for that student.

Teachers find that goal setting is more successful when parents, students, and teachers plan specific actions to achieve a goal. Figure 4.11 invites students, parents, and teachers to each establish a goal for the student and then list what they will do to assist in achieving the goal. In each case, it is important that the student

Figure 4.9: GOAL EXAMPLES

ACADEMIC SKILL GOALS

❏ Master math facts
❏ Understand and apply mathematical concepts (time, fractions, ratio, etc.)
❏ Effectively use the problem-solving process in math and science
❏ Create and solve story problems
❏ Implement the scientific method
❏ Transfer spelling skills into written work across the curriculum
❏ Effectively apply letter and sound relationships in reading and writing
❏ Increase written and oral vocabularies
❏ Develop independent reading habits
❏ Write neatly and with correct letter formation
❏ Complete a piece using all of the steps in the writing process
❏ Use more precise language and specific terminology in responses in science
❏ Develop a story with a beginning, middle, and end
❏ Incorporate unique analogies and symbols in writing
❏ Develop stronger summarization skills

STUDY OR RESEARCH SKILL GOALS

❏ Maintain a well organized portfolio
❏ Manage time well during independent assignments and complete quality work on time
❏ Improve the quality of work
❏ Improve the organization of information
❏ Manage materials more effectively
❏ Accept responsibility for achievement levels
❏ Effectively use a variety of resources to extend learning
❏ Use correct bibliographic references
❏ Develop critical thinking skills
❏ Improve application of problem-solving skills
❏ Appropriately apply more complex technology

BEHAVIOR OR SOCIAL SKILL GOALS

❏ Assume more leadership responsibilities in groups
❏ Encourage others
❏ Be an active listener
❏ Foster respect for others
❏ Interact more effectively with peers and adults
❏ Increase self-esteem and confidence
❏ Be persistent in learning tasks
❏ Improve self-control
❏ Increase intrinsic motivation
❏ Understand and accept behavioral consequences
❏ Participate more comfortably in large group discussions

Metacognitive Responses

Kingore, B. (2007). *Assessment,* 4th ed. Austin, TX: Professional Associates Publishing.

Figure 4.10: COLLABORATIVE GOAL SETTING

NAME _____   DATE _____

Student's goals for self:

Academic goal:

Social or behavior goal:

Study skills or research goal:

Parent's goals for student:

Academic goal:

Social or behavior goal:

Study skills or research goal:

Teacher's goals for student:

Academic goal:

Social or behavior goal:

Study skills or research goal:

Kingore, B. (2007). *Assessment,* 4th ed. Austin, TX: Professional Associates Publishing.

write a reaction after the parent and teacher have written their goal suggestions for the student. These student responses help maintain the student's ownership in the process. Goal setting is something educators do *with* students, not *to* them.

Figure 4.11: COLLABORATIVE GOAL SETTING PLAN

NAME _John_   DATE _October 28_

Student's goal for self:	**What I will do to accomplish my goal:**
I want to research the latest information about the Titanic. I want to write about it for my history report.	I will search new resources and the internet about Dr. Ballard and his explorations
	Date by which I want to reach my goal: _10-24_
Parent's goal for student:	**What I will do to assist my child in reaching this goal:**
I would like you to spell more accurately while you work on your Titanic project.	I will continue to help you study for spelling tests and buy a word book for you to use as you write.
	STUDENT'S RESPONSE: I'll use the word book when I write and spell check when I'm using the computer.
Teacher's goal for student:	**How I will assist my student in achieving this goal:**
I would like you to increase your independent learning skills.	Your titanic project is an excellent idea for independent learning. I will facilitate your search for resources and help you edit.
	STUDENT'S RESPONSE: Thanks. I want it to be really good.

Kingore, B. (2007). *Assessment*, 4th ed. Austin, TX: Professional Associates Publishing.

Goal Setting Plan

Figure 4.12 is a format successfully used in many classrooms of upper elementary, middle school, and high school students. The value of this graphic organizer is that it asks students to state a goal and then outline the specific steps to accomplish it. Planning is an important link to success for many students, as it requires them to establish a sequence to reach a goal. This plan has five steps indicated, but in reality, there is no predetermined number of steps to reach a goal. Students are encouraged to plan the number of steps most appropriate toward reaching their goal. At a later date, students revise their goal-setting plan to reflect the status of their goal. After recording the date, they state what they have

accomplished and reflect upon how they view that accomplishment.

GOAL SETTING WEEKLY PLAN

Figure 4.13 is a variation for inexperienced or less organized students who are not able to handle goal setting over a long period of time. With this form, students are guided to set a short-term goal and then plan the steps to achieve that goal. Students would typically complete the top two boxes of the form on Monday. Then on Friday of that week, students revisit their goal plan to reflect upon what they have accomplished. Initially, with students inexperienced in goal setting or students less task oriented, only part of the goal may be achieved. Students are encouraged to write how they feel about their accomplishment and plan what they will do next to continue their development. In many cases, students continue their goal setting process using another weekly plan.

Figure 4.13: GOAL SETTING WEEKLY PLAN

NAME _Colin_   DATE _February 12_

My goals for this week:	**My action plan:**
I won't talk as much, and I'll get my work finished before I mess around.	1. I will think!
	2. I will ask Jenny to give me our secret signal when I get too loud.
	3. I'll try to time myself and make it a game to get done faster.
	4. I will keep track of how many times Mrs. Francis smiles at me. She's going to smile when I do good work

REFLECTION DATE _February 16_

What I accomplished this week:
I did good every day except Thursday.

How I view this accomplishment:
I feel better about it because I don't talk as much and I get my work done.

What I will do next:
Try hard again.

Kingore, B. (2007). *Assessment*, 4th ed. Austin, TX: Professional Associates Publishing.

Figure 4.11: COLLABORATIVE GOAL SETTING PLAN

NAME _____   DATE _____

Student's goal for self:	What I will do to accomplish my goal: Date by which I want to reach my goal: _____
Parent's goal for student:	What I will do to assist my child in reaching this goal: STUDENT'S RESPONSE:
Teacher's goal for student:	How I will assist my student in achieving this goal: STUDENT'S RESPONSE:

Kingore, B. (2007). *Assessment,* 4th ed. Austin, TX: Professional Associates Publishing.

Figure 4.12: GOAL SETTING PLAN

Name _____   Date _____

My goals:	My action plan:
	1.
	2.
	3.
	4.
	5.

Reflection Date

What I accomplished:	My reflection:

Kingore, B. (2007). *Assessment,* 4th ed. Austin, TX: Professional Associates Publishing.

Metacognitive Responses

Figure 4.13: GOAL SETTING WEEKLY PLAN

NAME _____   DATE _____

My goals for this week:	My action plan:
	1.
	2.
	3.
	4.

REFLECTION DATE _____

What I accomplished this week:

How I view this accomplishment:

What I will do next:

Kingore, B. (2007). *Assessment,* 4th ed. Austin, TX: Professional Associates Publishing.

Monthly Goal Setting

Some teachers find it simpler to integrate goal setting with ongoing activities in the classroom. For example, elementary and secondary students can incorporate goals in their learning logs or journals. On the first school day of each month, students review previous goals written in their journals or logs, revise those goals, and reflect upon their progress. During some monthly reviews, students add a new goal.

Primary classrooms can combine goal setting with handwriting practice. Once a month, students determine the school-related goals they want to set and then write them on their lined handwriting paper. One student particularly revealed his need for organization when he set his goals as: 1) *To finish some of my writing pieces,* and 2) *To remember where I put my goals!*

Goal Setting Bud and Bloom

With more experienced or sophisticated students, the rose analogy is an effective goal setting device. Using Figure 4.14, students write a learning goal or goals for themselves and store those goals in their portfolios. At a later date, they revise their goals to reflect upon how much their learning has bloomed. If appropriate, develop the analogy further with the students.

A bud needs:	A goal needs:
Nutrients	Nurturing environment and collaboration with others
Soil	Content information, practice, positive attitude, and self-esteem
Light	Learning opportunities
Water	Task commitment

Metacognitive Responses

Figure 4.14: GOAL SETTING BUD AND BLOOM

NAME _____   DATE _____

Budding goal:

REFLECTION DATE _____

Idea in bloom:

Kingore, B. (2007). *Assessment,* 4th ed. Austin, TX: Professional Associates Publishing.

STUDENTS' METACOGNITIVE DEVELOPMENT OVER TIME

Teachers effectively employing authentic assessment report that students' metacognitive abilities mature with time and experience. The following are three changes teachers noticed.

1. ATTITUDE

With experience in reflection, students increase their willingness to complete captions or reflections on their learning. At first, many students are resistant because they lack experience in metacognition, they are not sure how to do it, and they are not certain why it is important. Later, students begin to enjoy the process and respect the value of their own voice in their work and progress. As one anonymous adage notes:

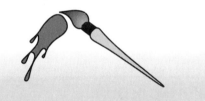

Attitude is the mind's paintbrush. It can color any situation.

2. SELF-MONITORING

With time and experience, students begin to use earlier works to compare how they have improved on specific goals and skills. As one fifth-grader commented after several months of product analysis: *It's cool to see how much my math has changed. I'm working harder problems now and getting them right most of the time.* As another example, a gifted first-grader stated during a student-involved conference with his mother and teacher: *This clearly shows how much I have improved in my punctuation when I write.*

3. BREADTH

With instruction and modeling, students' reflections increase in length and depth of content. Reflections stretch from a few words to sentences containing a more mature awareness of criteria for assessing the quality and value of students' learning. The second grader's and ninth grader's captions that follow are examples of this development from very simple to more thoughtful responses.

Second-Grade Examples

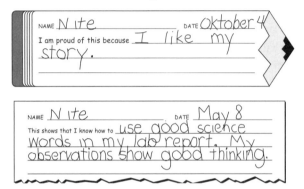

NAME Nite   DATE Oktober 4
I am proud of this because I like my story.

NAME Nite   DATE May 8
This shows that I know how to use good science words in my lab report. My observations show good thinking.

Ninth-Grade Examples

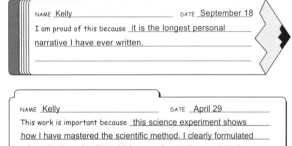

NAME Kelly   DATE September 18
I am proud of this because it is the longest personal narrative I have ever written.

NAME Kelly   DATE April 29
This work is important because this science experiment shows how I have mastered the scientific method. I clearly formulated a hypothesis and validated it by experimentation, analytical observation, and careful data recording.

Metacognition and the decision-making process of portfolios actually increase students' motivation to excel and be responsible for their learning.

Kingore, B. (2007). *Assessment,* 4th ed. Austin, TX: Professional Associates Publishing.

• CHAPTER 5 •
Conferences

The best way to learn about a child's thinking and learning is to ask the child

—*Ministry of Education, Canada*

Conversations from student to teacher, student to student, and student to parent continue spontaneously throughout the day to assist, encourage, and affirm students. However, structured conversations in the form of conferences also enhance learning. The objective of conferencing is to discuss with and listen to students in order to elicit their perceptions, gain insights into their learning, and facilitate their continued achievements. Through conferences, teachers and parents refine their understanding of the students' viewpoints, strengths, and needs as the students acknowledge that they have something worth saying and accomplishments worth honoring. The tone is interactive, and the information is supported and guided by specific examples of students' work.

Interactive conferences help students:
- Think about their learning,
- Engage in an ongoing information exchange,
- Achieve new levels of understanding,
- Experience the perspective of other participants,

- Affirm the value of their ideas and opinions,
- Self-assess,
- Acknowledge progress,
- Respond to comments and inquiry,
- Set learning goals, and
- Become more autonomous learners.

Traditional school conferences focused on information between teachers and parents. Now, conferences invite students, teachers, and parents to communicate with a collective attitude of mutual respect, cooperation, and shared responsibility to enrich the learning experiences of the students.

STUDENT-TEACHER CONFERENCES

Authentic assessment promotes students conferencing with teachers to directly share their perceptions. The quality of a student-teacher discussion is greatly enhanced by the thoughtful preparation completed by students before they conference with the teacher. Forms to guide students' conference preparation are included as Figures 5.1 and 5.2.

Kingore, B. (2007). *Assessment,* 4th ed. Austin, TX: Professional Associates Publishing.

Figure 5.1: CONFERENCE PREPARATION

NAME _____   DATE _____

Before coming to the conference, please prepare your portfolio for sharing.

❑   Ensure that all products have your name, the date completed, and a completed caption strip attached.

❑   Arrange the products in the predetermined order.

❑   Select one product added to your portfolio since your last conference that you especially want to discuss. Mark its place in your portfolio by attaching a sticky note that extends from the edge of the product to flag that piece.

Answer the following questions, please.

Why did you choose the product that you want to share first?

What was the goal you set during our last conference? What have you accomplished toward that goal?

List two or three questions that you want to discuss.

Figure 5.2: CONFERENCE PREPARATION

NAME _____   DATE _____

Areas of study this reporting period:

* _____
* _____
* _____
* _____

Number of products assigned: _____   Number of products I completed: _____

What I am proud of:

What I would like to improve:

The one thing I especially enjoyed learning:

One change I suggest:

My questions are:

Kingore, B. (2007). *Assessment,* 4th ed. Austin, TX: Professional Associates Publishing.

Conferences

Questioning is another important component of successful, interactive conferences. Teachers plan questions, such as those in Figure 5.3, to help the conference proceed without the pauses that inevitably occur when people try to think of what to ask. Many teachers find that having prepared questions helps them better focus on relevant assessment information and use time with students more productively. When conferencing with a student, the questions become guides to select among as needed.

Assessment Questioning Guidelines

* Effective questions are high-level and open-ended to encourage students to think. Those questions are more valuable to assessment and provide richer information than recall-level quizzing.

* Develop a list of possible leading and probing questions ahead of time, but unless assessment standards require identical questions for all students, be flexible in which ones you actually use with different students at different times.

* Conferences are more productive when students are prepared for the questions to be discussed. Provide students with a list of possible questions before conferencing with them. Allow them to ponder their responses rather than feel put on the spot.

* Invite students to prepare questions they think are significant. *What do you want someone to ask you? What would you like to ask others?*

* Provide wait time during the conference to allow students to be more thoughtful in their responses.

* Follow the student's lead. Let the student's information naturally guide the questioning responses.

* A brief written record of observations and conclusions may be more appropriate and informative than a simple checklist.

End the conference with a moment for both the student and teacher to write a brief note about the conference and future goals. These notes are valuable memory prompts before the next conference. Provide the student with a blank paper, conference note, or reflection form (Figures 5.4 through 5.6) to write notes of her or his perception of the conference. On another paper, simultaneously record important notes for guiding the student's continued growth.

Duplicate a conference form front and back so the same paper can be used for multiple conferences. If the students' copies are duplicated on colored paper, the paper is more easily found when it is needed again. The student usually files the conference notes in the back of the portfolio and thus the colored page signals that the work in front of it has already been discussed in a conference. The teacher typically stores conference notes in an instructional file.

To find the time for student conferences, write one student's name on each day or so of the class or section planner. Rotating among the students will yield a five to ten minute conference with each student once every six to nine weeks.

Kingore, B. (2007). *Assessment,* 4th ed. Austin, TX: Professional Associates Publishing.

Figure 5.3: CONFERENCE QUESTIONS

1. What have you chosen to share with me first?
   - Why did you choose this product?
   - How did you think of that idea?
   - What could you say to your parent about this to explain what you've learned?

2. What questions or concerns do you want to discuss today?
   - What is the problem as you see it?
   - Who can best help you? How can they help?

3. What should I learn about you from your work?
   - How is that important?
   - What else do you want me to know?

4. Are your learning achievements satisfying or not satisfying to you? Why do you feel that way?
   - What do you feel is a strength?
   - What would you like to change?

5. What product shows something important you've learned?
   - Why is this important?
   - What did you do to learn it?

6. What is something in your portfolio that you think we should do again?
   - What do you like about it?
   - How is it important to next year's class?
   - How could we change it to make it better?

7. What is on your reading review that you would like to share?
   - Have you encouraged others to read this?
   - Have you read anything else like it?
   - What do you plan to read next?

8. What is something you can do now that you could not do well before?
   - What did you do to learn it?
   - How did you use this ability?

9. Which product do you feel is not your best work?
   - Why are you not satisfied with it?
   - What would you change about it?

10. What changes have you noticed in your work?
    - How do you feel about these changes?
    - What additional help or resources do you need?

11. What was the goal you set during our last conference?
    - How have you progressed toward that goal?
    - How or when did you achieve it?

Kingore, B. (2007). *Assessment,* 4th ed. Austin, TX: Professional Associates Publishing.

Figure 5.4: CONFERENCE NOTES

NAME _____   DATE _____

What I would like to learn:

How I feel about our conference:

Kingore, B. (2007). *Assessment,* 4th ed. Austin, TX: Professional Associates Publishing.

✂ -

Figure 5.5: CONFERENCE NOTES

NAME _____   DATE _____

What we discussed at the conference:

How I have improved:

My next goal to achieve:

Kingore, B. (2007). *Assessment,* 4th ed. Austin, TX: Professional Associates Publishing.

Figure 5.6: CONFERENCE REFLECTION

NAME _____   DATE _____

What I did:	What I will do next time:

What I enjoyed:	What I would change:

Kingore, B. (2007). *Assessment,* 4th ed. Austin, TX: Professional Associates Publishing.

When conferencing or observing, develop simple codes and formats to monitor students' progress and goals. These enable you to jot ideas faster and provide a consistent format for data. Primary teachers in Hurst-Euless-Bedford schools in Texas share the following example of a quick note code.

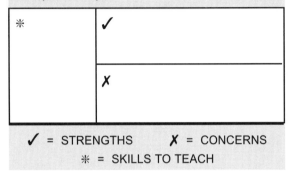

✓ = STRENGTHS   ✗ = CONCERNS
          ✳ = SKILLS TO TEACH

Teachers do not want students to think the only time they can meet with the teacher is when a conference is scheduled. Provide a form, such Figure 5.7, which allows students to request a conference. This particular form helps students think through what they need to discuss so the conference time is more productive.

PARENT-TEACHER CONFERENCES

Teachers are experienced with traditional conferences between teachers and parents. A portfolio enhances the information exchange

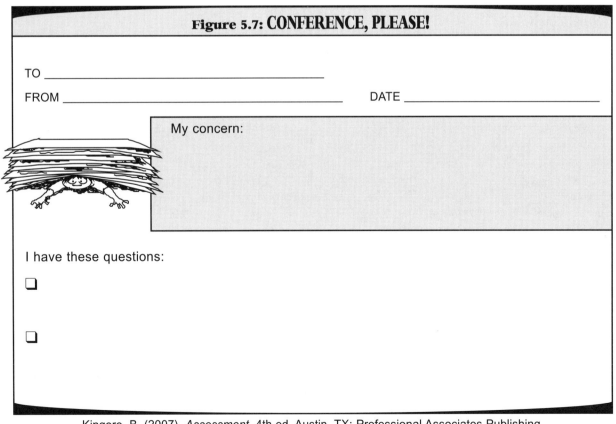

Figure 5.7: CONFERENCE, PLEASE!

TO _____

FROM _____   DATE _____

My concern:

I have these questions:

❑

❑

Kingore, B. (2007). *Assessment,* 4th ed. Austin, TX: Professional Associates Publishing.

during a conference because teachers use specific product examples from the portfolio to support and clarify each point regarding the student's growth and potential.

When sharing information, the parent and teacher must sit side by side to more comfortably review pieces from the portfolio. This seating arrangement also signals a more collaborative rather than a confrontational environment.

Guidelines for Parent-Teacher Portfolio Conferences

1. Establish rapport by first showing the parents a successful product their child chose from the portfolio and wanted them to see.

2. Accent students' growth and the strengths of the work rather than only comment on deficiencies.

3. Use specific product examples to share information more concretely and to document major instructional conclusions. Avoid educational jargon.

4. Use a triplet to focus the discussion.[36]

5. Elicit and actively listen to the parent's comments and their questions.

6. Do not overwhelm parents by attempting to discuss every item in the portfolio. Pre-plan and be selective.

7. Remind parents that they will have other opportunities to review the portfolio, such as a portfolio conference with their child, and that the bound portfolio will be sent home at the end of the school year.

8. Offer specific suggestions regarding how parents might support their child's continued development at home.

9. Conclude by summarizing major points and inviting continued collaboration.

[36] See Chapter 2 for more information about triplets.

Kingore, B. (2007). *Assessment,* 4th ed. Austin, TX: Professional Associates Publishing.

STUDENT-INVOLVED CONFERENCES

Most student-involved conferences are conducted at the school. One type of student-involved conference involves only the student and a parent or other significant adult of the student's choosing. This type of conference involves less school or teacher time because multiple student-parent conferences occur simultaneously while the teacher facilitates. These conferences can also add depth and authenticity to a parents' night at school.

A second type of conference is a three-way conference where the student, parent, and teacher are all participants. This type of conference requires significantly more teacher time, as only one conference is completed at a time. However, the three-way conference produces valuable communication as all three people vested in the student's needs and achievements sit down to learn and share together.

Model a student-involved conference during a parent meeting early in the year by having a parent and former student or two teachers role-play the conference in front of the parents. Then, parents know what to expect when they have a conference with their child later.

Objectives of Student-Involved Conferences

Successful student-involved conferences intend to:
- Elicit the students' perspectives of their learning.
- Showcase what students have produced and accomplished.

Conferences

- Accent the students' active role in their assessment.
- Require students' to plan, organize, present, respond, and self-evaluate.
- Encourage students to set goals for their learning.
- Provide authentic audiences for students' work.
- Increase students' accountability.

The process of students sharing their portfolios with adults vests the students with status and accents their responsibility for their own learning. When students are truly accountable, they become self-motivated to improve.

Students' Preparation for the Conference

Student preparation is necessary for productive and successful student-involved conferences. Students will not be confident communicators unless they are well prepared and have practiced the procedure. Their preparation encourages them to focus on a few specific items from their portfolios that they most want or need to share since it is not practical to conference on every piece in most portfolios. Parents also appreciate knowing their child has worked to prepare for their conference together.

SEQUENCE FOR STUDENTS' PREPARATION

1. Students list how they have changed as a learner and select specific portfolio products to support those changes. They prepare for the conference by completing the student section of Figure 5.8 to help them synthesize their work and focus on what their achievements represent.

2. Students select the first product they want to share and plan what they want to say about it to communicate their perceptions about their learning.

3. Students then select two or three additional products and prepare what to say about each of them.

4. The teacher selects one or more pieces to include. These products represent district learning standards, skills, and achievement levels that the teacher believes every parent should review. Parents need to be informed which of the pieces they discuss during the conference are selected by the student and which are required by the teacher.

5. As a class, discuss the Procedures for Students (Figure 5.9) and incorporate any additional procedures brainstormed by the students.

6. A student volunteer and the teacher model in front of the class what a student-involved conference looks and sounds like. This demonstration gives students a better idea of the process and a better ability to prepare.

7. Next, students work in pairs to role-play their portfolio conferences and practice the specific procedures listed in Figure 5.9 that will be used for student-parent conferences. One student role-plays a parent while the other student shares and discusses her or his portfolio. Then, the two reverse roles and continue role-playing a conference using the second student's portfolio. Role-playing develops students' confidence and increases their fluency for a conference with their parent or family representative. It is fascinating to observe this role-playing as students are surprisingly perceptive when playing adults' roles.

8. Student committees can be formed to complete any needed arrangements for

Figure 5.8: STUDENT-INVOLVED CONFERENCE

NAME _____   DATE _____

STUDENT

While you look at my work, I want you to notice:

* _____

* _____

* _____

* _____

These are things I think I do well:

* _____

* _____

* _____

* _____

My next academic and study skill goals are:

* _____

* _____

* _____

* _____

PARENT/GUARDIAN

After looking at your work and listening to your explanations, I want to comment:

GUARDIAN _____   DATE _____

the conferences. Some examples include arranging for refreshments, organizing the classroom space, preparing welcome signs, and duplicating needed papers.

9. Students write a letter to their parent or family representative asking them to attend the conference.

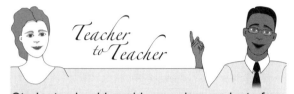

Students should avoid removing products from their portfolios during conferencing; it is difficult for them to get the pieces back in the correct order, even when the pages are numbered. Instead, have students place sticky notes on the edge of each selected piece so the note stands out like a flag. Then, the student simply turns to each piece as the portfolio is shared.

[37] DeBono, 1993.

Student Closure

Debrief the experience with students after each conference by asking them to reflect on the process orally or in writing. A PMI format[37] or one of the various conference forms in this chapter effectively prompt individual or small group conference reflections. For three-way conferences, Figure 5.11 provides an effective format for debriefing.

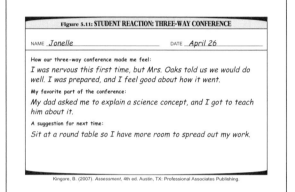

Figure 5.11: STUDENT REACTION: THREE-WAY CONFERENCE

NAME *Jonelle*   DATE *April 26*

How our three-way conference made me feel:
I was nervous this first time, but Mrs. Oaks told us we would do well. I was prepared, and I feel good about how it went.

My favorite part of the conference:
My dad asked me to explain a science concept, and I got to teach him about it.

A suggestion for next time:
Sit at a round table so I have more room to spread out my work.

Kingore, B. (2007). *Assessment*, 4th ed. Austin, TX: Professional Associates Publishing.

Figure 5.9: PROCEDURES FOR STUDENTS

❏   1. Have your prepared portfolio at your desk or conference site.

❏   2. Introduce your parent(s) or family representative to your teacher.

❏   3. Sit between your parents if both are present, or sit in a close circle.

❏   4. Share your work in the order and manner you planned.

❏   5. Ask your parent(s) if they have any questions or other items that they want to discuss.

❏   6. Invite your parent(s) to join you in goal setting what you should accomplish next.

❏   7. Show your parent(s) around the room and use the entire classroom environment to support your learning process and achievements.

❏   8. Invite your parent(s) to complete a Portfolio Response Letter (Figure 5.10).

❏   9. Thank your parent(s) for attending.

Kingore, B. (2007). *Assessment,* 4th ed. Austin, TX: Professional Associates Publishing.

Figure 5.10: PORTFOLIO RESPONSE LETTER

DATE _____

DEAR _____,
                        Name of the student

The product that impressed me the most:

I learned from your portfolio sharing:

I enjoyed:

I would like you to work on:

Comments:

Sincerely,

Kingore, B. (2007). *Assessment,* 4th ed. Austin, TX: Professional Associates Publishing.

Conduct a class discussion to combine responses and allow students to share anecdotes about their conferences. Elicit their perceptions about the conference process and develop a list of suggestions for refining the process next time.

Discuss how the students feel about the Portfolio Response letters they receive from their parents. (Most students choose to file those responses in their portfolios because parents' written notes of positive feedback and compliments are highly valued by the students.) Encourage students to write a follow-up letter to their parents thanking them for attending the conference and sharing their learning experiences.

Conference Factors for Teachers to Consider

Multiple school faculties conduct debriefing sessions to discuss the values and problems associated with implementing student-involved conferences. A synthesis of their comments is presented on a PMI chart[38] (Figure 5.12). When implementing or refining the use of student-involved conferences, refer to the PMI chart and consider those observations and responses from others experienced with the process.

The concept of student-involved conferences is difficult at first for many educators to adopt because it requires a significant shift from the traditional conference procedures. The following nine factors help guide the

[38] DeBono, 1993.

Figure 5.11: STUDENT REACTION: THREE-WAY CONFERENCE

NAME _____   DATE _____

How our three-way conference made me feel:

My favorite part of the conference:

What I suggest for next time:

Kingore, B. (2007). *Assessment,* 4th ed. Austin, TX: Professional Associates Publishing.

Figure 5.12: PMI CHART ON STUDENT-INVOLVED CONFERENCES

PLUS (+)	MINUS (-)	INTERESTING (?)
It is student-centered; students are responsible, accountable, and involved.	Students need to be taught conferencing skills.	It promotes positive interactions between a student and parent.
It encourages students to organize, communicate, and evaluate their work.	Not all parents attend the conference.	A majority of the parents do attend.
It provides an opportunity for teachers to observe students in a new light.	It is time intensive with young children.	It is a self-esteem builder for students.
The portfolio products demonstrate progress to parents more concretely than grades alone.	Some teachers doubt that students have the verbal skills to lead conferences.	Many students seem excited and surprised that their parents are responsive and interested.
The process demonstrates the value of the information from authentic assessment.	There are communication issue with ELL families; translators may be needed.	Working parents are willing to take off from work to attend.
It encourages a positive parental response; they like the specific academic examples to discuss.	Parents need information about their role; they are sometimes unsure how to appropriately interact and question their child.	Students are empowered; their leadership role gives them status.
It motivates students to do their best because of the authentic audience of the conference.	Teachers may have little if any experience with this process; training is needed.	Teachers are amazed how positive an experience it is for parents and students.
It provides multiple opportunities for students to use analytical thinking.	Students need more thoughtful captions for more in-depth parent communications.	Students have many specific ideas about how they can improve next time.

Kingore, B. (2007). *Assessment,* 4th ed. Austin, TX: Professional Associates Publishing.

Conferences

preparation for conducting student-involved parent conferences.

1. The teacher's role changes from being the authority to becoming a facilitator and a supportive commentator.

2. Clarify to students that the teacher plays a critical role in guiding learning and helping students prepare for conferences but that they will be the leaders responsible for the meeting. The intent during the actual conference is for the teacher to remain in the background as much as possible and observe so the spotlight is clearly focused on the students.

3. Encourage the parents to direct their attention and responses to the student rather than the teacher.

4. When initiating student-involved conferences, provide the parents with a list of sample questions they can use to discuss products with their child.[39] In this way, parents can prompt their child if needed during the conference. Also, include a reminder to parents that their child is learning and that they will see mistakes in products as well as growth in learning. Specify that the conference is to celebrate the student's accomplishments and understand achievement levels rather than to criticize.

5. Avoid giving *canned* information to parents. Each student-parent conference should reflect the unique learning of the student and address the concerns of the parent.

6. Avoid interrupting any student-involved conferences. If the teacher frequently intervenes, the students typically stop leading and expect the teacher to take over.

7. Understand that traditional parent-teacher conferences may also be scheduled when deemed necessary. Teachers may want to conference alone with parents at another time when an adult's perception of the student's learning is different from the student's or when special student needs should be privately addressed with parents.

8. Understand that some parents may still want to request a teacher conference. Teachers generally find, however, that holding the student-involved conferences provides most parents with so much information that few request a parent-teacher conference.

9. At the conclusion of a conference, encourage the parents to debrief with each other and share their opinions. Provide them with a copy of Figure 5.13 to record their ideas.

While student-involved conferences may seem a difficult process to attempt, teachers and parents both express surprise at how well students rise to the occasion. Even primary students can conduct conferences with their parents and delight the participants with how much they have to say about their school work. Kindergarten teachers suggest that children are more successfully involved in three-way conferences when they rotate with their parents among the learning centers or learning stations set up in the room. This process is more concrete and comfortable to young students. Their work and the class activities prompt what children want parents to know about school.

Students can also conference at home. Students simply take the portfolio home overnight and have a portfolio conference with a parent or parents. The parents then record their reactions on the Portfolio Response Letter shared earlier (Figure 5.10).

---

[39] Refer to the questions in the parent letter, Figure 10.3.

Kingore, B. (2007). *Assessment,* 4th ed. Austin, TX: Professional Associates Publishing.

Figure 5.13: PARENT REACTION: STUDENT-INVOLVED CONFERENCE

STUDENT _____ DATE _____

RELATIONSHIP TO STUDENT _____

1. How do you feel about having your child involved in the conference?

2. What did you notice about your child's reactions to the conference?

3. What information or which part of the conference was most helpful to you?

4. Were your concerns and interests addressed?

5. Were the arrangements and setting comfortable for you? Is there anything that would work better for you in the future?

6. What are your comments or suggestions to make future conferences more effective?

Kingore, B. (2007). *Assessment,* 4th ed. Austin, TX: Professional Associates Publishing.

This procedure alarms some educators because they assume the portfolio contents will be lost or damaged. However, when the home environment supports learning, teachers can send portfolios home for conferences and have the portfolios returned safely the next day.[40] It is vital to schedule portfolio sharing at home after students have grown to value their work and take pride in the portfolio. That pride motivates them to handle their portfolio with care.

PEER REQUEST FOR HELP

Students know that their teacher is there to help them, but they also need to view their classmates as sources of assistance. Often, both students benefit when one helps another clarify an idea or process. Consider providing a small area where students post messages and requests. This procedure is particularly useful in departmentalized situations where multiple sections of a course meet in the same room but the students do not have opportunities to see or talk with one another about class topics. The Peer Request for Help form (Figure 5.14) and the Response to Peer Request form (Figure 5.15) are one way to organize this interaction.

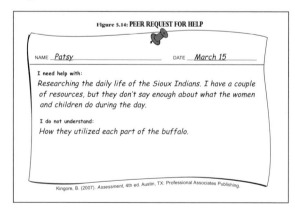

Figure 5.14: PEER REQUEST FOR HELP

NAME *Patsy*   DATE *March 15*

I need help with:
Researching the daily life of the Sioux Indians. I have a couple of resources, but they don't say enough about what the women and children do during the day.

I do not understand:
How they utilized each part of the buffalo.

Kingore, B. (2007). *Assessment*, 4th ed. Austin, TX: Professional Associates Publishing.

PEER REVIEW

Encourage students to help each other refine their work through peer conferences. Allow each student to select a product that is in process and then collaborate with another student to review the work. Math story problems, written compositions, and science lab reports are examples of products for student review. Encourage each student to read the piece aloud. This process enables both the ear and the eye to guide the review for editing and revision. Figures 5.16 and 5.17 help students organize their responses.

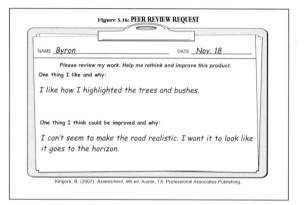

Figure 5.16: PEER REVIEW REQUEST

NAME *Byron*   DATE *Nov. 18*

Please review my work. Help me rethink and improve this product.
One thing I like and why:
I like how I highlighted the trees and bushes.

One thing I think could be improved and why:
I can't seem to make the road realistic. I want it to look like it goes to the horizon.

Kingore, B. (2007). *Assessment*, 4th ed. Austin, TX: Professional Associates Publishing.

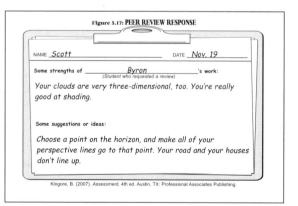

Figure 5.17: PEER REVIEW RESPONSE

NAME *Scott*   DATE *Nov. 19*

Some strengths of _____ *Byron* _____'s work:
                    (Student who requested a review)
Your clouds are very three-dimensional, too. You're really good at shading.

Some suggestions or ideas:
Choose a point on the horizon, and make all of your perspective lines go to that point. Your road and your houses don't line up.

Kingore, B. (2007). *Assessment*, 4th ed. Austin, TX: Professional Associates Publishing.

---

[40] A sample letter informing parents about portfolio sharing at home is included in Chapter 10.

Figure 5.14: PEER REQUEST FOR HELP

NAME _____ DATE _____

I need help with:

I do not understand:

Kingore, B. (2007). *Assessment,* 4th ed. Austin, TX: Professional Associates Publishing.

- -

Figure 5.15: RESPONSE TO PEER REQUEST

NAME _____ DATE _____

My suggestion for _____ :
                              (Student who requested help)

A resource that might help:

Let's meet at: _____ on _____

Kingore, B. (2007). *Assessment,* 4th ed. Austin, TX: Professional Associates Publishing.

Conferences

Figure 5.16: PEER REVIEW REQUEST

NAME _____ DATE _____

Please review my work. Help me rethink and improve this product.

One thing I like and why:

One thing I think could be improved and why:

Kingore, B. (2007). *Assessment,* 4th ed. Austin, TX: Professional Associates Publishing.

Figure 5.17: PEER REVIEW RESPONSE

NAME _____ DATE _____

Some strengths of _____ 's work:
(Student who requested a review)

Some suggestions or ideas:

Kingore, B. (2007). *Assessment,* 4th ed. Austin, TX: Professional Associates Publishing.

• **CHAPTER 6** •
Rubrics

*Rubrics represent not only scoring tools but also,
more importantly, instructional illuminators.*
—W. James Popham

Rubrics are a significant assessment and evaluation tool. The ongoing process of constructing effective rubrics invites professional conversations among grade-level teams and across grade levels of educators. These conversations clarify the instructional priorities that precede assessment. Together, educators analyze the key attributes of learning tasks, discuss which criteria can be measured and taught, and construct rubrics that reflect those decisions. Thus, thoughtfully developed rubrics contribute to the quality of instruction.

Well-constructed rubrics can be used three ways: goal setting, teacher evaluation, and students' self-assessment. Initially, provide a copy of a rubric and ask students to set goals before they begin by checking the levels they intend to achieve. When the task is complete, students use the same rubric copy, marking with a second color of pen, to self-assess their achievement level. Finally, teachers use the same rubric copy and a third color of pen to mark their evaluation of the achievement. Many teachers report that achievement increases when students use a rubric to goal set their levels of success before they begin the task. Setting their own target increases the students' determination to reach it.

UNDERSTANDING RUBRICS

Rubrics are:
- **Guidelines to quality** that describe the requirements for various levels of proficiency on a learning task. They challenge students to think about the characteristics of quality work and how to plan for success. They enable teachers to clarify to students what is expected in a learning experience and what to do to reach higher levels of achievement.
- **Standards for evaluation,** providing clear, quantified criteria that state the parameters of quality work. They specify evaluation criteria and describe each level on a scoring scale. Thus, a rubric is a scoring guide that distinguishes acceptable from unacceptable responses and establishes a clearer standard to more accurately and fairly determine grades.

Kingore, B. (2007). *Assessment,* 4th ed. Austin, TX: Professional Associates Publishing.

- **Task specific or generalizable.** Specific rubrics relate to one topic or task and assess a particular learning experience. Generalizable rubrics can be used with repeated applications and conserve preparation time; they can be modified as needed. While both are useful, generalizable rubrics are more practical for busy teachers.

- **Holistic or analytical.** Holistic rubrics aggregate all of the evaluative criteria into a single qualitative score. The format of a holistic rubric is hierarchically arranged statements or paragraphs. The evaluation is based on a consensus of the entire work and is useful when the objective is to focus on the process or product as a whole.

To initially develop holistic scoring, sort students' work into stacks that represent different levels of quality, such as *strong, adequate, below level,* and *inadequate.* Then, describe each stack in terms of the attributes common to those works and hierarchically arrange those descriptions on a holistic rubric. Holistic rubrics are useful in many instructional situations. Students use Figure 6.1 or Figure 6.2 to self-evaluate their learning behaviors as they complete a classroom task. Reviewing Figure 6.3 helps students to focus their goals

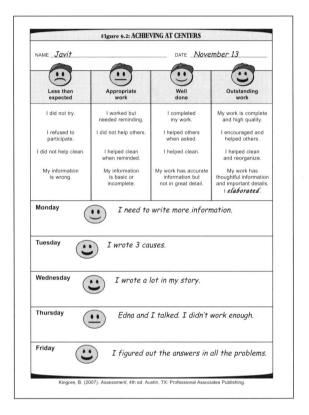

Kingore, B. (2007). *Assessment,* 4th ed. Austin, TX: Professional Associates Publishing.

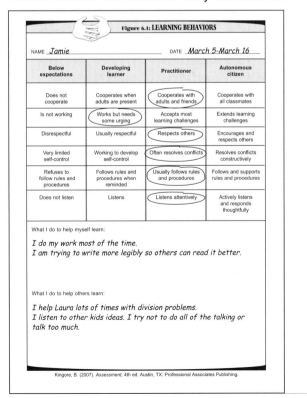

Kingore, B. (2007). *Assessment,* 4th ed. Austin, TX: Professional Associates Publishing.

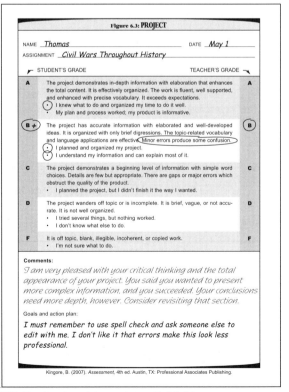

Kingore, B. (2007). *Assessment,* 4th ed. Austin, TX: Professional Associates Publishing.

Kingore, B. (2007). *Assessment,* 4th ed. Austin, TX: Professional Associates Publishing.

Figure 6.1: LEARNING BEHAVIORS

NAME _____ DATE _____

Below expectations	Developing learner	Practitioner	Autonomous citizen
Does not cooperate	Cooperates when adults are present	Cooperates with adults and friends	Cooperates with all classmates
Is not working	Works but needs some urging	Accepts most learning challenges	Extends learning challenges
Disrespectful	Usually respectful	Respects others	Encourages and respects others
Very limited self-control	Working to develop self-control	Often resolves conflicts	Resolves conflicts constructively
Refuses to follow rules and procedures	Follows rules and procedures when reminded	Usually follows rules and procedures	Follows and supports rules and procedures
Does not listen	Listens	Listens attentively	Actively listens and responds thoughtfully

What I do to help myself learn:

What I do to help others learn:

Kingore, B. (2007). *Assessment,* 4th ed. Austin, TX: Professional Associates Publishing.

Rubrics

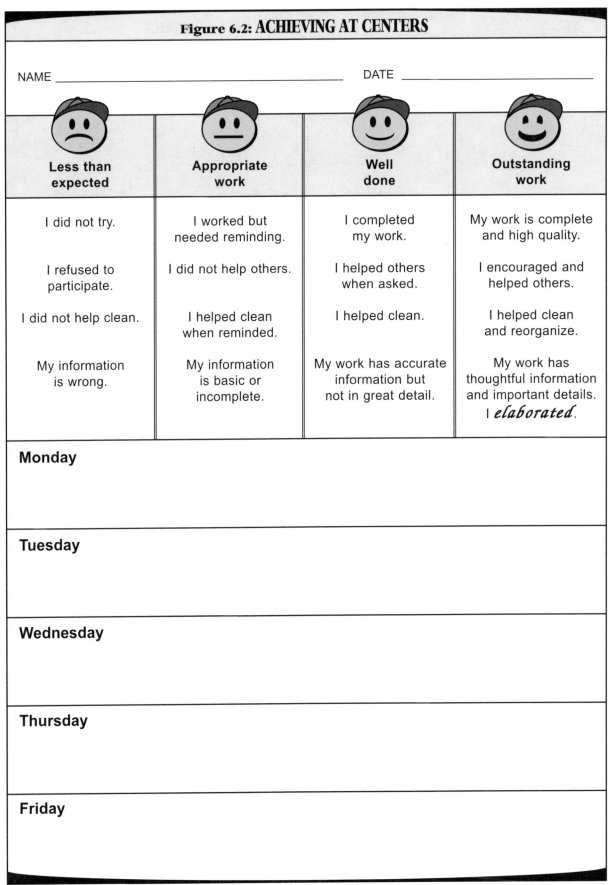

Figure 6.2: ACHIEVING AT CENTERS

NAME _____   DATE _____

Less than expected	Appropriate work	Well done	Outstanding work
I did not try. I refused to participate. I did not help clean. My information is wrong.	I worked but needed reminding. I did not help others. I helped clean when reminded. My information is basic or incomplete.	I completed my work. I helped others when asked. I helped clean. My work has accurate information but not in great detail.	My work is complete and high quality. I encouraged and helped others. I helped clean and reorganize. My work has thoughtful information and important details. I *elaborated*.

Monday

Tuesday

Wednesday

Thursday

Friday

Kingore, B. (2007). *Assessment,* 4th ed. Austin, TX: Professional Associates Publishing.

before they begin; teachers and/or students use the same rubric to analyze students' levels of achievement at the completion of the task.

Analytical rubrics allow an evaluation of each criterion instead of scoring the product as a whole. An analytical rubric lists specific criteria with the characteristics for degrees of success listed as separate levels beside or under each criterion. Thus, analytical rubrics enable teachers and students to recognize that a student's degree of proficiency may vary among the different criteria of the work. For example, a student might score at grade level on several criteria and slightly higher or lower on another criterion. Figure 6.4 and Figure 6.5 are examples of analytical rubrics. The Rubric Generator at the end of this chapter (Figure 6.9) enables teachers to effectively develop analytical rubrics for any learning task.

There are no absolutes in terms of how many levels best communicate the different

degrees of success for each criterion. The goal is a valid differentiation of levels that is more broad than just right or wrong yet is not so broad that differences seem minute.[41] An even number of degrees helps avoid the problem of someone just settling on the center too often instead of more carefully analyzing levels.

To challenge advanced and gifted students, use a rubric with six levels. Level four represents grade-level standards and scores an *A* in terms of a grade. Five and six also score an *A* but delineate what a student can do to achieve the next levels of expertise. This hierarchy encourages many advanced students to set higher expectations and challenge themselves to excel beyond grade-level standards.

Figure 6.5: WRITING

NAME *Jullian*　　　　　　　　　　DATE *April 5*
PROJECT *Persuasive Letter*

	Below standard	Apprentice	Developing	Proficient
Conventions •Capitalizing •Grammar •Paragraphs •Punctuation •Spelling Points *17*¦20	Serious errors makes reading and understanding difficult *below 14* points	Frequent errors are present but content is readable; emerging skills *14-15* points	Minimal errors; mechanical and spelling are typical and appropriate for grade level *16-17* points	The product is enhanced by the skillful application of mechanics; fluid *18-20* points
Idea development Points *19*¦20	No clear focus or main idea; details are confusing *below 14* points	Stated main idea; most details relate to it *14-15* points	Clear focus; appropriate main idea; details relate and clarify ideas *16-17* points	Cohesive; well defined and elaborated main idea; details increase interest and meaning *18-20* points
Vocabulary Points *20*¦20	Some words are inappropriate or used incorrectly *below 14* points	Words and phrases are simple or vague *14-15* points	Descriptive and interesting language is used appropriately with elaboration *16-17* points	Uses specific terminology; precise, advanced language; rich imagery *18-20* points
Organization Points *18*¦20	Unclear; lacks organization *below 14* points	Attempts to organize and sequence but the writing is hard to follow *14-15* points	Organized effectively; a good beginning and end; clear sequence; well structured *16-17* points	Coherent; skillfully planned; logically sequenced and organized to communicate well *18-20* points
Sentence fluency Points *17*¦20	Short, choppy, or incomplete sentences *below 14* points	Generally complete; simple sentences; some run-on sentences *14-15* points	Well-constructed and varied sentences; smooth transitions *16-17* points	Crafted with a variety in sentence length and structure that enhances the total effect; fluid *18-20* points

TOTAL: *91*¦100

Kingore, B. (2007). *Assessment,* 4th ed. Austin, TX. Professional Associates Publishing

Figure 6.4: OPEN-ENDED PRODUCT

NAME *Candy*　　　　　　　　　　DATE *November 11*
PRODUCT OR LEARNING EXPERIENCE *Diorama of the Solar System*

	Information	Writing conventions	Vocabulary	Organization
Getting started	Little information not accurate Points: Below 28	Serious errors make it hard to understand Points: Below 14	Incorrect Points: Below 14	Unorganized Points: Below 14
On the right track	Basic facts; needs elaboration Points: 28• 29• 30 •(31)	Frequent errors but readable; emerging skills Points: 14 • 15	Simple words and phrases Points: 14 • 15	Hard to follow at some places Points: 14 • 15
Got it	Develops topic well; includes most of the key ideas and concepts; some substantiation Points: 32• 33 • 34 • 35	Few errors; appropriate in __capitalization __punctuation __spelling __complete sentences __grammar Points: 16 • 17	Descriptive; uses interesting and varied word choices Points: 16 •(17)	Organized; a clear sequence Points: 16 • 17
Wow!	In-depth information; well supported ideas; elaborates Points: 36• 37 • 38 • 39 • 40	Skillful application of mechanics in ✓capitalization ✓punctuation ✓spelling ✓complete sentences __grammar Points:(18) 19 • 20	Advanced; uses specific terms and multiple-syllable words; rich adjectives Points: 18 • 19 • 20	Skillfully planned, organized, and sequenced; fluent Points: 18 •(19) 20

Total Grade Points *85*/100	COMMENTS *This is carefully done and shows your time and preparation. You incorporate a good depth of content in a clearly organized manner. Read Elliot's Mission to Neptune to expand your understanding of the relationships among the planets.*

Kingore, B. (2005). *Assessment,* 3rd ed. Austin: Professional Associates Publishing.

[41] Parents and students often associate a five-degree rubric with the traditional A-B-C-D-F of letter grades. Hence, it is best to avoid a five-degree rubric if letter grades are not the intent.

Kingore, B. (2007). *Assessment,* 4th ed. Austin, TX: Professional Associates Publishing.

Figure 6.3: PROJECT

NAME _____ DATE _____

ASSIGNMENT _____

STUDENT'S GRADE		TEACHER'S GRADE
A	The project demonstrates in-depth information with elaboration that enhances the total content. It is effectively organized. The work is fluent, well supported, and enhanced with precise vocabulary. It exceeds expectations. • I knew what to do and organized my time to do it well. • My plan and process worked; my product is informative.	**A**
B	The project has accurate information with elaborated and well-developed ideas. It is organized with only brief digressions. The topic-related vocabulary and language applications are effective. Minor errors produce some confusion. • I planned and organized my project. • I understand my information and can explain most of it.	**B**
C	The project demonstrates a beginning level of information with simple word choices. Details are few but appropriate. There are gaps or major errors which obstruct the quality of the product. • I planned the project, but I didn't finish it the way I wanted.	**C**
D	The project wanders off topic or is incomplete. It is brief, vague, or not accurate. It is not well organized. • I tried several things, but nothing worked. • I don't know what else to do.	**D**
F	It is off topic, blank, illegible, incoherent, or copied work. • I'm not sure what to do.	**F**

Comments:

Goals and action plan:

Kingore, B. (2007). *Assessment,* 4th ed. Austin, TX: Professional Associates Publishing.

Rubrics

Figure 6.4: OPEN-ENDED PRODUCT

NAME _____ DATE _____

PRODUCT OR LEARNING EXPERIENCE _____

	Information	Writing conventions	Vocabulary	Organization
Getting started	Little information not accurate Points: Below 28	Serious errors make it hard to understand Points: Below 14	Incorrect Points: Below 14	Unorganized Points: Below 14
On the right track	Basic facts; needs elaboration Points: 28• 29 • 30 • 31	Frequent errors but readable; emerging skills Points: 14 • 15	Simple words and phrases Points: 14 • 15	Hard to follow at some places Points: 14 • 15
Got it	Develops topic well; includes most of the key ideas and concepts; some substantiation Points: 32• 33 • 34 • 35	Few errors; appropriate in __capitalization __punctuation __spelling __complete sentences __grammar Points: 16 • 17	Descriptive; uses interesting and varied word choices Points: 16 • 17	Organized; a clear sequence Points: 16 • 17
Wow!	In-depth information; well supported ideas; elaborates Points: 36 • 37 • 38 • 39 • 40	Skillful application of mechanics in __capitalization __punctuation __spelling __complete sentences __grammar Points: 18 • 19 • 20	Advanced; uses specific terms and multiple-syllable words; rich adjectives Points: 18 • 19 • 20	Skillfully planned, organized, and sequenced; fluent Points: 18 • 19 • 20

Total Grade Points	COMMENTS
/	

Kingore, B. (2007). *Assessment,* 4th ed. Austin, TX: Professional Associates Publishing.

Figure 6.5: WRITING

NAME _____ DATE _____

PROJECT _____

Conventions •Capitalizing •Grammar •Paragraphs •Punctuating •Spelling Points __/___	Serious errors makes reading and understanding difficult _____ points	Frequent errors are present but content is readable; emerging skills _____ points	Minimal errors; mechanical and spelling are typical and appropriate for grade level _____ points	The product is enhanced by the skillful application of mechanics; fluid _____ points
Idea development Points __/___	No clear focus or main idea; details are confusing _____ points	Stated main idea; most details relate to it _____ points	Clear focus; appropriate main idea; details relate and clarify ideas _____ points	Cohesive; well defined and elaborated main idea; details increase interest and meaning _____ points
Vocabulary Points __/___	Some words are inappropriate or used incorrectly _____ points	Words and phrases are simple or vague _____ points	Descriptive and interesting language is used appropriately with elaboration _____ points	Uses specific terminology; precise, advanced language; rich imagery _____ points
Organization Points __/___	Unclear; lacks organization _____ points	Attempts to organize and sequence but the writing is hard to follow _____ points	Organized effectively; a good beginning and end; clear sequence; well structured _____ points	Coherent; skillfully planned; logically sequenced and organized to communicate well _____ points
Sentence fluency Points __/___	Short, choppy, or incomplete sentences _____ points	Generally complete; simple sentences; some run-on sentences _____ points	Well-constructed and varied sentences; smooth transitions _____ points	Crafted with a variety in sentence length and structure that enhances the total effect; fluid _____ points

TOTAL:

Kingore, B. (2007). *Assessment,* 4th ed. Austin, TX: Professional Associates Publishing.

CHARACTERISTICS OF A QUALITY RUBRIC

Quality rubrics:

- Reflect the most significant elements related to success in a learning task. The criteria focus on the *main ideas* of the work rather than a narrow list of skills or procedures. Each level of a criterion elaborates the *details* of successful achievement by describing important aspects that represent the best thinking in the field.[42]
- Organize elements in a progression from least developed to most stellar (or most to least, if preferred).[43]
- Are practical and easily used by students and teachers to accurately and consistently identify the level of competency or stage of development.
- Promote a standard for more accurate and fair grading.
- Encourage students' self-evaluation, high expectations, and achievement.
- Are shared with students prior to beginning the task so they know the characteristics of quality work.
- Are demonstrated to students with accompanying examples of products representing very different levels of responses that clarify a range of quality from low to high for that assignment..

Product Descriptors and Rubrics

Product descriptors and rubrics are distinct but related assessment and evaluation tools. A product descriptor is an inventory or checklist of the components of the assignment. Even when points are included, however, it does not explain the degree of quality for any requirement on the list. Hence, using product descriptors increases subjectivity when grading (*I guess this report gets a B*) and fails to guide students' thinking about how to demonstrate higher achievement. A product descriptor or checklist of components is best used to guide students' process as they complete assignments. A rubric is needed to guide students' level of quality and evaluate the results of their work. Rubrics need to accompany product descriptors for assessment and evaluation. A comparative analysis of product descriptors and rubrics is developed in Figure 6.6.

Everyone Benefits from Rubrics

Rubrics provide teachers, students, and parents with standards of achievement instead of relying on more subjective decisions.

TEACHERS BENEFIT

- Use rubrics to set clear expectations for assignments and to assess learners' current levels of proficiency.
- Carefully constructed rubrics are relevant to instruction and guide teachers in designing lessons that enable students to reach higher levels of proficiency.
- Rubrics provide a standard by which to explain grades to parents and students.
- Once fully established, rubrics can make the grading process more interesting and efficient.

STUDENTS BENEFIT

- Rubrics help students set individual goals and provide students with a clearer view of the merits and demerits of their work than grades alone communicate.
- Rubrics communicate to students that they are responsible for the grades they *earn*

---

[42] Stiggins, 2005. Stiggins stipulates that rubrics must be *on target* which he defines as clear, complete, and compelling to represent the best thinking in the field.

[43] Experience in rubric applications suggests that either progression is effective and simply a matter of teacher/student preference.

Kingore, B. (2007). *Assessment,* 4th ed. Austin, TX: Professional Associates Publishing.

Figure 6.6:
PRODUCT DESCRIPTORS AND RUBRICS

Evaluation Tool	Example	Advantages	Disadvantages
Product descriptor	**SCIENCE LAB REPORT** ☐ Components ☐ Procedure ☐ Data ☐ Conclusions ☐ Appearance	• It lists the different components or attributes of the product • It is a useful checklist for students to determine which components to include.	• It fails to clarify that there are degrees of achievement. • It is vague. Teachers and students are less likely to agree on the ratings.
Product descriptor with a grading scale	**SCIENCE LAB REPORT** Components 10 ·· 7 ·· 4 ·· 0 Procedure 20 ·· 15 ·· 10 ·· 0 Data 30 ·· 20 ·· 10 ·· 0 Conclusions 30 ·· 20 ·· 10 ·· 0 Appearance 10 ·· 7 ·· 4 ·· 0	• It has all of the advantages of a product descriptor. • It provides points or a scale to clarify that there are different degrees of quality.	• The points do not explain to students what to do to improve their grade or achievement. • It is vague. It fails to specify what constitutes differences among the points on the scale so teachers and students are less likely to agree on ratings.
Rubric	Figure 6.7: Science Lab Report	• It lists the evaluative criteria and elaborates the ascending or descending levels of achievement for each criterion so students see what to do to increase achievement. • Well-constructed rubrics require teachers to carefully analyze and communicate the learning task and the teacher's objectives. • Well-constructed rubrics clarify the characteristics of quality work so teachers and students are more likely to agree on the ratings.	• It is more time-consuming to produce.

Kingore, B. (2007). *Assessment*, 4th ed. Austin, TX: Professional Associates Publishing.

NAME _____   DATE _____   EXPERIMENT _____

Comments:

Goals and action plan:

A Lab Report should include: Heading, Title, Problem, Hypothesis, Materials, Procedures, Data, Drawings/diagrams, and Conclusions.

Figure 6.7: SCIENCE LAB REPORT

TOTAL POINTS: ____ /	Components	Procedures	Data	Conclusions	Appearance/ Mechanics
Below standard	Comments are missing or flawed Below 7 points	Steps are missing or not accurate Below 14 points	Inaccurate and/or incomplete Below 21 points	Illogical or not accurate Below21 points	Inadequate; not neat; little care is evident Below 7 points
Apprentice	One or more components are missing or poorly developed 7 points	Not sequential; confusing 14-15 points	Measurements and observations are accurate; lacks graphs or tables 21-23 points	Limited understanding of scientific concepts underlying the lab; simple or vague 21-23 points	Adequate; needs more careful attention to detail; frequent errors present but readable 7 points
Proficient	Required components are complete and appropriate 8 points	Adequate; in logical order but lacks detail 16-17 points	Accurate representation of data in tables, graphs, and written form 24-27 points	Accurate understanding; addresses problem and states knowledge gained 24-27 points	Attractive; neatly completed; typed; mechanics and spelling are appropriate 8 points
Exceeding	All required components are complete and add to the effectiveness of the report 9-10 points	Logical; numbered; detailed; complete sentences 18-20 points	Professional and accurate graphs, charts, drawings and written form; specific terminology 28-30 points	Accurate and thorough interpretation; logical explanation clearly addresses the questions 28-30 points	Professionally completed; aesthetically pleasing; typed; skillful application of mechanics 9-10 points

Kingore, B. (2007). *Assessment*, 4th ed. Austin, TX: Professional Associates Publishing.

Rubrics

rather than to continue to view grades as something someone *gives* them.

- Quality rubrics affect achievement. Marzano's (2000) research supports that rubrics' directly effect student learning, and increase achievement by fourteen to thirty-two percentile points. Rubrics encourage teachers to analyze the higher and lower qualities of desired knowledge and skills and then pass this perspective on to students in the form of rubrics that, in turn, improve student achievement by helping them think more clearly about the characteristics of quality and success.

PARENTS BENEFIT

- Rubrics inform parents about which learning concepts and skills are required at a specific grade level.
- Rubrics more concretely explain students' learning capabilities and achievement levels.
- Rubrics communicate more clearly the standard supporting grades so parents understand why a student earns certain grades.

Rubrics are effective preassessment tools. Teachers or students use a rubric to goal set or preassess before instruction begins and then revisit the rubric after instruction to assess growth and continuing learning needs.

The Accuracy of Rubrics

Some adults are suspicious of the assessment validity of rubric applications and assume that rubrics introduce grading subjectivity. Marzano argues that the current system based upon points and percentages is inherently *more* subjective. His research found that the correlation between the rubric score and a standardized test was much higher than the correlation between a point or letter-grade and a standardized test.[44]

Conduct the following experiment to illustrate the efficacy of rubrics. At a faculty meeting or workshop, ask teachers to independently grade a provided paper. Invariably, the responses lack consensus and cover a wide range of grades. The obvious problem is that if teachers are unclear of a common standard of quality, students are also likely to be confused. A rubric defuses this dilemma by providing a shared standard of quality. Rubrics are essential to help ensure consistency and fairness in evaluation so different educators assign similar grades to a work sample. Without a rubric, a grade of *A* may not mean the same thing in different classes.

Rubrics are standard in life situations. Increase parents', students' and other professionals' confidence in rubrics by reminding them of the large number of situations in addition to education in which rubrics are consistently used.

STUDENT SELF-ASSESSMENT AND PEER ASSESSMENT

Students take more ownership in learning when they are expected to assess their work using provided criteria for success.[45] Teachers develop students' self-assessment skills through modeling in class sessions. Questions, such as the metacognitive questions in Chapter 4, focus students' reflection and prompt them to analyze and discuss multiple aspects of their work. Help students cultivate self-assessment as a habit by expecting them to engage in self-assessment and evaluation regularly.

---

[44] Marzano, 2000.

[45] Leahy, Lyon, Thompson, & Wiliam, 2005; McTighe & O'Connor, 2005; Stiggins, 2005.

Kingore, B. (2007). *Assessment,* 4th ed. Austin, TX: Professional Associates Publishing.

Implementing peer assessment also helps students develop self-assessment habits. Experienced teachers know that students spot errors in other's work much more quickly and energetically than in their own work. Peer editing and peer evaluation in small groups can be productive in teaching students to understand and more conscientiously use rubrics. Leahy, Lyon, Thompson, & Wiliam (2005) caution that "...students should not be giving another student a grade that will be reported to parents or administrators. Peer assessment should be focused on improvement, not on grading" (p. 21).

To be effective, assessment feedback needs to cause students to think.[46] Self-assessment, using a rubric written in student-friendly language or developed by the class with teacher guidance, causes students to be more engaged in assessment and to think about their own achievement.

Self-assessment is quite valuable for students and adults. It is essential to any student's progress toward being a responsible learner, and it provides a window for adults to learn about students' perspectives of learning. To engage in self-evaluation, students complete the learning assignment and use a provided rubric to assess each level they earned before handing the product to the teacher. When teachers grade the same task, they use a different color to evaluate on the same form. Ideally, the two evaluations match. Increase students' thinking by including a section on the bottom of a rubric for comments and for students' goal setting and action planning. With the addition of this space, McTighe and O'Conner (2005) conclude that "...the rubric moves from being simply an evaluation tool for 'pinning a number' on students to a practical and robust vehicle for feedback, self-assessment, and goal setting" (p.13).

Educators who provide regular opportunities for self-assessment report valued changes in the learning culture. Students become increasingly capable of monitoring, adjusting learning, and setting significant goals. They also more honestly and accurately engage in self-appraisal. Indeed, some students' evaluations are harder on themselves than the teacher's evaluation.

When Students Aren't Accurate

Some teachers report that not all students are accurate or honest when using rubrics. The following suggestions guide responses to this problem.

- Review the assessment tools in use. Some teachers refer to product descriptors as rubrics. Product descriptors are a fine tool to provide students with a list of the components to include in the product but they are less likely to produce accurate student self-evaluations for the reasons compared in Figure 6.6. Clearly articulated levels of proficiency produce more accurate student responses.
- Refine the language used to delineate levels. Strive to replace generalized words, such as *good* or *excellent* and *frequently* or *sometimes,* with more precise words to clarify intended traits.
- Invest time in thoroughly training students to use rubrics. Providing a rubric to students before beginning an assignment is necessary but insufficient to support learning. Students may lack the teacher's clear conception of what constitutes quality work.[47]
  - Conduct mini-lessons demonstrating the process of accurately evaluating with rubrics.
  - Provide examples from weak to strong learning responses.
  - Direct the class through the process of evaluating each work using a rubric.
  - Emphasize procedural steps.

[46] Leahy, Lyon, Thompson, & Wiliam, 2005; Wiggins,1998.
[47] McTighe & O'Connor, 2005.

Kingore, B. (2007). *Assessment,* 4th ed. Austin, TX: Professional Associates Publishing.

– Later, small groups of students work together using a rubric to evaluate another set of products.

- Model a *think aloud.* Teachers or students share with others the cognitive processes or thinking that they go through as they evaluate a product with a rubric.

- Actively follow through on the accuracy of students' self evaluations. If only one or two students have accuracy issues, meet with each individually to briefly review specific use of a self-assessment rubric. Ask the student to justify each level response with examples in the product. Actively listen and clarify when misunderstandings exist.

- Continue discussing the process with the class. Model and share specific examples.

Teachers have found a place for both product descriptors and rubrics in their instruction. Some teachers prefer a product descriptor to introduce the learning experience and concretely outline the components of the learning task. Then, they combine the descriptors into major category criteria and clarify each degree of success to construct a rubric for the task. Thus, the product descriptor becomes a checklist for students to mark their progress and inclusion of the requirements as they work; the rubric is their evaluation tool.

Guidelines for Constructing Quality Rubrics

1. Articulate what is meant by quality work. Discuss with other professionals the measurable characteristics that distinguish stellar from mediocre responses.
2. Collect samples of rubrics as models to adapt as needed.
3. Determine potential criteria by collecting a wide quality range of students' work

and then analyzing attributes common to performances at different levels of achievement.

4. As often as appropriate, limit the number of criteria so the rubric fits on one page. Lengthy rubrics appear more overwhelming and therefore less practical to use. Limit the number of criteria by focusing on the main ideas of the learning task.
5. For each criterion, write descriptors for the levels of quality exhibited in students' work. Circle words that can vary and adjust them during revisions of the levels.
6. As often as possible, accent *what to do* in the proficiency levels of each criterion rather than just relating what is wrong or calculating the number of errors. In other words, try to tell the student how to achieve a higher level instead of just label the problem.
7. The first priority is to clearly determine and communicate the degrees of success for each criterion. It is tempting to lapse into humorous or clever phrases (*1st base, 2nd base, 3rd base, and home run*), but save those ideas for later.
8. As much as possible, avoid generalities such as *good-better-best* or *little-some-frequently.* When generalities are evident, review the rubric to refine terminology.
9. Use points, percentages, or grades to weight each criterion. Weighting designates the relative importance of each criterion so students understand where to focus their learning time and effort.
10. Ask colleagues to read or use constructed rubrics and offer improvement suggestions.
11. When feasible, use the rubric in more than one class. Rewrite specific word choices based on those applications. When appropriate, elicit ideas for clarification and change from students.
12. The process of creating rubrics can seem difficult and time-consuming. It is often developmental–using a rubric reveals ways to change it. Be comfortable reevaluating, revising, and rewriting rubrics.

Kingore, B. (2007). *Assessment,* 4th ed. Austin, TX: Professional Associates Publishing.

THE RUBRIC GENERATOR: TIER II AND TIER III

The Rubric Generator is a device I began developing in 1990 to enable teachers to create rubrics in less time and with less frustration by duplicating, cutting, and pasting components. It has evolved and greatly expanded into the rubric generator shared as Figure 6.9. Skim the Rubric Generator and other collected rubrics to determine the criteria crucial to contents, processes, and products typical in the curriculum. Photocopy or print[48] the applicable criterion strips–a criterion and levels of achievement. When planning a specific learning experience and evaluation, select which criterion strips apply to that task. Rewrite and adapt each as needed, organize and paste them on the form, and complete the new rubric. In this manner, customize and construct needed rubrics for learning assignments without starting from scratch each time. Figure 6.9 is designed so that the criterion strips fit the template. Figure 6.8 highlights the process for using the Rubric Generator.

The criteria apply to multiple content areas, so the generator is presented as an alphabetical listing of criterion strips. *Complexity* and *organization*, for example, are criteria applicable to products in science, social studies, language arts, and math.

Rubric Tiers

The Rubric Generator has three tiers of complexity to accommodate different learning levels.[49] Tier II is a simplified version. It is useful when brief rubrics are preferred or when more simple language would better communicate to a specific student population. Tier III presents expanded descriptors to more specifically communicate what constitutes quality work and how to incorporate depth and

Figure 6.8:
Using the Rubric Generator

1. **Select applicable criteria.**
   Skim the Rubric Generator and any collected rubrics to determine the specific criteria that are crucial to intended content, process, or product evaluation.

2. **Copy criteria strips.**
   Photocopy the applicable criteria and levels of proficiencies. Cut each criterion as a separate strip to more easily maneuver into a new rubric.

3. **Organize the criteria.**
   Place the criteria strips on one or more copies of the blank rubric template (Figure 6.8).

4. **Review and rewrite the criteria strips.**
   When planning a specific learning experience evaluation, rewrite and adapt any of the descriptors to increase quality as well as more specifically address the assignment and student population.

5. **Weight each criterion.**
   Use points, percentages, or grades to weight each criterion and designate its relative importance within the total learning task.

Process

---

[48] The *Assessment Interactive CD-ROM* is a tool to digitally compile rubrics (Kingore, 2007).
[49] See Chapter 3 for the Rubric Generator: Tier I.

Kingore, B. (2007). *Assessment,* 4th ed. Austin, TX: Professional Associates Publishing.

Tier II Example

Figure 6.9: RUBRIC GENERATOR

NAME _____ DATE _____

ASSIGNMENT __Mathematics Problem Solving__

	Math application	Math communication	Math concepts	Math strategies
Started	Failed attempt at a solution	Incorrect or missing	Incorrect; misunderstood	Inappropriate; flawed application
	Below 21 points	Below 21 points	Below 14 points	Below 14 points
On the right track	Needed prompting; errors present	Minimal explanation; basic terminology	Understands the problem but the solution or procedure has flaws	Generally correct but too simple
	21-23 points	21-23 points	14-15 points	14-15 points
Got it!	Correct solution; minimal prompting or errors	Appropriate terminology and labels	Correct problem and solution	Correct; efficient strategies; correctly applied
	24-26 points	24-26 points	16-17 points	16-17 points
WOW!	Correct solution; precise application;high-level response	Precise terminology and clearly labeled graphics	Correctly interprets and clearly explains concepts	Innovating and high level; above expectations
	27-30 points	27-30 points	18-20 points	18-20 points

Total Points / **Comments:**

Goals and action plan:

Kingore, B. (2007). *Assessment*, 4th ed. Austin, TX: Professional Associates Publishing.

Tier III Example

Figure 6.9: RUBRIC GENERATOR

NAME _____ DATE _____

ASSIGNMENT __Mathematics Problem Solving:__

	Math applications	Math communication	Math concepts	Math strategies
Below standard	Attempts a solution; limited mathematical applications	Incorrect or no explanation provided	Misunderstood; process and/or solution are incorrect	Inappropriate; no apparent logic to the solution
	Below 21 points	Below 21 points	Below 14 points	Below 14 points
Apprentice	Hesitant to proceed independently; computational errors are present	Explanation is minimal; basic terminology and/or no graphic support	Generally correct; problem is understood but solution and/or procedure has flaws	Approach is oversimplified; strategies are partially flawed in application
	21-23 points	21-23 points	14-15 points	14-15 points
Proficient	Correct solution is achieved; minimal prompting or errors	Appropriate terminology and graphics; clear explanation	Problem and intended solution are correct; uses relevant information correctly	Appropriate, effective strategies; applied correctly and logically
	24-26 points	24-26 points	16-17 points	16-17 points
Exceeding	Formulas are executed correctly; precisely applied; higher-level response than expected	Exceptional explanation; uses advanced, precise terminology and graphics	Correctly interprets all important elements of the problem; integrates advanced concepts independently	Innovative and advanced strategies; independently implemented; sophisticated approach and thinking
	27-30 points	27-30 points	18-20 points	18-20 points

Total Points / **Comments:**

Goals and action plan:

Kingore, B. (2007). *Assessment*, 4th ed. Austin, TX: Professional Associates Publishing.

complexity. This version is most useful when communicating with mature students, adults, or when detailed rubrics are needed.

Determining Point Values

On this page, the analytical rubrics for mathematics are constructed with four criterion strips from the Rubric Generator: Tier II and then from the Tier III generator to compare the levels. Each criterion is weighted by determining point values and then multiplying by the grading scale to determine the range for each achievement level. Specifically, if 90 percent is an *A*, then 0.9 times 20 points equals 18 to 20 points for the highest level on the rubric; if 80 is a *B,* then 0.8 times 20 equals 16 to 17 points.

Numerical adjustments are frequently needed after calculating the point range for each level. Adjust the points to:
1. Compensate for values rounded up or down when not whole numbers.
2. Ensure that each of the levels of quality totals as close as possible to the points appropriate to that grading scale. For example, the level for an A should total 90 to 100 points (or whatever the point spread for the preferred grading scale).
3. Balance the range of points within each potential score so that each range is approximately the same. For example, when a criterion, such as strategies, is worth 20 points, the points for each score have to range from two to three points: 14 to 15, 16 to 17, and 18 to 19 points.

Point values are an effective communication tool because they clarify the total grade to students and parents. Teachers or students circle the score earned within each range of points and then total them to compute the final grade. This process, for example, clearly communicates why a student earns an 82 and which criteria require changes if the student intends to earn a higher score.

Kingore, B. (2007). *Assessment,* 4th ed. Austin, TX: Professional Associates Publishing.

STUDENT-DEVELOPED RUBRICS

After students are experienced using rubrics, increase their involvement in rewriting or developing rubrics. The objectives are:
- To promote students' ownership in their assessment;
- To increase students' involvement in interpreting levels of achievement for each criterion on a rubric; and
- To customize a rubric more directly to a specific learning assignment.

The following procedure is easily implemented and typically takes twenty to twenty-five minutes of class time to complete.

1. To control the time required for the decision-making process, the teacher preselects five to eight criteria strips from the Rubric Generator that are applicable to the intended learning experience.
2. The teacher provides copies of the selected criteria strips to the class and involves them in determining which four to six criteria they think are most important for the assignment. Frequently, the teacher designates that one or two of the criteria are required. For example, a teacher may announce that *content depth* is vital to the assignment and must be one of the final five criteria.
3. Divide the class into groups and provide each group one criterion strip to evaluate and rewrite for five to ten minutes. Some teachers allow informal and clever but classroom-appropriate phrases instead of more formal terminology. To facilitate class sharing, give each group a strip of an overhead transparency sheet on which to copy their final criterion levels.
4. Place the rewritten criteria strips on the overhead or document camera to facilitate review and organization by the entire class. Consider additional suggestions and responses before adopting the final copy.
5. The edited criteria strips are then photocopied or typed by one student on the computer and distributed to the class as the rubric for that assignment. The research project rubric below is an example of a student-developed rubric with edited criteria strips.

Figure 6.9: RUBRIC GENERATOR

NAME _____ DATE _____

ASSIGNMENT ___Research Project___

	Resources	Content depth	Critical thinking	Diagram
Beginner	Inappropriate, did not search very much	Inaccurate or missing information	Brain dead	Messy; wrong
Assistant	Minimal resources but used correctly	Valid but basic information	General understanding; limited examination of one viewpoint	Neat and accurate but not very informative
Researcher	Appropriate in quantity, quality, and application; accurately documented	Covers topic effectively; well developed and supported; goes beyond basic facts	Understands scope of topic; conclusion reflects analysis of information	Carefully prepared; accurate; adds to a reader's understanding
Einstein	Extensive, varied, and high caliber; professionally documented; uses advanced technology and most current data	Precise data; in-depth; well supported with details and examples; develops complex relationships	Clearly understands scope and issues; conclusions based upon thorough examination of evidence; analyzes alternatives	Artfully prepared; labeled and accurate; clarifies and embellishes a reader's understanding
Total Points /	Comments:			
Goals and action plan:				

Kingore, B. (2007). *Assessment*, 4th ed. Austin, TX: Professional Associates Publishing.

With time and experience, students become surprisingly sophisticated in their understanding of the value of rubrics. Kim Cheek, a teacher of gifted students at Wylie Middle School, verified that her students truly understood the process when they were asked to judge a writing contest for young children. Her students decided that they should write a rubric so their judging would be more fair. They then created a rubric to guide their decisions before they proceeded to judge the contest.

Rubrics have been successfully used for years in the Olympics, Wall Street stock analysis, beauty and talent contests, state and national level tests, and many professional competitions.

Kingore, B. (2007). *Assessment,* 4th ed. Austin, TX: Professional Associates Publishing.

Figure 6.9: RUBRIC GENERATOR

NAME _____ DATE _____

ASSIGNMENT _____

Total Points	Comments:
/	

Goals and action plan:

Kingore, B. (2007). *Assessment,* 4th ed. Austin, TX: Professional Associates Publishing.

RUBRIC GENERATOR: TIER II [50]

Consider using the following descriptive terms to label the achievement levels. The descriptors describe the ascending levels of achievement as well as the desired behaviors of the students.

| Below standard | Intermediate | Advanced | Exceeds standard |

| Beginning | Developing | Competent | Distinguished |

| Below expectations | Basic | Proficient | Advanced |

| Started | On the right track | Got It! | WOW! |

| Novice | Apprentice | Practitioner | Expert |

| Emerging | Developing | Proficient | Exemplary |

[50] See Chapter 3 for the Rubric Generator: Tier I in which the achievement levels are presented in a pictorial form for learners with beginning reading skills.

Carried out plan	Calculations	Application	Appearance
No plan; not complete	Not correct	Little effort	Not neat
Completed with frequent help	Some errors	Not able to complete independently; errors	Needs more careful detail
Good plan; completed with little help	Some calculations shown; correct results; labeled	Correct; little prompting; few if any errors	Attractive; neat
Well planned; followed through well; self-motivated	All calculations shown; correct results; appropriately labeled	High-level; skillful	Eye-catching; beyond expectation

Kingore, B. (2007). *Assessment,* 4th ed. Austin, TX: Professional Associates Publishing.

Communication	Complexity	Components	Comprehension	Conclusions	Constructs meaning
No discussion	Too simple	Missing or flawed	Does not understand	Incorrect	Nonsense
Needs prompting and focus	Simple information; little critical thinking	One or more parts are missing or poorly developed	Beginning level of understanding	Accurate but simple or vague	Unclear; rambles
Explains or discusses	Uses critical thinking; compares and contrasts	Required parts are complete	Adequate understanding; good details	Accurate; addresses problem and states knowledge gained	Clear and understandable
Clear; confident; strong vocabulary	Beyond expected level; analyzes from multiple points of view	All required parts are complete and effective	Thorough understanding; uses precise vocabulary, details, and concepts	Accurate; thorough explanation; addresses all of the questions	Meaningful; clear focus; well developed

Kingore, B. (2007). *Assessment,* 4th ed. Austin, TX: Professional Associates Publishing.

Content depth	Cooperation	Creativity	Critical thinking	Diagram	Discussion
Lacks correct information	Does not cooperate; bothers others	Copied	Basic	Incorrect; poorly illustrated	No discussion
Needs depth or elaboration	Cooperates when adults are present	Little creativity	General understanding	Neat and correct; not very informative	Needs prompting
Develops topic well; goes beyond basic facts	Cooperates with adults and friends; helps others when asked	Creative; expanded typical ideas	Understands problem and considers issues; examines evidence	Carefully illustrated; correct; aids understanding	Appropriate nonverbal and verbal interaction
In-depth information; well-supported content; elaborates	Cooperates with adults and all classmates; assists others	Unique; novel; fresh perspective	Clear understanding; thorough examination of evidence and alternatives	Artfully illustrated; thoroughly labeled and accurate; adds to reader's understanding	Verbally and nonverbally shows analysis and active listening

Rubrics

Effort/task commitment	Fluency	Graph	Idea development	Independent work	Integration of skills
Did not try	Choppy; incomplete	Incorrect	Confusing	Did not work	Unable to apply skills
Little effort	Simple sentences; some run-on sentences	Hard to understand	States a main idea; most details fit	Works but interrupts others	Applies some skills; inconsistent
Works and completes task	Well-constructed sentences	Adequate use of data; some labels	Appropriate main idea and details; clear	Works well; helps others; shares; completes task	Accurately applies skills in multiple subject areas; minor errors
Works productively; uses time well; self-motivated	Sentences vary in length and structure; fluid	Plots the data well; easy to interpret; clearly labeled	Well developed main idea with meaningful details	Engaged; encourages and redirects others back to the task; goes beyond the assignment	Consistently integrates skills and information effectively

Kingore, B. (2007). *Assessment,* 4th ed. Austin, TX: Professional Associates Publishing.

Knowledge	Math application	Math communication	Math concepts	Math strategies	Note taking
Little knowledge; not accurate	Attempts a solution	Incorrect or missing	Incorrect; misunderstood	Inappropriate; flawed application	Minimal; missing information
Basic facts	Errors are present	Minimal explanation; basic terminology	Understands the problem but the solution or procedure has flaws	Generally correct but too simple	Records important information
Offers most key ideas and concepts; some substantiation	Correct solution; minimal prompting or errors	Clearly explains; appropriate terminology, labels, and graphics	Correct problem and solution	Correct; efficient strategies; correctly applied	Determines what is most important; a clear picture of the subject
In-depth knowledge; well supported ideas	Correct solution; precise application; high-level response	Exceptional explanation; precise terminology and clearly labeled graphics	Correctly interprets and clearly explains concepts	Innovating and high level; above expectations	Covers subject well; shows which information is more important; rereads notes

Kingore, B. (2007). *Assessment,* 4th ed. Austin, TX: Professional Associates Publishing.

Rubrics

Oral presentation	Organization	Participation	Personal connection	Problem interpretation	Problem solving
Needs help to proceed	Unorganized; unable to follow	Does not participate	Lacking	Misunderstands	Inappropriate or flawed
Needs some help; lacks fluency, eye contact, or gestures	Hard to follow but sequenced	Responds when asked	Limited	Only a basic understanding	Incomplete; limited understanding
Prepared; good gestures and eye contact; well paced	Organized; a clear sequence	Volunteers and responds when necessary	Relates topic to self	Generally correct interpretation and explanation	Appropriate process and application
Exceptional; fluent; mannerisms add to the total effect	Skillfully planned, organized, and sequenced; logical	Volunteers, responds, and elaborates information willfully; includes others	Clearly explains and supports connection between self and topic	Well analyzed interpretation; clearly understands and explains problem	High-level solution; analyzes well

Kingore, B. (2007). *Assessment,* 4th ed. Austin, TX: Professional Associates Publishing.

Procedure	Resources	Scientific data	Strategies	Summarization	Technology
Steps are missing or flawed	Inappropriate	Inaccurate and/or incomplete	Inappropriate or flawed	Not well done; unclear or inaccurate	Does not apply technology
Sequence is correct but has some errors	A few resources used appropriately	Accurate data but lacks graphs or tables	Incomplete; uses limited strategies	Describes part of the information	Limited success; needs assistance
Accurate and complete; in sequence	Appropriate in number, kind, and use; reliable; correct form	Accurate data in tables, graphs, and written form	Applies strategies appropriately	Summarizes information accurately	Independently uses suggested internet sites; applies technology
Complete and clearly developed; well sequenced	Extensive and varied; reliable; accurately documented; independently uses technology	Precise graphs, charts, drawings and written form; specific terminology	Effective use of advanced strategies; flexible	Summary is inclusive, appropriately brief, and clearly developed	Advanced; accesses information with ease; explains technology to others

Kingore, B. (2007). *Assessment,* 4th ed. Austin, TX: Professional Associates Publishing.

Rubrics

Time management	Visual aids	Vocabulary	Voice/style	Writing conventions	Written reflection
Did not complete task	Inappropriate; misused	Incorrect	Not original	Serious errors make it hard to understand	Lacks content
Needed frequent prompting	Little value; limited use	Simple words and phrases	A little style	Frequent errors but readable; emerging skills	Beginning content level
Used time appropriately	Appropriate in number, kind, and appearance; appropriately used	Descriptive; interesting; uses elaboration	Interesting	Few errors; appropriate for grade level	Appropriate content and effort
Mature management; self-motivated	Very attractive; varied; enriches information; well used	Advanced; uses specific terms; rich imagery	Original, personal, and interesting	Skillful application of mechanics; exceeds grade level	High-level response and effort; clear interpretation

Kingore, B. (2007). *Assessment,* 4th ed. Austin, TX: Professional Associates Publishing.

RUBRIC GENERATOR: TIER III [51]

Consider using the following descriptive terms to label the achievement levels. The descriptors describe the ascending levels of achievement as well as the desired behaviors of the students.

| Below standard | Intermediate | Advanced | Exceeds standard |

| Beginning | Developing | Competent | Distinguished |

| Below expectations | Basic | Proficient | Advanced |

| Started | On the right track | Got It! | WOW! |

| Novice | Apprentice | Practitioner | Expert |

| Emerging | Developing | Proficient | Exemplary |

[51] See Chapter 3 for the Rubric Generator: Tier I in which the achievement levels are presented in a pictorial form for learners with beginning reading skills.

Carried out plan	Did not complete plan or lacked plan	Completed with frequent assistance and prompting	Completed plan; limited prompting needed	Followed through well; autonomous; exceeded expectations
Calculations	Inaccurate or mislabeled	Some calculations are shown; some errors	Calculations are shown; results are correct and labeled; minimal errors	All calculations are shown; results are correct and exceptionally well-labeled
Application	Attempts task with limited skill	Hesitant to proceed independently; errors are present	Correct response or solution with minimal prompting or errors	Skillful application; higher-level response than expected; unique
Appearance	Inadequate; not neat; little care evident	Adequate; needs more careful work and attention to detail	Attractive and visually appealing; neatly completed	Eye-catching; aesthetically pleasing; beyond expectations

Kingore, B. (2007). *Assessment,* 4th ed. Austin, TX: Professional Associates Publishing.

Rubrics

Category	Level 1	Level 2	Level 3	Level 4
Communication	Not able to discuss; confused or disjointed	Needs prompting to explain or discuss; lacks a clear focus	Adequate explanation or discussion; appropriate vocabulary	Explains independently, clearly, and confidently; precise vocabulary
Complexity	Insufficient or irrelevant information	Simple and basic information; limited critical thinking is evident	Critical thinking evident; compares and contrasts; integrates topics across time or disciplines	Beyond expected level; analyzes multiple perspectives and issues; abstract thinking
Components	Components are missing or flawed	One or more components are missing or poorly developed	Required components are complete, appropriate, and well developed	All required components are complete, effective, and add to the final product
Comprehension	No comprehension is demonstrated	Response reflects a beginning level of understanding of some information	Appropriate use of details and vocabulary; adequate understanding	Precise vocabulary; supportive ideas; related concepts; demonstrates thorough understanding
Conclusions	Illogical or inaccurate understanding	Accurate but limited understanding of concepts; simple or vague	Accurate understanding; clearly addresses problem and states knowledge gained; some documentation	Accurate and thorough interpretation; logical explanation addresses all of the questions; well documented
Constructs meaning	Needs clarity and focus; undeveloped	Attempts to construct meaning, but rambles; unclear	Information is generally clear and understandable	Cohesive; meaningful; clearly focused; in-depth analysis

Kingore, B. (2007). *Assessment,* 4th ed. Austin, TX: Professional Associates Publishing.

Content depth	Cooperation	Creativity	Critical thinking	Diagram	Discussion
Inaccurate or incomplete information	Does not cooperate; disrespectful; disturbs others	Used others' ideas or responses	Vague; basic	Inaccurate; poorly illustrated	No verbal or nonverbal participation demonstrated
Valid but little depth or elaboration; sparse	Cooperates when adults are present; usually respectful	Typical or cliched responses; little original thinking	General understanding; focuses on single issue; limited examination of evidence	Neat and accurate but minimally informative	Some participation with prompting
Covers topic effectively; well developed and supported; explores the topic beyond facts	Cooperates with adults and friends; respectful; assists others when prompted	Creative integration; enhances more typical ideas or responses	Understands scope of problem and more than one of the issues; conclusion reflects examination of information	Carefully prepared; accurate; aids understanding of the topic	Nonverbally interacts; appropriate verbal participation
Precise data; in-depth; well supported with details and examples; develops complex concepts and relationships	Cooperates with adults and all classmates; respectful and encouraging; assists others independently	Unique ideas or responses; insightful; fresh perspective; novel; imaginative	Clearly understands scope and issues; conclusions based upon thorough examination of evidence; explores reasonable alternatives; evaluates consequences	Artfully prepared; thoroughly labeled and accurate; clarifies and embellishes the content	Nonverbally encourages others; verbal responses reflect analysis and active learning

Kingore, B. (2007). *Assessment,* 4th ed. Austin, TX: Professional Associates Publishing.

Rubrics

Effort/task commitment	Fluency	Graph	Idea development	Independent work	Integration of skills
Apathetic; resistant; inadequate for task	Short, choppy, or incomplete sentences	Messy; incorrectly plotted	No clear focus or main idea; details are confusing	Inappropriate; resistant	Unable to apply skills; weak
Incomplete or limited	Generally complete; simple sentences; some run-on sentences	Distorts the data	States main idea; most details relate to it	Works but interrupts others and needs some prompting to stay on task	Attempts to integrate information and skills; inconsistent
Appropriate effort; successful	Well-constructed and varied sentences; smooth transitions	Adequate, but the data is somewhat difficult to interpret; some labeling	Clear focus; appropriate main idea; details relate and clarify ideas	Works effectively; attentive; helps others; shares appropriately; completes assignment	Demonstrates skill mastery by applying skills in multiple subject areas; minor errors
Extensive commitment; rigorous effort; autonomous	Crafted with a variety in sentence length and structure that enhances the total effect; fluid	Plots the data well and is easy to interpret; labeling clarifies the information	Cohesive; well defined and elaborates main idea; details increase interest and meaning	Engaged; encourages and redirects others back to task; negotiates; resolves conflict; goes beyond the assignment	Consistently integrates information and skills in process and product; masterfully applied

Kingore, B. (2007). *Assessment,* 4th ed. Austin, TX: Professional Associates Publishing.

Knowledge	Math applications	Math communication	Math concepts	Math strategies	Note taking
Little knowledge evident; reiterates facts without complete accuracy	Attempts a solution; limited mathematical applications	Incorrect or no explanation provided	Misunderstood; process and/or solution are incorrect	Inappropriate; no apparent logic to the solution	Minimal information; major omissions
Provides basic facts; lacks key ideas; fair degree of accuracy	Hesitant to proceed independently; computational errors are present	Explanation is minimal; basic terminology and/or no graphic support	Generally correct; problem is understood but solution and or procedures is flawed	Approach is oversimplified; strategies are partially flawed in application	Records important information
Accurately relates major ideas and concepts; some appropriate substantiation and analysis	Correct solution is achieved; minimal prompting or errors	Appropriate terminology and graphics; clear explanation	Problem and intended solution are correct; used relevant information correctly	Appropriate, effective strategies; applied correctly and logically	Determines the most important aspects of the information; brief but complete
Relates in-depth knowledge of concepts and relationships; well supported; examines issues	Formulas are executed correctly; precisely applied; higher-level response than expected	Exceptional explanation; uses advanced, precise terminology and clearly labels graphics	Correctly interpreted all important elements of the problem; integrates advanced concepts independently	Innovative and advanced strategies; independently implemented; sophisticated approach and thinking	Synthesizes; indicates relative importance of information; summarizes and forms conclusions; reviews notes to correct misconceptions

Kingore, B. (2007). *Assessment,* 4th ed. Austin, TX: Professional Associates Publishing.

Rubrics

Oral presentation	Organization	Participation	Personal connection	Problem interpretation	Problem solving
Needs prompting and assistance	Unclear; lacks organization	Does not participate; resistant	Lacking, insufficient, or irrelevant	Misunderstands the problem	Inappropriate process or solution; logic is flawed
Addresses topic; needed prompting; lacked fluency, eye contact, or gestures	Attempts to organize and sequence but is hard to follow	Does not volunteer but responds when asked	Limited attempt to relate the topic to self	Basically understands the problem; interpretation is limited	Incomplete or limited in application
Well prepared; clear; well paced; generally effective speaking techniques	Organized effectively; a good beginning and ending; a clear sequence; well structured	Volunteers once or twice and willingly responds when asked	Credible connection made between self and topic; analysis is evident	Generally correct interpretation and explanation; appropriate response	Appropriate process and application; analytical thinking is evident
Exceptional; dynamic; fluent; speech and mannerisms enhance communication	Coherent; skillfully planned; logically sequenced and organized to communicate well	Routinely volunteers; responds and elaborates information; includes others	Fully supported and cohesive connection; complex analysis demonstrated	Well analyzed and explained interpretation; clearly understands the problem	High-level solution; innovative; synthesizes; evaluates

Kingore, B. (2007). *Assessment,* 4th ed. Austin, TX: Professional Associates Publishing.

Procedure	Resources	Scientific data	Strategies	Summarization	Technology
Inaccurate sequence; steps are missing, inappropriate, or flawed	Inappropriate, unrelated, or no resources used for documentation	Inaccurate and/or incomplete	Inappropriate, flawed, or incomplete	Inadequate and/or inaccurate; unclear	Does not apply technology
Sequence is correct but minimal; some errors	Minimal resources used appropriately; some resources are not reputable	Measurements and observations are accurate; lacks graphs or tables	Limited application; not sure of process	Uses several sentences to describe part of the information	Limited success using internet links to find information; needs assistance to use technology
Accurate sequence in the procedure; complete	Appropriate in quantity, quality, and application; accurately documented; reliable; correct form	Accurate representation of data in tables, graphs, and written form	Successfully applies a limited number of strategies; appropriate process	Correct; accurately summarizes information	Independently uses suggested technology; accesses information effectively
Embellishes or adds steps to improve the procedure's efficiency or clarity	Extensive, varied, and appropriate; high caliber and reliable; complex information; accurately documented; incorporates advanced technology	Professional and accurate graphs, charts, drawings and written form; precise scientific terminology	Advanced strategies are independently implemented; flexible and innovative	Inclusive, clearly and succinctly describes the relevant information; thoughtfully developed	Advanced application; exceeds suggested resources; uses complex technology; accesses information; independently; clarifies for others

Kingore, B. (2007). *Assessment,* 4th ed. Austin, TX: Professional Associates Publishing.

Time management	Visual aids	Vocabulary	Voice/style	Writing conventions	Written reflection
Did not complete task	Incomplete or inappropriate; ineffective	Words are inappropriate or used incorrectly	Formalized	Serious errors makes reading and understanding difficult	Content lacks understanding; no effort evident
Needed frequent assistance	Minimal visual aids; limited application; misuses visual aids	Words and phrases are simple or vague	Some personal style	Frequent errors present but content is readable; emerging skills	Content reflects a beginning level of understanding; tried to address the topic
Used time appropriately	Appropriate in quantity, quality, and appearance; appropriately used to support information	Descriptive language is appropriate with elaboration	Personal; evokes feelings and interest in the topic	Minimal errors; mechanics and spelling are typical and appropriate for grade level	Addresses major content points; some interpretation; appropriate effect
Autonomous; mature time management	High visual appeal; extensive and varied; enhances and integrates information; skillfully used	Interesting, uses specific terminology; precise, advanced language; rich imagery	Personal voice enhances appeal and interest; the originality of the ideas linger in your mind	Product is enhanced by the skillful application of mechanics; fluid; above expectations	Clearly interprets and synthesizes content; high-level response and effort

Kingore, B. (2007). *Assessment,* 4th ed. Austin, TX: Professional Associates Publishing.

· CHAPTER 7 ·
Open-Ended Techniques

The same classroom experience often affects different learners in different ways.
—Carol Ann Tomlinson.

Open-ended techniques for assessment and evaluation promote multiple processes and diverse responses because they allow more than one way to proceed and more than one way to be correct. They are less restrictive and elicit the student's perceptions of learning through an invitation for high-level thinking. Open-ended techniques increase both students' and teachers' comfort levels with different responses and different ways of learning. Inasmuch as these techniques can be used multiple times, they save instruction time and simplify the assessment process.

In order to incorporate a variety of effective open-ended assessment and evaluation techniques, teachers need format examples to prompt their own development of procedures and assessment tools. Effective open-ended formats with less writing are requested by teachers in primary through secondary classrooms to prompt students' reflections and scaffold their thinking. Open-ended techniques include observation, inquiry, checklists, inventories, interviews, and self-assessment devices.

When implementing more open-ended assessment techniques:
*   Be flexible.
*   Maximize students' involvement and responsibilities for recordkeeping.
*   Take a risk and try something different.
*   If a tool does not meet your needs or provide valid diagnostic information, try a different one.

After using an open-ended form, store the responses and consider repeating the task at a later date to assess students' growth and changes.

Open-Ended Techniques

Kingore, B. (2007). *Assessment,* 4th ed. Austin, TX: Professional Associates Publishing.

ASSESSMENT THROUGH ANALYTICAL OBSERVATION

Dynamic teachers, determined to better understand the multiple facets of students' learning, continually analyze students' behaviors to interpret what is occurring in learning situations. Documented observations during authentic learning experiences enable educators to verify and respond to students' capacities and potential. Analytical observation infers that teachers do more than merely watch; they analyze as they observe to guide instructional decision-making.

Values of Analytical Observation

- Analytical observation helps teachers to interpret students' levels of development, acquired proficiencies, learning needs, and multiple facets of potential.
- It enables teachers to assess the *process* of students' learning as well as the *products* they produce.
- It signals the students' integration and transfer of skills taught in previous learning experiences.
- It helps teachers understand and support special populations and students' learning needs that may be clouded by standardized tests results.
- It supports and integrates with other authentic assessments and evaluations.
- It substantiates teachers' interpretations and insights about their students.
- It encourages teachers to focus on each student at reoccurring intervals so quiet children do not slip through the cracks.

What do Teachers Observe?

- *Skill mastery*
  Which skills have specific students mastered? Which students would benefit from support, reteaching, continued guided practice, or acceleration of instruction?
- *Skill integration*
  Are students appropriately applying targeted skills? How effectively are students transferring the skills into new learning situations? How have advanced students extended the skill applications?
- *Modality preferences*
  What categories of learning experiences do specific students most enjoy? Which enable specific students to best succeed?
- *Needs for instructional accommodations*
  - Which learning experiences might better promote needed practice and continuous learning?
  - What flexible grouping implications might better accommodate needs?
  - What pacing or level adjustments might be beneficial?
  - Is a student frequently demonstrating behaviors typical of students with learning differences or disabilities? Does the portfolio document these differences? What additional assessment information should be requested?
  - Which children consistently demonstrate responses that exceed age-level expectations? What are their areas of advanced capabilities? Does the portfolio document these responses? What assessment information should be requested?

Documenting Observations

Teachers document analytical observations to increase validity and enable other educators to understand what a teacher has come to know about a student. A combination of assessment procedures effectively documents learning.

- Observers document children's behaviors and processes because how students' proceed when learning can be as significant

Kingore, B. (2007). *Assessment,* 4th ed. Austin, TX: Professional Associates Publishing.

at the results. Processes reveal students' attitudes, strategies, frameworks of knowledge, sequencing, and skill integration.

– Documentation: Checklists, lists of learning standards, and anecdotal records[52] are effective.

• Observers document conversations among children involved in learning assignments. Listening to them as they work and brainstorm together provides insight into each student's attitudes and motivations as well as their prior knowledge, interests, strategies, vocabulary, achievement, and social skills.

– Documentation: Written anecdotes, recordings, and checklists are effective.

INQUIRY

As students engage in learning tasks, teachers frequently interpret and respond to what students are trying to by questioning and probing for clarity of their thinking. As teachers analyze behaviors, they talk with the students because children often have significant information to share if only we know to ask. Talking with children about what they are doing or how they feel about their work provides a window that increases adults' understanding of students' behaviors and invites students to bring their thinking to a conscious level. Hence, teachers use inquiry to interpret and respond to what students are trying to do when engaged in learning tasks. The objective is for teachers to model and guide the reflective process so metacognitive or self-monitoring strategies are an internalized part of students' learning.

Inquiry allows teachers to assess the process involved in students' learning rather than only evaluating the product. Inquiry probes are suggested in Figure 7.1 to prompt questions that would most enhance an understanding of

students' learning. Consider which probes might help guide instructional decisions, and write other questions as they occur.

When teachers question students about an answer, students frequently change that answer. We infer from this response that students are used to being questioned when they are wrong. Hence, they respond by thinking of another answer. It is more productive to students' thinking skills and self-confidence if we question them more when they are correct! That invites students to model to other students the thinking behaviors that work.

Exciting moments and increased mental engagement occur in a lesson when teachers encourage students to produce their own questions. As producers, students are more motivated to offer original ideas, suggest solutions, and reflect upon what they have heard, seen, and done. Model inquiry and prompt students to develop questions to ask one another.

CHECKLISTS

Checklists are an assessment tool of choice for many teachers. At their best, checklists provide a succinct means of documenting learning and focusing on important learning standards. The caution however, is to avoid checklists that have such an infinite list of isolated skills that the marking is laborious and consumes extensive instructional time. Brief

---

[52] A set of dated, specific anecdotes for each student guides instruction and enhances the information shared at conferences and in report card narratives. See Kingore, 2008, for a discussion of an observation folder to systematically and efficiently organize anecdotes for all children.

Kingore, B. (2007). *Assessment,* 4th ed. Austin, TX: Professional Associates Publishing.

Figure 7.1: INQUIRY PROBES

Communicating with Young Students

Tell me about your picture.
Tell me about your work.
Explain more so I understand.
How did you figure that out?
What are you thinking about now?
What did you do to begin this work?
What do you plan to do next?
What did you think was easy or difficult?

What would you like to ask about this work?
What changes do you want to make?
Show me something you did well.
If you did not know something, what would you do to learn?
How would you share this information with others?
How is this like (previous content) ?
What is the most important thing you learned from this?

Communicating with Older Students

Talk with me about the work you are doing right now.
What aspect of this work is most effective?
What is your next step or idea?
What is another way to approach that?
How did you figure that out?
Why do you think that is so?
What evidence do you have to support that?
What in the text led you to infer or conclude that?
What question is essential to this topic?
What if this happened in a different order or sequence?

How would you explain this to another?
If this had not worked, what would you have done?
What did you want to happen?
What changes do you suggest?
If you did not know, what would you ask to get the most information?
How is this like (previous content) ?
What is a possible relationship between _____ and _____?
What is the most important thing you learned from this?
How would you share this information with others?
What might you do differently next time?

lists can guide assessment and provide a quick notation system. Figure 7.2 is an example of such a checklist. After listing the names of the students in the group, use this checklist to jot down observed skill applications while working with the group.

Students can use checklists to guide their self-assessment. For example, after teaching revision techniques, a simple checklist, such as Figure 7.3, reminds students which techniques to apply during a particular revising session. It is most productive to check one to three of the items at a time for students' to attend to. This use of checklists guides students and allows them to take responsibility for their continued achievements.

Checklists are also effective as assessments of students' work ethic and learning behaviors. One example is Figure 7.4. This assessment tool encourages the student, a peer, and the teacher to collaboratively analyze that student's work habits and learning behaviors. Using different colors, each person marks the same copy of the form for comparison.

Figure 7.2: SMALL GROUP CHECKLIST

Jot down observations and insights. Check *proficient* when applicable.

Students:	Skill:	Skill:	Skill:
	❑ PROFICIENT	❑ PROFICIENT	❑ PROFICIENT
	❑ PROFICIENT	❑ PROFICIENT	❑ PROFICIENT
	❑ PROFICIENT	❑ PROFICIENT	❑ PROFICIENT
	❑ PROFICIENT	❑ PROFICIENT	❑ PROFICIENT
	❑ PROFICIENT	❑ PROFICIENT	❑ PROFICIENT
	❑ PROFICIENT	❑ PROFICIENT	❑ PROFICIENT
	❑ PROFICIENT	❑ PROFICIENT	❑ PROFICIENT
	❑ PROFICIENT	❑ PROFICIENT	❑ PROFICIENT

Kingore, B. (2007). *Assessment,* 4th ed. Austin, TX: Professional Associates Publishing.

Open-Ended Techniques

Figure 7.3: REVISING CHECKLIST

❑   Make the beginning catchy to grab a reader's attention.

❑   Add a powerful adjective.

❑   Combine two ideas or two sentences.

❑   Delete a word that is overused or not needed.

❑   Circle two words. Use a thesaurus and substitute stronger, sophisticated, and more interesting words.

❑   Substitute an action verb with more punch.

❑   Elaborate by adding an appropriate and interesting detail.

❑   Elaborate by using one or more wonder words.
   ❑ Who   ❑ When   ❑ What
   ❑ Where   ❑ Why   ❑ How

❑   Vary sentence beginnings and types of sentences.

❑   Make the ending unique and interesting.

Kingore, B. (2007). *Assessment,* 4th ed. Austin, TX: Professional Associates Publishing.

✂ -

In classroom environments that characterize positive, respectful interactions, teachers suggest that peer feedback is welcomed and often viewed as very important to their students. In addition, it is helpful in preparation for a parent conference to ask parents to complete this form and then compare their perceptions with the teacher or student's responses.

INVENTORIES AND INTERVIEWS

Understanding the interests and preferences of everyone in a classroom is important. The more teachers and students know about each other, the more comfortable they tend to be with each other. Students are certainly more likely to risk sharing a divergent question or response in a group with whom they are comfortable.

Teachers want to understand students' interests and preferences so they can more effectively match instructional tasks to students' needs. Thus, teachers incorporate interest inventories and interviews that provide insights into students' interests and learning passions. The problem, however, is that many instruments that elicit students' interests are time-consuming, labor intensive and require extensive hand writing. To ease that difficulty for students, this section features simplified formats that often integrate art with written responses and even invite students to collaborate. Many of these forms are appropriate for young children and special-needs learners.

Figure 7.4: LEARNING CHARACTERISTICS: A COLLABORATIVE ASSESSMENT

STUDENT _____   DATE _____

PEER _____   DATE _____

PARENT _____   DATE _____

TEACHER _____   DATE _____

Work and Study Habits	Consistently	Sometimes	Not Yet
Stays on task			
Manages time well			
Organizes work			
Uses multiple, appropriate resources			
Reorganizes and returns materials			
Sets goals for self			
Seeks help when needed			
Does not call undue attention to self			
Completes quality work			
Persistence			
Shows patience			
Self-monitors and checks own work			
Edits and revises work			
Is willing to try something new			
Accepts responsibility for own learning			
Social Skills			
Communicates diplomatically			
Works cooperatively			
Listens attentively			
Helps others as needed			
Encourages others			
Respects others' ideas and property			
Works and interacts with others quietly			

Comments:

Goal or action plan:

Adapted from: Kingore, B. (2004). *Differentiation: Simplified, Realistic, and Effective.*
Austin: Professional Associates Publishing.

Open-Ended
Techniques

Effective inventories and interviews:

- Encourage respect and appreciation for students' differences.
- Help teachers learn more about every student.
- Build students' self-esteem.
- Promote high achievement by incorporating students' interests.[53]
- Enable teachers to form flexible groups based upon interests.
- Encourage independent study responding to students' interests.
- Enable teachers to establish mentorships for students.

Guidelines

- Before students begin, inform students if the inventories will be displayed in the room for all to view. The inventories make an interesting and often visually intriguing display for students to compare and contrast information, but they should know in advance that this personal work will be shared.

- Consider asking students to complete an interest inventory or interview at the beginning of the year and then again later in the year; store both forms in their portfolios. It is interesting for students to realize how their interests can change with time.

- To a point, encourage students to highlight interests that are school applicable and appropriate. Interests applicable to school enable teachers to plan school experiences that incorporate and extend what students know about their favorite topics. For example, a student's interest in rain forests would often have more future learning connections at school than a student's interest in an arcade game.

- Inventories and interviews provide teachers with the information to incorporate better learning options. Many students perform at a higher level when they have some power of choice. *Choice* does not provide students with a license that anything goes. Rather, inventories and interviews should help teachers and students negotiate learning experiences that are appealing to the student and applicable to the desired learning outcomes.

- Have the interviewer and the interviewee sign the interview when the information is completed. The signatures assure that both people understand and accept responsibility for their thoughts. The responses should never appear to be secret or something to be used against a student.

Picture Interest Inventory

Picture interest inventories, such as Figure 7.5, invite students to illustrate and write about things they most like and want to learn. Miriam Winegar in Oregon shares the idea of integrating art with an investigation of a student's interests. This application results in a great visual display for the room and is particularly an asset for spatial and visual learners who benefit from using art to communicate their ideas.

PROCEDURE

To begin, ask students to brainstorm and list what most interests them and what they want to learn more about at school. Encourage them to think about their preferences and add to their list over several days. Teachers have found that these inventories are more valid when students have time to reflect and respond rather than complete the inventory at one time.

[53] Research from Amabile (1983) and Csikszentmihalyi (1997) support that motivation to achieve increases when a student's interests are incorporated.

Kingore, B. (2007). *Assessment,* 4th ed. Austin, TX: Professional Associates Publishing.

NAME _____   DATE _____

PICTURE OR SELF-PORTRAIT:

Kingore, B. (2007). *Assessment,* 4th ed. Austin, TX: Professional Associates Publishing.

Open-Ended Techniques

Next, ask students to revisit their list of interests and prioritize them. With primary students, ask them to put a check or a star by the ones that they most like. With older students, ask them to rate each as a one, two, or three to denote the level of interest. Secondary students can rank their lists with one being their greatest interest and continue numbering to their lowest interest. Prioritizing is a life skill; students cannot time manage or make decisions unless they learn to prioritize. This step effectively applies that high-level thinking skill.

Finally, students choose their highest-rated interests to illustrate and scribe on their picture interest inventory. They paste their photograph into the box and then illustrate one interest in each of the ovals. The largest oval is for their greatest interest; descending oval sizes represent descending priorities in interests. For the best success, have students draw one picture and then write about it before beginning another illustration. When students complete all of the art first, their written explanations are less expansive and show less thinking than when they go back and forth between drawing and completing their written explanations.

Applications Involving Teachers
*   Develop picture inventories as a class project to celebrate individual interests, similarities, and differences.
*   Develop a personal interest inventory. Students enjoy knowing more about their teacher.

Applications Involving Families
*   For young children, encourage an adult family member to assist in developing a picture interest inventory at home.
*   All family members can develop individual inventories to share together as a family or to use in planning family activities or vacations in which everyone's interests are actively incorporated.

With primary-aged students, use Big Buddies[54] to more efficiently complete picture interest inventories. Arrange for upper-elementary students to work with the younger children in one or more sessions to individualize and complete the inventories. Teachers are then free to facilitate the process and conduct analytical observations rather than complete most of the writing for the children.

I'm Good At... I'm Not Good At... I Want to Learn...

This inventory is particularly useful in mixed-ability classrooms with a wide range of student abilities. It is an effective way to accent that all students have something they do well, something they perceive they do not do well, and something they want to learn this year at school.

Students fold a large piece of paper into thirds and label each third: *I'm Good At..., I'm Not Good At...,* and *I Want to Learn...* Encourage students to draw and write one or more responses in each column.

One insightful teacher had her class silently walk around the room to view what other students had included on their forms. Her challenge to her students: *Find a classmate who wants to learn what you know well and another classmate who is good at an area in which you need help. We are the best we can be, and we are here to learn together and help each other.*

---

[54] See Chapter 3 for a discussion of Big Buddies as facilitators.

Kingore, B. (2007). *Assessment,* 4th ed. Austin, TX: Professional Associates Publishing.

Students have an active role as interviewees and interviewers. Figure 7.6 discusses multiple ways to successfully involve students in interviews.

I Want to Learn About _____.

Figures 7.7 provides an alternative inventory that appeals to visual and spatial learners. Encourage the students to draw multiple responses and add words or phrases, almost graffiti style, to clarify their choices. When appropriate, suggest that students create symbols for their interests instead of just drawing literal pictures. Explaining the symbols often invites students to discuss their inventories at greater length with each other.

Project Interview

One way to respond to the individual learning differences of students is to use a project interview, such as Figure 7.8. Rather than all students completing the same project, the results of these interviews will suggest a wide variety of projects to maximize student interest and motivation.

The project interview in this chapter requires students to think about their priorities and plan an appropriate project that is interesting to them but also applies related skills and learning standards. Thus, the project is a defensible learning experience rather than just fun and creative. Ask students to plan a sequence for completing the project so they are more likely to succeed in a timely fashion.

In most cases, the student should complete a response to each item on the

---

Figure 7.6:
WAYS TO COMPLETE INTERVIEWS

Student's self-reflection

A student writes responses on an interview form and then briefly meets with the teacher to discuss the results or shares the responses in a class discussion.

Student's self-taped interview

A student tape records responses to the interview questions. This option is especially helpful for special-needs students for whom handwriting is difficult. It is also effective with young students when an older student or adult is available at a later time to transcribe the recording. With this option, older students can also transcribe the recording in their own classroom as an exercise to practice skills in the mechanics of writing.

Student to student interview

Students interview one another and write responses for each other as the interview proceeds. This process invites interaction, discussion and comparative thinking between the students.

Teacher to student interview

The teacher interviews a student and writes the student's responses.

Adult to student interview

A parent at home, a parent volunteer at school, or another significant adult interviews a student and writes the student's responses.

Open-Ended Techniques

Kingore, B. (2007). *Assessment,* 4th ed. Austin, TX: Professional Associates Publishing.

Figure 7.7: I WANT TO LEARN ABOUT _____.

Figure 7.8: PROJECT INTERVIEW

INTERVIEWER _____ DATE _____

SUBJECT AREA OR TOPIC _____

1. What are you interested in doing?

2. How is this project relevant to your topic?

3. Which learning standards and skills can be incorporated in this project?

4. What important skills or information can you gain from this project?

5. What do you plan to be your final product?

6. What resources will you need, and how will you access them?

7. How may I or others help?

8. On the back of this page, sketch a time line or flow chart of your project showing dates and steps from the beginning to the completion of your work.

STUDENT'S SIGNATURE _____

INTERVIEWER'S SIGNATURE _____

Open-Ended Techniques

Kingore, B. (2007). *Assessment,* 4th ed. Austin, TX: Professional Associates Publishing.

interview and then briefly meet with the teacher to discuss and brainstorm further. Having students complete the interview first requires them to organize their thoughts and enables a more productive use of time when the teacher and student meet to discuss the project plan.

As a foreign language application, conduct an interview in a language other than English for a learning task incorporating vocabulary, fluency and grammar.

Reading or Math Interview

Interviewing is a valuable way to gain information about students' learning processes and strategies. Interviews also help students become more aware of their thinking as they discuss their learning process. After an interview is complete, the teacher and student use the recorded information to analyze the student's capabilities and potentials to determine the most productive instructional decisions.

The questions in Figures 7.9 and 7.10 are intended to be used flexibly. Vary each as is appropriate to increase students' understanding or to reword for use with young students.

Reading and math Interviews are particularly effective as repeated tasks. Students complete the interview at the beginning of the year and then again later in the year to compare the changes and growth in their perceptions about learning.

Peer Interviews

Students enjoy talking to and learning more about peers. Figure 7.11 is a form to use between students. For more authentic interviews, students select and create their own interview questions. However, many students are inexperienced interviewers and have difficulty composing questions that elicit more than single-word answers. Figure 7.12 categorizes several question options. Encourages students to select the questions most appropriate to their interviewing situation and then plan additional questions. Discuss the value of open-ended questions that encourage multiple-word responses. These questions also apply to research projects and family-history interviews.

Combine completed classmate interviews into a class Who's Who Book. Add a photograph or the interviewed student's original artwork on an accompanying page to illustrate each interview. Arrange the pages so that the illustration and the interview are on the same two-page spread as the book is read.

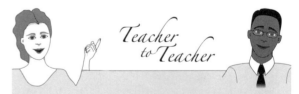

Teacher to Teacher

Teachers using open-ended techniques suggest that students' reflective thinking is more important than spelling and handwriting during interviewing or any self-assessment process. Focus on students' analysis of the merits of their work and encourage them to be thoughtful in their responses. This emphasis produces more fruitful information and motivates students to be reflective.

Kingore, B. (2007). *Assessment,* 4th ed. Austin, TX: Professional Associates Publishing.

Figure 7.9: READING INTERVIEW

INTERVIEWER _____ DATE _____

SUBJECT AREA OR TOPIC _____

1. Are you a good reader? Why do you think so?

2. What do you like to read most?

3. How do you choose something to read?

4. When are you most likely to read something?

5. What do you do when you come to a word you do not know?

6. What do you do when you do not understand the meaning of what you read?

7. How do you help yourself remember what you read?

8. How would you explain "reading" to a young child who asks you how to read?

STUDENT'S SIGNATURE _____

INTERVIEWER'S SIGNATURE _____

Open-Ended Techniques

Kingore, B. (2007). *Assessment,* 4th ed. Austin, TX: Professional Associates Publishing.

Figure 7.10: MATH PROBLEM SOLVING INTERVIEW

INTERVIEWER _____ DATE _____

SUBJECT AREA OR TOPIC _____

On the back of this paper, copy a complex story problem and solve it.

1. What can you tell me about this problem?

2. Which words are most important? Why are they?

3. Is there something that can be eliminated, or is there something missing?

4. How might a diagram or a sketch be helpful?

5. Tell me the sequence of steps you went through to solve this problem.

6. What would you caution someone else about this problem? Is there a part where one should be especially careful?

7. What is a way to check your solution?

STUDENT'S SIGNATURE _____

INTERVIEWER'S SIGNATURE _____

Kingore, B. (2007). *Assessment,* 4th ed. Austin, TX: Professional Associates Publishing.

Figure 7.11: CLASSMATE INTERVIEW

INTERVIEWER _____ DATE _____

Peer's name _____   Nickname _____

Birth date _____   Birth place _____

Brothers and sisters _____

Pets _____

Two favorite authors _____

Two favorite books _____

Favorite TV show _____   Favorite movie _____

Favorite song or group _____

Favorite place on Earth _____

What are your hobbies, collections, and interests?

Who is your role model? How does that person influence you?

What is your favorite memory?

If you could meet and talk with anyone, who would it be? Why do you choose that person?

What four words best describe you?

• _____   • _____

• _____   • _____

What would you like everyone to know about you?

What is something you have done that made you especially proud?

What is the best gift you have ever received?

Kingore, B. (2007). *Assessment,* 4th ed. Austin, TX: Professional Associates Publishing.

Open-Ended Techniques

Figure 7.12: BANK OF INTERVIEW QUESTIONS, Page 1

Check the questions you want to incorporate in your interview.
Then, write additional questions that are appropriate to your interview situation.

TELL ME ABOUT YOURSELF
- ❑ Nickname
- ❑ Family members
- ❑ Birth place
- ❑ Birth date
- ❑ Pets
- ❑ Hobbies
- ❑ Special interests

FAVORITE THINGS
- ❑ What is your favorite sport?
- ❑ What kind of TV programs do you like to watch?
- ❑ What is your favorite style of music?
- ❑ What are your three favorite books?
- ❑ What do you collect? What got you started with your collection?
- ❑ What is your favorite season? Why is it your favorite?
- ❑ What kind of weather do you like best? Why is that your favorite?
- ❑ What is your favorite memory?

SCHOOL
- ❑ What is your favorite subject at school?
- ❑ What would you most like to learn?
- ❑ What do you like best and least about school?
- ❑ If you were a teacher, how would you teach your class?
- ❑ What changes would you make to improve the school?
- ❑ What would the perfect classroom look like?
- ❑ Do you most enjoy working alone or with others? Why is that so?
- ❑ What is the best book you have read?
- ❑ If you wrote a book, what would it be about?
- ❑ What is the most interesting non-fiction book you have read?
- ❑ What is the most interesting problem you have solved at school?
- ❑ What is the hardest thing for you at school?

PERSONAL CHOICES
- ❑ What is the best thing about being you? What is the worst thing?
- ❑ What is your idea of a schedule for a perfect Saturday?
- ❑ Have you ever invented anything or had an idea for an invention? What is it?
- ❑ What do you think is the most important invention ever created? Why do you think that?
- ❑ Which five words best describe you?
- ❑ Which two words are least like you?

Figure 7.12: BANK OF INTERVIEW QUESTIONS, Page 2

- ❏ What is the best news you could get?
- ❏ What is something you heard on the news that interests you? Why is it interesting?
- ❏ What is the best thing that has ever happened to you?
- ❏ What is something important others should know about you?
- ❏ Who is the person you would most like to meet?
- ❏ Who is a person you hope to never meet?
- ❏ What do you think is the perfect age to be? Why is it perfect?
- ❏ How do you best express yourself?
- ❏ When alone, what do you most like to do?

FEELINGS
- ❏ What is the most beautiful thing you have ever seen?
- ❏ What makes you feel grouchy or annoyed?
- ❏ What fascinates you?
- ❏ What do you most like about TV or the movies? What do you least like?
- ❏ What do you feel is the most important thing about living in the U.S.A.?
- ❏ What time of the day do you feel your best? Why is that so?
- ❏ Which feeling is the most important? Why do you think that?
- ❏ Who or what makes you laugh?

FUTURE CHOICES
- ❏ What is something you really want but cannot afford right now?
- ❏ What do you think is the best thing about being an adult?
- ❏ What will you be doing _____ years from now?
- ❏ What would you change if you could change the world?
- ❏ What is your greatest hope for the future?
- ❏ In the future, where would you most like to explore? Why does that interest you?
- ❏ What profession do you think you could do really well? Why does that career interest you?

IMAGINING
- ❏ If you had three wishes what would they be?
- ❏ If you had three wishes that had to be used to help others, what would they be?
- ❏ If you could invite four famous people to dinner, who would you invite? What would you discuss? What would you serve?
- ❏ What would your perfect bedroom look like?
- ❏ Where is another place you would like to live? Why is that appealing to you?
- ❏ What would you do with $1000?
- ❏ If you could meet and talk with anyone in the world right now, who would it be? Why is that?
- ❏ If you could participate in any event in history, what would it be? What is your role?
- ❏ In which time in history would you prefer to live? Why is that your choice?

Kingore, B. (2007). *Assessment,* 4th ed. Austin, TX: Professional Associates Publishing.

Open-Ended Techniques

SELF-ASSESSMENT TOOLS

The assessment and evaluation tools presented in this section promote students' analysis of their own work as well as the collaborative process of students and teachers analyzing proficiencies. As Costa and Kallick (1992) accent,[55] *We must constantly remind ourselves that the ultimate purpose of education is to have students become self-evaluating. If students graduate from our schools still dependent upon others to tell them when they are adequate, good, or excellent, then we've missed the whole point of what education is about (p. 279).*

Students use Figure 7.13 as an alternative to reading logs. On the form, students periodically reflect about a book they have read or are reading. The students' favorite part of the task is creating their own graphics for rating the book.

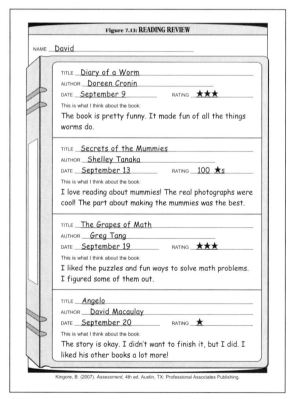

Kingore, B. (2007). *Assessment,* 4th ed. Austin, TX: Professional Associates Publishing.

Share with your class several examples of written reviews, such as television,

movie, and book reviews. After discussing different kinds of ratings, allow students to create their own rating systems. Most students base their ratings on large numbers, such as *one million stars.* Some students, however, create more symbolic or abstract rating systems, like Kourtney's weather ratings and Michael's brain connections.

Graphic Organizers for Self-Assessment

Students' self-assessments can take many forms. Graphic organizers that teachers use for instruction can also be effective forms to prompt students' reflection. In the following example, the PMI strategy[56] is used to evaluate the first year of implementing portfolios in

[55] Costa, & Kallick, 1992.
[56] De Bono, 1993.

Figure 7.13: READING REVIEW

NAME _____

Great Books!

TITLE _____

AUTHOR _____

DATE _____   RATING _____

This is what I think about the book:

TITLE _____

AUTHOR _____

DATE _____   RATING _____

This is what I think about the book:

TITLE _____

AUTHOR _____

DATE _____   RATING _____

This is what I think about the book:

TITLE _____

AUTHOR _____

DATE _____   RATING _____

This is what I think about the book:

Kingore, B. (2007). *Assessment,* 4th ed. Austin, TX: Professional Associates Publishing.

Open-Ended Techniques

one middle school. The student's response shared here illustrates how the plus, minus, and interesting columns prompt critical thinking.

The PMI strategy is easily implemented by having students fold plain paper into thirds to create areas for organizing their responses. Students can turn paper horizontally for handwriting ease.

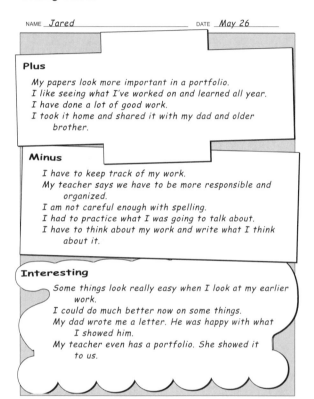

NAME *Jared*   DATE *May 26*

Plus

My papers look more important in a portfolio.
I like seeing what I've worked on and learned all year.
I have done a lot of good work.
I took it home and shared it with my dad and older brother.

Minus

I have to keep track of my work.
My teacher says we have to be more responsible and organized.
I am not careful enough with spelling.
I had to practice what I was going to talk about.
I have to think about my work and write what I think about it.

Interesting

Some things look really easy when I look at my earlier work.
I could do much better now on some things.
My dad wrote me a letter. He was happy with what I showed him.
My teacher even has a portfolio. She showed it to us.

The remaining templates in this chapter provide the open-ended formats with less writing that are more effective for primary students and students with special learning needs. Figure 7.14 and Figure 7.15 invite teachers to list the criteria specific to a group task. The same forms can be used more than once as different criteria are listed when the tasks vary. The Teamwork Assessment uses thumbs-up graphics for students' assessments. The Discussion Assessment has blank places so a teacher can use a variety of assessment icons or words. Working individually on the Discussion Assessment or as a group on the Teamwork Assessment, students

assess the quality of their work when the task is complete. The discussion that ensues is reflective and often encourages the refinement of group interaction skills for future group work.

Figure 7.14: DISCUSSION ASSESSMENT

NAME *Gretchen*   DATE *March 15*
TOPIC *What can we do to help protect the environment?*

CRITERIA:	Below standard	C	B	A
1. *I read the assignment and prepared two key points.*				✓
2. *I made a positive contribution.*				✓
3. *I gave others a chance to participate, too.*			✓	
4. *I respected my classmates' ideas.*				✓
5. *I made my point promptly.*		✓		
6. *I asked questions that helped others think.*			✓	

How I prepared for the discussion:
I read the assignment and tried to think of two points and a question to share.

Something I liked:
Piggy-backing on each others' ideas worked well and was fun.

What I will do next time:
I will try to let other people talk more. I rambled, and others stopped listening to me.

Kingore, B. (2007). Assessment, 4th ed. Austin, TX: Professional Associates Publishing.

Figure 7.15: TEAMWORK ASSESSMENT

TEAM *Brian, Logan, Scott, Amelia, and Jess*
ASSIGNMENT *Building a newspaper bridge*
DATE *December 6*

CRITERIA:	👍	👊	👎
1. *We followed directions and planned well.*		✓	
2. *We helped each other problem solve.*	✓		
3. *We worked quietly together.*			✓
4. *We cooperated and encouraged each other.*	✓		
5. *We all gave ideas and helped each other.*	✓		
6. *Our bridge test was successful.*	✓		

What we enjoyed:
We liked working together to build and test the bridge.

What our team did well:
We all tried hard, and it was so much fun designing and building the bridge exactly like we planned. We really did well at being thoughtful and nice to each other.

How we need to improve:
We need to be more considerate to other groups. We got into trouble for being too noisy, but we were mostly loud because we got so excited about what we were doing.

Kingore, B. (2007). Assessment, 4th ed. Austin, TX: Professional Associates Publishing.

Figure 7.14: DISCUSSION ASSESSMENT

NAME _____   DATE _____

TOPIC _____

CRITERIA:				
1.				
2.				
3.				
4.				
5.				
6.				

How I prepared for the discussion:

Something I liked:

What I will do next time:

Kingore, B. (2007). *Assessment,* 4th ed. Austin, TX: Professional Associates Publishing.

Open-Ended Techniques

Figure 7.15: TEAMWORK ASSESSMENT

TEAM _____

ASSIGNMENT _____

DATE _____

CRITERIA:	 👍	 🤙	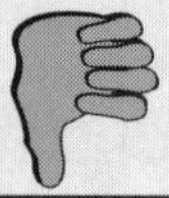 👎
1.			
2.			
3.			
4.			
5.			
6.			

What we enjoyed:

What our team did well:

How we need to improve:

Kingore, B. (2007). *Assessment,* 4th ed. Austin, TX: Professional Associates Publishing.

Graphic Organizers for Evaluation

In addition to diagnosing students' strengths and needs, open-ended formats can be adapted to establish grades. Figure 7.16 and Figure 7.17 illustrate that adding a scoring scale allows a holistic conclusion to be reached about the quality of the work. The teacher, with input from the students as appropriate, lists statements on the numbered lines of the form that describe the task and designate the attributes of the task. When the assignment is complete, the student self-evaluates by filling out the checklist, finishing the sentence-stem reflections, and circling a holistic interpretation of the level of quality attained. Then, the teacher uses the same copy of the form to complete an evaluation of the quality of the work. Figure 7.18 illustrates that evaluative scales can also be included on assessments composed of sentence stems for students' self-assessment.

Adapt the forms to student needs by varying the scoring scale at the bottom of each

Figure 7.17: PROJECT CHECKLIST EVALUATION

NAME _Lauren_   DATE _January 29_
TOPIC/TITLE _Asteroids_

		Yes	No
1.	_I researched five characteristics about asteroids._	☑	☐
2.	_I explained why we usually do not see the asteroids._	☑	☐
3.	_I compared meteor showers to raindrops._	☑	☐
4.	_I shared my information in a video._	☑	☐
5.	_I used magazines, the internet, text, and a museum._	☑	☐
6.	_I incorporated: • point of view._	☑	☐
7.	_• substantiation._	☑	☐
8.	_• summary._	☑	☐
9.		☐	☐
10.		☐	☐
11.		☐	☐
12.		☐	☐

My favorite part of the project:
I loved going to the Air and Space Museum to research my topic. A man who works there let me go in the back to see things not on display. It was really fun.
What I would change:
I have to change the way the video ends because I forgot to have the credits like they do in the movies.
How others can help:
I need everybody to give some ideas on how I could make the credits and help me do it. I would let them add their names.
How I am improving:
I used technology and used more than one resource.

	Novice	Apprentice	Practitioner	Distinguished
STUDENT'S SCORE:	Below passing	C	(B)	A
TEACHER'S SCORE:	Below passing	C	B	(A)

Kingore, B. (2007). *Assessment,* 4th ed. Austin, TX: Professional Associates Publishing.

form. Possible variations are included in the examples to prompt thinking. Additional examples of descriptive terms for achievement levels are listed on the first page of the Rubric Generator (Tier II and Tier III) in Chapter 6.

Figure 7.16: EDITING CHECKLIST EVALUATION

NAME _William_   DATE _October 3_
TOPIC/TITLE _Narrative writing assignment-Fable_

		Yes	No
1.	_I stated my main idea or moral._	☑	☐
2.	_My sentences are complete with subject-verb agreement._	☑	☐
3.	_I have an effective beginning, middle, and ending._	☑	☐
4.	_I used a variety of sentence types._	☑	☐
5.	_I used interesting and related details._	☑	☐
6.	_I clearly organized my ideas._	☑	☐
7.	_I used strong verbs._	☑	☐
8.	_I used correct punctuation and capitalization._	☑	☐
9.	_I checked my spelling._	☑	☐
10.	_I read this to myself, and it makes sense._	☑	☐
11.	_I read this to a classmate for comments._	☑	☐
12.		☐	☐

What I am most proud of:
I am proud of my characters and surprise ending. None of my friends figured out what would happen.

How I am improving:
My spelling is better. My sentences are also longer and more detailed.

What I need help with:
I need to use better vocabulary. I use too many little words in my writing.

	Below standard	Developing	Proficient	Exceptional
STUDENT'S SCORE:	1	2	(3)	4
TEACHER'S SCORE:	1	2	(3)	4

Kingore, B. (2007). *Assessment,* 4th ed. Austin, TX: Professional Associates Publishing.

Teacher to Teacher

Using these forms as examples, encourage intermediate, middle school, and high school students to create their own open-ended assessment and evaluation forms. Shifting students from consumers to producers increases their involvement and sense of ownership in assessment procedures. Enhance their enjoyment of the task by allowing them to incorporate illustrations with clever or humorous phrases instead of more formal terminology.

Kingore, B. (2007). *Assessment,* 4th ed. Austin, TX: Professional Associates Publishing.

Figure 7.16: EDITING CHECKLIST EVALUATION

NAME _____ DATE _____

TOPIC/TITLE _____

	Yes	No
1. _____	☐	☐
2. _____	☐	☐
3. _____	☐	☐
4. _____	☐	☐
5. _____	☐	☐
6. _____	☐	☐
7. _____	☐	☐
8. _____	☐	☐
9. _____	☐	☐
10. _____	☐	☐
11. _____	☐	☐
12. _____	☐	☐

What I am most proud of:

How I am improving:

What I need help with:

STUDENT'S SCORE:				
TEACHER'S SCORE:				

Kingore, B. (2007). *Assessment,* 4th ed. Austin, TX: Professional Associates Publishing.

Figure 7.17: PROJECT CHECKLIST EVALUATION

NAME _____   DATE _____

TOPIC/TITLE _____

		Yes	No
1.	_____	☐	☐
2.	_____	☐	☐
3.	_____	☐	☐
4.	_____	☐	☐
5.	_____	☐	☐
6.	_____	☐	☐
7.	_____	☐	☐
8.	_____	☐	☐
9.	_____	☐	☐
10.	_____	☐	☐
11.	_____	☐	☐
12.	_____	☐	☐

My favorite part of the project:

What I would change:

How others can help:

How I am improving:

STUDENT'S SCORE:				
TEACHER'S SCORE:				

Kingore, B. (2007). *Assessment,* 4th ed. Austin, TX: Professional Associates Publishing.

Open-Ended Techniques

Figure 7.18: LITERATURE EVALUATION

NAME _____   DATE _____

TITLE _____

AUTHOR _____

I would compare this book to _____

by _____ because:

The best things about this book:

How I demonstrated my learning:

Skills I used in my work:

STUDENT'S SCORE:				
TEACHER'S SCORE:				

Kingore, B. (2007). *Assessment,* 4th ed. Austin, TX: Professional Associates Publishing.

· CHAPTER 8 ·
Products:
Assessing and Differentiating

Tell me I forget. Show me, I remember.
Involve me, I understand.
—Chinese Proverb

Products result from content (the complexity of what students are to know) and process (how students use key skills and relate ideas as they make sense of the content). Students create products to demonstrate and extend what they learn. Thus, products are both learning activities and assessments. Well-designed product assignments respond to how students best demonstrate their learning. These assignments motivate students to excel and encourage students to process information and apply skills in meaningful ways.[57] The results assess students' learning and inform teachers.

Products include responses in the form of concrete items, physical actions, and verbal conclusions or summaries of understanding. Inherent within these products are more abstract outcomes from the students' work. These abstract products consist of enduring learning qualities, such as frameworks of knowledge, strategies, attitudes, and self-efficacy.[58]

Products impact assessment and evaluation in varied and significant ways.

- As students are completing a product task, teachers assess students' process and confirm work habits, strategies, and both verbal and nonverbal responses.

- Through an effectively designed and completed product, students communicate their level of understanding and document their achievement of the learning objective.

- Teachers assess products to monitor and adjust instruction and ensure all students experience continuous learning success.

- Students use products to celebrate and share their learning with others through informal discussions and more formal student-led conferences.

- Products provide a concrete tool to support conference conclusions. Over time, students, families, and teachers use the products in a portfolio to assess how a child is progressing and changing as a learner.

- Products become an evaluation tool when teachers evaluate the quality of the products and assign grades.

[57] McTighe & O'Connor, 2005.
[58] Tomlinson, et.al., 2002.

Kingore, B. (2007). *Assessment,* 4th ed. Austin, TX: Professional Associates Publishing.

PRODUCT OPTIONS

Product options abound. To have value as assessment tools, however, product assignments must align to learning objectives and result from a threefold concerted effort: collect appropriate evidence to document learning, involve options that merit the time and energy required, and balance realistically between a single learning pathway and an excessive plethora of choices.[59]

Some educators worry about providing a balance of product offerings to students inasmuch as adults may inadvertently teach using products most related to their own strengths and passions. Still other teachers spend exorbitant amounts of time and energy seeking new products that their students have not experienced. They misinterpret *variety* to mean fun and end up on a product treadmill trying to find something new, sadly, sometimes inviting more fluff than the substance that might interest students. Exemplary products have an audience beyond the grading pen and stem from authentic tasks–representing the work of practitioners in a field. Teachers also seek product assignments that can be efficiently prepared and involve students in respectful, equitable work.[60]

To increase efficiency when determining appropriate product assignments, create a list of products applicable to the curriculum and learning standards. Reflect upon the developing list and ponder which product options:
- Are most appropriate for the students' ages, learning profiles, and interests.
- Are most applicable to the content.
- Actively engage students in applying and transferring acquired skills.

- Promote depth and complexity of content.
- Have diagnostic value.
- Are respectful, equitable work.
- Promote continuous learning success.
- Stem from authentic problems and audiences.
- Require available materials and appropriate amounts of time.
- Encourage variety in applications.
- Are most enjoyable to facilitate.[61]

Students vary dramatically in their learning modalities and intelligences. To engage more students more of the time, classroom-learning tasks need to offer as wide a variety in the types of products assigned as the variety represented by the students' learning profiles. Assessment becomes responsive when appropriate options present students with choices for demonstrating what they know and are able to do.[62] Research supports that students are more successful in learning tasks that respond to their readiness levels and incorporate their modality and intelligence strengths. McTigue and O'Connor (2005) advise, however, that teachers "allow choices–but always with the intent of collecting needed and appropriate evidence based on goals" (p.12).

Hence, products promote assessment and differentiation opportunities when they integrate students' best ways to learn and when they evolve from the curriculum and selected learning standards as authentic ways to demonstrate applications.

THE PRODUCT GRID

Teachers need a system for product options that enables them to customize assignments effectively and efficiently. A product grid

---

[59] McTigue and O'Connor, 2005.

[60] Kingore, 2004. Appendix B: Product Options for Differentiated Instruction presents a lengthy list of products designed for teachers to skim as a visual checklist to guide selection of the most appropriate product options for students.

[61] Adapted from Kingore, 2004, p 23.

[62] Erickson, 2007.

Kingore, B. (2007). *Assessment,* 4th ed. Austin, TX: Professional Associates Publishing.

is one example of such a system. Participating teachers compliment the product grid system as a tool that helps more efficiently differentiate learning experiences and product assignments.

A product grid customizes a list of multiple products appropriate to a class by encoding each product to learning modalities and multiple intelligences.[63] As product options are determined, they are listed in alphabetical order for quick reference. Each product is then coded to the modalities and intelligence preferences primarily required by the student to complete the product.

In addition to matching the best ways for students to learn, the objective of a product grid is to replace simple answer sheets that require little thinking with tasks that encourage active participation and challenge students to generate responses. To advance learning, the products must connect to content and invite students to apply and transfer acquired skills. The intent is not to entertain students but rather to engage them so appropriately in learning experiences that enjoyment results. Experienced teachers report that these products also serve as springboards for increased discussion and interaction among students.

The following codes appear in the product grid examples in this chapter. As appropriate, vary the product grid so it is more applicable to students' needs by developing additional codes, such as codes for students' interests.

Modality codes		
V	=	Visual
O/A	=	Oral/auditory
W	=	Written
K	=	Kinesthetic

Multiple Intelligence codes		
L	=	Linguistic
L-M	=	Logical-mathematical

N	=	Naturalist
S	=	Spatial
M	=	Musical
B-K	=	Bodily kinesthetic
Inter	=	Interpersonal
Intra	=	Intrapersonal

The products are coded to include the logical-mathematical and naturalist intelligences if the content of the products can incorporate specific logical-mathematical or naturalist content in the task. For example, the creation of a flow chart engages naturalistic intelligence when a student explains the life cycle of a rainforest Nursery Frog.

Most products incorporate interpersonal intelligences when completed by a group of students; products encourage intrapersonal intelligence when completed by an individual. Hence, the grid marks both interpersonal intelligence and intrapersonal intelligence for any product that could be completed equally well by either a group or an individual. As often as is appropriate, a teacher may begin a task assignment by stating to the class: *You may work by yourself or with one or two other people.* Thus, students are sometimes given the choice to work alone or with others. As one wise gifted student observed: *You can't work with others all of the time without compromising what you could really do.*

A Product Grid Blank

A blank form for a product grid is provided (Figure 8.1) so teachers can organize their instructional product options. Alphabetically list the products that are developmentally appropriate to the students, most applicable to teaching, and useful to integrate learning standards. Then, code each product to the learning modalities and multiple intelligences primarily required by students to complete and present that product.

---

[63] See Appendix B for a brief discussion of multiple intelligences.

Kingore, B. (2007). *Assessment,* 4th ed. Austin, TX: Professional Associates Publishing.

Figure 8.1: PRODUCT GRID FOR _____

	MODALITIES				MULTIPLE INTELLIGENCES							
	V	O/A	W	K	L	L-M	N	S	M	B-K	Inter	Intra

Kingore, B. (2007). *Assessment,* 4th ed. Austin, TX: Professional Associates Publishing.

PRODUCT GRID APPLICATIONS TO DIFFERENTIATE INSTRUCTION

Six Differentiation Options

PRODUCT-STUDENT MATCH

The teacher develops and uses a general product grid, such as Figure 8.2, to more accurately prescribe a specific product appropriate to a student's learning profile, product preferences, and learning objective. The intent is to match product assignments to students' prior knowledge and learning rate.

LEARNING TASK EXTENSION

When a teacher skims a general product grid and a desired modality or intelligence is not engaged, the teacher ponders how the task might be varied to incorporate that need. For example, when a student makes a booklet about a topic, oral/auditory modes are not required. To address the needs of a highly auditory learner, a teacher might vary the task by: 1) Allowing the student to record the booklet as a read-along book for others, 2) Inviting the student to read the booklet to another class, or 3) Arranging for the student to work together with another student to produce the booklet. In this manor, a product grid assists teachers' objective to select product assignments that orchestrate all of the modes of learning and intelligence preferences.

PRODUCT CHOICE

When preparing a lesson, the teacher may skim a list of products and select more than one option for students to use, all of which are appropriate to the learning task and the students. Product options allow each student some choice in how to demonstrate their learning, and the power of choice increases students' motivation to excel.

Figure 8.2: GENERAL PRODUCT GRID[64]

64 Full-sized versions of the general product grid pages are included on the CD-ROM (Kingore, 2007).

Kingore, B. (2007). *Assessment,* 4th ed. Austin, TX: Professional Associates Publishing.

CONTENT-SPECIFIC PRODUCTS

Instead of a general product grid, teachers frequently request product grid examples that are specifically related to one subject area and/or grade level. To develop a content-specific product grid, the teacher brainstorms and organizes a list of products most applicable to a specific content area or topic for the class.

For example, which specific math products might increase critical thinking responses and help balance the use of computational exercises? In response to requests for content-specific product grids, five examples follow. These grids are customized for beginning readers and writers (Figures 8.3A and 8.3B), primary students (Figure 8.4A and 8.4B), and the subject areas of language arts and social studies (Figure 8.5A and 8.5B), math (Figure 8.6A and 8.6B), and science (Figure 8.7A and 8.7B).

Most list products are self-explanatory; however, some merit examples for clarification and to prompt additional application ideas. While many different content-related applications are possible, some suggestions are offered for specific products on each content list.

Avoid losing a good instructional possibility when brainstorming product ideas alone or with others. Write quick notes of any application ideas that emerge. Focus on what students should learn and demonstrate as a result of this product experience.

LEARNING OPTIONS POSTERS

Learning options posters list potential product assignments. To save planning time and promote diversity in product responses, consider the following sequence to develop them.

1. One or more teachers work as a team to prepare a list of content-specific products appropriate to the age, readiness levels, and learning profiles of the students.
2. The teachers review their curriculum and teaching objectives to determine which products have the potential for rich instructional applications to the content.
3. Narrow the list to products that are open-ended and generalizable in order to match multiple learning topics, accommodate different learning styles, and allow multiple applications throughout the school year. The exact number of products is determined by the flexible thinking of the teacher.
4. Elaborate the products into clearly explained learning tasks students select as appropriate to document their learning.
5. Organize the tasks to post in the classroom for product assignments throughout the year or to provide teacher-approved options for students who need replacement tasks when they have mastered the concepts and skills in the core curriculum.

Figure 8.8 is one example with nine options for elementary and middle school students to select to demonstrate their understanding of a book they have read. Figure 8.9 provides six product options for elementary writing. Figure 8.10 is a math example for young children. Figure 8.11 lists options for secondary history products.[65]

The learning options can be weighted for thinking level, complexity, and depth to align with the simple to more complex applications that are needed by specific students in mixed-ability classrooms. The objective is to focus on a variety of product options useful over an extended period of time rather than to suggest that students have to select multiple products and complete multiple tasks for the same segment of learning.

---

[65] For additional prepared learning options posters, see Kingore, 2004.

Kingore, B. (2007). *Assessment,* 4th ed. Austin, TX: Professional Associates Publishing.

INDIVIDUALIZED PRODUCT GRIDS

To maximize student autonomy, use a copy of the class product grid to provide personalized product lists. To develop these lists, the teacher or the student assesses the student's modalities and pattern of intelligences.[66] On a copy of the class product grid, the teacher or the student then highlights three or four of the product grid columns that match the student's pattern of strengths. Next, the student skims down the list of products looking for those that are interesting and incorporate many highlighted strengths. Finally, the student lists those selected products to create an individualized product list.

Upper elementary and secondary students use individualized product lists when it is appropriate for them to choose which products they will complete to document their learning. The tool simplifies differentiation and the determination of replacement tasks when a student has mastered the concepts and skills in the core curriculum. The products options can be weighted for depth and complexity to align with tiering objectives.

This option allows open-ended product selection as each student has a list of appropriate products to choose from to demonstrate achievement on any learning task. With this option, a student can use the list as appropriate all year. In a mixed-ability classroom, these product lists particularly help advanced and gifted students proceed independently with projects and self-directed study when pre-assessment validates that they have already mastered the core curriculum.

Use your individualized product list to choose how you will demonstrate your next learning achievement.

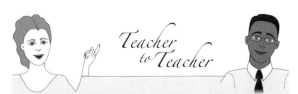

Teachers question: *How do we determine grades when students are completing different products?* Product options for students do affect grading procedures. Seldom is an answer-key as effective as a rubric when different products are involved to demonstrate learning. Chapter 6 provides several rubric examples and a tool for generating rubrics appropriate for product assignments. Chapter 3 includes a pictorial rubric generator that is applicable for evaluating young or ELL students.

Many products have the potential to serve as effective preassessments when used as repeated tasks. Acrostics, concept maps, flow charts, graphs, reports, time lines, and Venn diagrams are examples of products that can be completed and then repeated in the following manner for achievement comparisons.

1. Each student initially completes a product and records name, date, and score or grade on the product.
2. The student stores the product for comparison at a later date.
3. At teacher-designated times during instruction and/or after instruction is completed, the student retrieves the initial product and uses a different colored pen to embellish, delete, or correct items on the product. The use of a different color clarifies changes in the student's knowledge and understanding over time.
4. These products prompt productive achievement discussions between teacher and student, student to student, and between parent and child.

[66] See Appendix B for a simple, informal tool to assess multiple intelligences.

Kingore, B. (2007). *Assessment,* 4th ed. Austin, TX: Professional Associates Publishing.

Figure 8.3A: PRODUCT GRID FOR BEGINNING READING AND WRITING SKILLS

	MODALITIES				MULTIPLE INTELLIGENCES							
	V	O/A	W	K	L	L-M	N	S	M	B-K	Inter	Intra
acrostic	•		•		•	•	•	•			•	•
alphabet chart for a topic	•		•		•	•	•	•			•	•
audio tape		•			•	•	•	•	•		•	•
chart	•		•		•	•	•	•				•
choral reading/readers theater	•	•	•		•	•	•		•			
collection collage	•			•		•	•	•		•	•	•
comic strip	•		•		•	•	•	•			•	•
concept or story map (web)	•		•		•	•	•	•				
dance	•	•		•					•	•	•	•
demonstration	•	•	•	•	•	•	•	•	•	•	•	•
diorama	•			•		•	•	•		•	•	•
experiment	•		•	•	•	•	•	•			•	•
flannel board presentation	•	•		•	•	•	•			•	•	•
graph	•		•		•	•	•	•			•	•
illustration	•					•	•	•			•	•
interview		•	•		•	•	•				•	
jigsaw puzzle	•			•		•	•	•		•	•	•
list			•		•	•	•				•	•
mobile	•			•		•	•	•		•	•	•
mural/banner	•			•		•	•	•		•	•	•
museum exhibit/display	•		•	•	•	•	•	•		•	•	•
oral report		•		•	•	•	•			•	•	•
painting	•			•				•		•	•	•
pantomime				•		•				•	•	•
photograph or photo sequence	•			•		•	•	•		•	•	•
picture dictionary/scrapbook	•		•		•	•	•	•			•	•
picture book	•		•		•	•	•	•			•	•
play/puppet show	•	•	•	•	•	•	•	•	•	•	•	•
pop-up book	•	•	•	•	•	•	•	•		•	•	•
poster	•		•	•	•	•	•	•		•	•	•
rap/song		•		•	•				•	•	•	•
rebus story or sentence	•		•		•	•	•	•			•	•
riddle or rhyme		•	•		•	•					•	•
role play	•	•		•	•					•	•	
scavenger hunt	•		•	•	•	•	•			•	•	
scrapbook	•		•	•	•			•		•	•	•
sculpture	•			•				•		•		•
wordless book	•							•			•	•

Kingore, B. (2007). *Assessment*, 4th ed. Austin, TX: Professional Associates Publishing.

Figure 8.3B:
PRODUCT EXAMPLES FOR BEGINNING READING AND WRITING SKILLS

Examples of potential products

- ACROSTIC–Using a concept or topic word, such as *families*, students brainstorm ideas as an adult writes significant words or phrases related to the topic that begin with each letter in the word.

- ALPHABET CHART FOR A TOPIC–For each letter of the alphabet, students brainstorm and list information to organize important facts and ideas about a topic.

- AUDIO TAPE–Record students retelling a folk tale or well-known story at the beginning, middle, and end of the year to hear and celebrate skill acquisitions and growth in story structure, vocabulary, and language fluency.

- CHORAL READING/READERS' THEATER–Divide well-known poems or rhymes into parts for students to perform.

- COLLECTION COLLAGE–Students make a collage of items found in even numbers or items of a certain color, texture, size, or other category.

- DANCE–Students create a dance that demonstrates how different animals move, eat or communicate,

- DEMONSTRATION–Students demonstrate a simple sequence or task, such as how to get to school when it is raining.

- DIORAMA–Students: 1. Make a diorama illustrating a problem or solution in a story the class is reading, or 2. Make a social studies diorama interpreting life in a past or current culture.

- FLANNEL BOARD PRESENTATION–Students glue small velcro or sandpaper pieces to paper illustrations and place them on a flannel board to retell a story or sequence.

- GRAPH–Students graph how many classmates are: 1. Eating turkey on Thanksgiving or eating something else, 2. Having company at their house during the holidays or not having company, or 3. Getting to school by walking, car, bus, bike, or another way.

- INTERVIEW–Students: 1. Tape record interviews with other students, 2. Interview family members to learn about family history, or 3. Interview people in school to learn about them and their jobs. Photograph the people being interviewed and display the photo as information is shared with others.

- MOBILE–Students create mobiles for different textures, such as rough, smooth, and tough, or for different categories, such as oviparous animals.

- PAINTING–Students paint: 1. A rainbow and explain its color sequence, or 2. A geometric figure with dots inside. *I painted a _____ with _____ dots inside.*

- PHOTOGRAPH OR PHOTO SEQUENCE–1. Using digital photographs of items around school, students describe a photo for others to identify. 2. Using several photographs of a learning experience at school, students place the photos in sequence as they retell the task.

- POSTER–Students create a poster using words and pictures to show others what they learned as they researched.

- RAP/SONG–Students use the tune for common songs, such as *The Farmer and the Dell*, to make up songs about math facts.

- REBUS STORY OR SENTENCE–Students use stickers or small cutouts of pictures in place of nouns in a sentence. Have them begin using simple patterns: *I want a [picture]. The [picture] can run.*

- RIDDLE OR RHYME–Students create riddles for others to solve about a topic being studied or people in the class. *I am the tallest and oldest person in the class. Who am I?*

- SCAVENGER HUNT–Students compute how many times a certain word appears on one page of the newspaper by highlighting that word each time they find it. Then, they compare results from several scavenger hunts.

- WORDLESS BOOK–1. Students tape record their version of a story for a wordless book and place their tape with the book in the reading center for others to enjoy. 2. Students dictate or write the words to accompany each page of a wordless book.

Kingore, B. (2007). *Assessment,* 4th ed. Austin, TX: Professional Associates Publishing.

Products

Figure 8.4A: PRODUCT GRID FOR PRIMARY GRADES

	MODALITIES				MULTIPLE INTELLIGENCES							
	V	O/A	W	K	L	L-M	N	S	M	B-K	Inter	Intra
acrostic	•		•		•	•	•	•			•	•
alphabet book for a topic	•		•		•	•	•	•			•	•
audio tape		•			•	•	•		•		•	•
book or booklet	•		•		•	•	•	•			•	•
chart	•		•		•	•	•	•			•	•
choral reading/readers theater	•	•	•		•	•	•		•		•	
collection collage	•			•	•	•	•	•		•	•	•
comic strip	•		•		•	•	•	•			•	•
concept or story map (web)	•		•		•	•	•	•			•	•
demonstration	•	•	•	•	•	•	•	•	•	•	•	•
diorama	•			•	•	•	•	•		•	•	•
experiment	•		•	•	•	•	•	•		•	•	•
fable		•	•		•	•	•	•			•	•
flannel board presentation	•	•		•	•	•	•			•	•	•
graph	•		•		•	•	•	•			•	•
illustration	•					•	•	•			•	•
interview		•			•	•	•				•	
invitation	•	•	•		•			•			•	•
jigsaw puzzle	•			•	•	•	•	•		•	•	•
journal/diary/learning log			•		•	•	•					•
letter			•		•	•	•				•	•
list			•		•	•	•				•	•
mobile	•			•	•	•	•	•		•	•	•
mural/banner	•			•	•	•	•	•		•	•	•
museum exhibit/display	•		•	•	•	•	•	•		•	•	•
newspaper	•				•	•	•	•			•	•
oral report		•		•	•	•	•				•	•
painting	•			•		•	•	•		•	•	•
photograph or photo sequence	•			•	•	•	•	•		•	•	•
picture dictionary/scrapbook	•		•		•	•	•	•			•	•
play/puppet show	•	•	•	•	•	•	•	•		•	•	•
poem/bio poem		•	•		•	•	•		•		•	•
pop-up book	•			•	•	•	•	•			•	•
poster	•			•	•	•	•	•		•	•	•
rap/performed rhyme/song		•		•	•				•	•	•	•
rebus story or sentence	•		•		•	•	•	•			•	•
riddle or rhyme		•	•		•	•					•	•
role play	•	•		•						•	•	
scavenger hunt	•		•	•	•	•	•				•	•
sculpture	•			•					•	•		•
story (with illustrations)	•	•	•		•	•	•	•			•	•
Venn diagram	•		•		•	•	•	•			•	•
wordless book	•						•				•	•

Kingore, B. (2007). *Assessment,* 4th ed. Austin, TX: Professional Associates Publishing.

Figure 8.4B:
PRODUCT EXAMPLES FOR PRIMARY GRADES

Examples of potential products

- ACROSTIC–1. Using a concept or topic word, such as *cooperation,* students brainstorm and write a significant word or phrase related to the topic that begins with each letter. 2. Using the title of a book the class is reading, students write events and details from the book.

- ALPHABET BOOK–Students write and illustrate an individual or small group alphabet book showing what they have learned about the topic being studied.

- AUDIO TAPE–Students record a book for the reading center and include a sound to designate when to turn the page.

- COLLECTION COLLAGE–Students work with others to create a collage for each color of the rainbow.

- COMIC STRIP–Students draw a comic strip in which one or two characters tell how to complete a simple process and sequence.

- CONCEPT STORY MAP (WEB)–Students create symbols for characters, settings, problems, and solutions and use them to map a book.

- FABLE–Students write and illustrate a fable using their favorite animal as the character and carefully plan their main idea as the moral of the story.

- INTERVIEW–Students interview five people to learn how they feel about spiders or insects and organize the results to share in class.

- INVITATION–Students write an invitation to the principal or other school personnel to come to their room to read the stories they created or to view other important completed work.

- JOURNAL / DIARY / LEARNING LOG–Each student compares three entries in his or her journal and explains one observation about his or her growth as a learner.

- LIST–As a class, list more precise words to say or write instead of simple, over-used words, such as *nice, said, good,* or *like.*

- MUSEUM EXHIBIT/DISPLAY–The class creates a three-dimensional museum exhibit to show what each student has learned while researching life in the oceans. Students complete cards to display beside each portion of the exhibit to explain and interpret the exhibit.

- PHOTOGRAPH OR PHOTO SEQUENCE–Students use a digital or regular camera to take photographs of items around school and write descriptions of their photographs. Students then ask others to read the description and draw a picture of what was described without seeing the photograph. The students compare the drawing to the photograph and discuss similarities and differences.

- POSTER–Students make a poster called *Pairs* that shows different pairs of common things, such as hands, eyes, button holes, and twins.

- REBUS STORY OR SENTENCE–Students write a summary or retelling of the beginning, middle, and end of a book by drawing pictures or symbols to substitute for several nouns that are important to the story.

- ROLE PLAY–Read <u>Chrysanthemum</u>[67] by Kevin Henkes. With others, students role play different behaviors at school that would be *absolutely dreadful* and *absolutely perfect.*

- SCAVENGER HUNT–Students create a scavenger hunt for words on a cereal box, such as: *Find a word that means 'good;' Find a word that rhymes with 'cat;'* and *Count how many times the word 'in' is on the box.* They then challenge others to complete the scavenger hunt.

- SCULPTURE–Students make a paper sculpture using nineteen sizes of paper and five geometric shapes.

- VENN DIAGRAM–Students compare addition to subtraction, two dinosaurs, two characters, or two stories using an illustration for the Venn, such as a bow tie, a penguin with outstretched wings, or outlines of two dinosaurs overlapping slightly to create three areas for writing similarities and differences.

[67] Henkes, 1996.

Kingore, B. (2007). *Assessment,* 4th ed. Austin, TX: Professional Associates Publishing.

Figure 8.5A: PRODUCT GRID FOR LANGUAGE ARTS AND SOCIAL STUDIES

	MODALITIES				MULTIPLE INTELLIGENCES							
	V	O/A	W	K	L	L-M	N	S	M	B-K	Inter	Intra
acrostic	•		•		•	•		•			•	•
advertisement/brochure	•	•	•	•	•			•		•	•	•
analogy/simile/metaphor		•	•		•	•	•				•	•
audio tape		•			•	•			•		•	•
book or illustrated story	•		•		•	•		•			•	•
bulletin board	•		•	•	•			•			•	•
cartoon or caricature	•				•			•			•	•
center (student made)	•	•	•	•	•	•	•	•		•	•	•
choral reading/readers theater	•	•	•	•	•	•		•	•	•	•	•
comic strip	•		•		•			•			•	
concept or story map (web)	•		•		•	•	•	•			•	
debate		•			•	•					•	
demonstration (labeled artifacts)	•	•	•	•	•	•		•		•	•	•
dialogue		•	•		•	•					•	
diorama	•			•	•			•		•	•	•
documentary film	•	•	•	•	•	•	•	•		•	•	•
editorial/essay/persuasive writing		•	•		•	•		•			•	•
fable (illustrated)	•	•	•		•	•	•	•			•	•
family tree	•		•		•			•			•	•
flannel board presentation	•	•		•	•	•	•	•		•	•	•
flow chart	•		•		•	•	•	•			•	•
game (original)	•	•	•	•	•	•					•	
interview		•	•		•	•					•	
jigsaw puzzle	•		•	•	•	•		•			•	•
journal/diary/learning log			•		•	•						•
letter/e-mail			•		•						•	•
magazine article			•		•						•	•
map/salt map (with legend)	•		•	•	•	•	•	•			•	•
mobile	•			•	•			•		•	•	•
model	•			•	•			•			•	•
mural	•			•	•		•	•		•	•	•
museum exhibit	•		•	•	•	•		•			•	
newscast/TV program	•	•	•	•	•	•				•	•	•
newspaper	•				•	•	•	•			•	
oral report/persuasive speech		•	•	•	•	•				•	•	•
panel discussion		•			•	•					•	
pantomime	•			•						•	•	•
photo essay	•			•		•	•	•		•	•	
play/puppet show (with music)	•	•	•	•	•	•		•	•	•	•	•
poem/diamante/bio poem	•	•	•		•	•		•	•		•	•
pop-up book	•		•	•	•	•	•	•			•	•
poster/chart	•		•	•	•	•	•	•			•	•
rap/performed rhyme/song		•		•	•				•	•	•	
rebus story	•		•		•	•	•	•			•	
reverse crossword puzzle	•		•		•	•	•				•	•
role play	•	•		•	•						•	•
scavenger hunt	•		•	•	•	•	•				•	•
simulation	•			•	•	•					•	•
survey (with data graphed)	•		•		•	•	•	•			•	•
symbols	•					•	•	•			•	•
time line	•		•		•	•	•				•	•
travelogue			•		•	•	•	•			•	•
Venn diagram	•		•		•	•	•	•			•	•

Kingore, B. (2007). *Assessment,* 4th ed. Austin, TX: Professional Associates Publishing.

Figure 8.5B:
PRODUCT EXAMPLES FOR LANGUAGE ARTS AND SOCIAL STUDIES

Examples of potential products

- ACROSTIC–Students use a concept or topic word, such as *Africa* or *Apache*. They then brainstorm and write a significant word, phrase, or sentence related to the topic that begins with each letter.

- ADVERTISEMENT/BROCHURE–Students create: 1. An advertisement for an item used by a character or historical figure to solve a problem, including how it was used and its current value, or 2. An advertisement for a city or other location they have studied, using words and illustrations that will make others want to visit that area.

- ANALOGY/SIMILE/METAPHOR–Students write direct analogies comparing a historical person or book character to a common object. *Martin Luther King, Jr. is like a broken clock because he ran out of time before he completed all the possibilities within him.*

- BULLETIN BOARD–Individuals or small groups of students make a bulletin board to highlight the publications and life of a favorite author who lived in or wrote about the time period or location being studied.

- CHORAL READING/READERS THEATER–Small groups transform a classic fable, short story, or poem into a readers theater to perform for parents or other classes.

- DEBATE–Students debate the censorship of books in school libraries, citing references for their research.

- EDITORIAL/ESSAY/PERSUASIVE WRITING–Each student writes an essay to the librarian, persuading the school to place a copy of a new book in the library. Students include supportive arguments explaining the book's literary merit and relevance to the student body.

- FAMILY TREE–Students interview their family members and develop a family tree that includes four or more generations. They then surround the family tree with pictures and maps of where different family members were born.

- FLOW CHART–Each student draws and labels a flow chart describing the sequence of events in a story the class is reading.

- INTERVIEW–In pairs, students simulate an interview between a reporter and a famous explorer or writer.

- JOURNAL/DIARY/LEARNING LOG–Students write journal entries for the main character of a novel, an explorer, or a historical figure.

- LETTER/E-MAIL–Students write a sequence of letters or e-mails between main characters, discussing the book's main idea from the characters' perspectives.

- MAGAZINE ARTICLE–Students write an article about living in one city, state, or country. They also take photographs, collect pictures, or draw illustrations to include in the article.

- NEWSPAPER–As a class, create a newspaper for the historical event being studied. Prompt students' thinking: *What is on the front page? What are the ads and sport events? Which businesses need more help?*

- PHOTO ESSAY–Students read Russell Freedman's Lincoln: A Photobiography[68] and then create a photobiography of the life in their community or a historical building in their city.

- POEM/DIAMANTE/BIO POEM–Students: 1. Create a bio poem for a historical figure or a character in a book; or 2. Write a diamante revealing two diverse perspectives of Manifest Destiny.

- TIME LINE–Students create a time line of dates significant to the social studies topic being studied. They then challenge others to label the time line to test their understanding of the topic.

- TRAVELOGUE–Students write travelogues from the perspective of early explorers as they pursue their travels and make their most important discoveries.

- VENN DIAGRAM–Students compare two countries by overlapping the outlines of their borders, creating three areas for writing similarities and differences.

Products

[68] Freedman, 1989.

Kingore, B. (2007). *Assessment,* 4th ed. Austin, TX: Professional Associates Publishing.

Figure 8.6A: PRODUCT GRID FOR MATHEMATICS

	MODALITIES				MULTIPLE INTELLIGENCES							
	V	O/A	W	K	L	L-M	N	S	M	B-K	Inter	Intra
acrostic	•		•		•	•		•			•	•
bio poem			•		•	•					•	•
bulletin board	•		•	•	•	•	•	•		•	•	•
center (student made)	•	•	•	•	•	•		•	•	•	•	•
chart/poster	•		•		•	•		•			•	•
children's story (illustrated)	•		•		•	•		•			•	•
collage	•			•		•		•		•	•	•
content puzzles	•		•	•	•	•		•		•	•	•
demonstration	•	•	•	•	•	•	•	•		•	•	•
diagram (labeled)	•		•		•	•	•	•			•	•
encyclopedia entry			•		•	•					•	•
error analysis	•		•		•	•					•	•
flow chart	•		•		•	•		•			•	•
game	•	•	•	•	•	•		•	•	•	•	•
glossary			•		•	•					•	•
graph	•		•		•	•	•	•				•
jigsaw puzzle	•			•	•	•	•	•			•	•
learning log			•		•	•						•
letter (math process)	•		•		•	•					•	•
list			•		•	•					•	•
math tracks	•		•	•	•	•		•		•	•	•
metaphor or simile	•	•	•		•	•					•	•
model	•			•	•	•	•	•	•	•	•	•
number challenge	•	•	•	•	•	•		•		•	•	
number line	•		•	•		•		•		•	•	•
oral report/informative speech	•	•	•	•	•	•					•	•
patterns	•		•	•	•	•		•	•	•	•	•
questionnaire (data graphed)		•	•		•	•					•	
rap		•		•	•	•			•	•	•	•
recipe			•		•	•					•	•
reverse crossword puzzle	•		•		•	•		•			•	•
riddle		•	•		•	•					•	
scavenger hunt	•		•	•	•	•				•	•	
song (original)		•	•		•	•			•		•	
story problem (original)	•		•		•	•		•			•	•
survey (with data graphed)	•		•		•	•	•	•			•	•
test (original)	•	•	•		•	•		•			•	•
time line	•		•		•	•		•			•	•
Venn diagram	•		•		•	•		•			•	•
written report			•		•	•					•	•

Kingore, B. (2007). *Assessment,* 4th ed. Austin, TX: Professional Associates Publishing.

Figure 8.6B:
PRODUCT EXAMPLES FOR MATHEMATICS

Examples of potential products

- ACROSTIC–Use a concept or topic word, such as *division* or *factorials*. Students brainstorm and write for each letter a significant word, phrase, or sentence related to the topic that begins with that letter.

- BIO POEM–Students create a bio poem for *integer.*

- BULLETIN BOARD–Create a bulletin board for students to post mathematical applications, such as: *Ways to Make 78,* or *Examples of Geometry in Architecture.*

- CENTER (STUDENT MADE)–Students use tangrams to create the ten digits and all the letters of the alphabet.

- CHILDREN'S STORY (ILLUSTRATED)– Students write and illustrate a story to explain a math concept. As examples, read Cindy Neuschwander's Sir Cumference series.[69]

- COLLAGE–Small groups of students organize collages showing fractions in daily life.

- CONTENT PUZZLES–Students write math facts on a simple graphic outline and cut it into ten to fifteen puzzle pieces for others to put back together by correctly matching the problem and the solution.

- DEMONSTRATION–Students use manipulatives to demonstrate multiplication to a younger student.

- ERROR ANALYSIS–Students analyze a problem that is flawed, writing what is wrong and how to correct it.

- FLOW CHART–Students draw and label a flow chart that illustrates how to apply a specific math strategy or geometric proof.

- GAME–Students create a stock market game or math fact rodeo for others to play.

- LETTER (MATH PROCESS)–Students complete one math problem and then write a letter to someone explaining step-by-step how they completed that problem.

- MATH TRACKS–Students draw a long track on a paper and then write one number at the beginning of the track and a different number at the end. Starting at the first number, they use any appropriate operations (as simple as addition or complex as algebra) to create a continuous equation that concludes with the number at the end of the track.

- METAPHOR OR SIMILE–Students express a mathematical concept through a metaphor or simile, such as: *Addition is like compound words, and subtraction is like contractions.*

- NUMBER CHALLENGE–Set a challenge number for pairs of students to reach using dice and any appropriate math operation or formula (as simple as addition or complex as algebra).

- QUESTIONNAIRE–Students conduct questionnaires asking adults how math is needed in their jobs, and graph the results.

- REVERSE CROSSWORD PUZZLE–Provide the completed puzzle grid of numbers. Students write the math facts that resulted in those numbers.

- RIDDLE–Students develop simple or more complex riddles, such as: *I am an odd number larger than six and smaller than the square root of eighty-one.*

- SCAVENGER HUNT–Provide a list of math terms for students to find examples in the real world. Students then compare and discuss their findings.

- TEST (ORIGINAL)–Instead of taking a test, students write the test items for the math process or concept of study.

- WRITTEN REPORT–Students write: 1. A report about the authentic applications of a polygon; 2. A report regarding how and why different traffic and information signs are specific polygons; or 3. A report relating how geometry applies to baseball or some other sport.

[69] Neuschwander, 1997.

Kingore, B. (2007). *Assessment,* 4th ed. Austin, TX: Professional Associates Publishing.

Figure 8.7A: PRODUCT GRID FOR SCIENCE

	MODALITIES				MULTIPLE INTELLIGENCES							
	V	O/A	W	K	L	L-M	N	S	M	B-K	Inter	Intra
acrostic	•		•		•	•	•	•			•	•
audio tape		•			•	•	•		•		•	•
book/booklet	•		•		•	•	•	•			•	•
bulletin board	•		•	•	•	•	•	•		•	•	•
center (student made)	•	•	•	•	•	•	•	•	•	•	•	•
chart/poster	•		•	•	•	•	•	•		•	•	•
choral reading/readers theater		•	•	•	•	•	•		•	•	•	
collection collage	•			•	•	•	•	•			•	•
comic strip	•		•		•	•	•	•			•	•
concept or story map (web)	•		•		•	•	•				•	•
critique		•	•		•	•	•				•	•
cross section	•		•		•	•	•	•			•	•
debate		•	•		•	•	•				•	
demonstration (labeled artifacts)	•	•	•	•	•	•	•	•	•		•	
description			•		•	•	•				•	•
diagram (labeled)	•		•		•	•	•	•			•	•
documentary film/film strip	•	•	•	•	•	•	•	•	•	•	•	•
editorial/essay/persuasive writing		•	•		•	•	•				•	•
encyclopedia entry	•		•		•	•	•				•	•
essay			•		•							•
experiment/demonstration	•	•	•	•	•	•	•	•	•	•	•	•
flannel board presentation	•	•		•	•	•	•		•	•	•	•
flow chart	•		•		•	•	•				•	•
game (original)	•	•	•	•	•	•	•	•	•	•	•	•
glossary			•		•	•	•				•	•
graph	•		•		•	•	•	•			•	•
handbook	•		•		•	•	•	•			•	•
interview		•	•		•	•	•				•	
lab report with illustrations	•		•		•	•	•	•			•	•
learning log			•		•		•					•
letter (science process)			•		•	•	•				•	
list			•		•	•	•				•	•
mobile	•			•	•		•	•		•	•	•
model	•			•			•	•		•	•	•
museum exhibit/labeled display	•		•	•	•	•	•	•		•	•	•
panel discussion		•			•	•	•				•	
patterns	•		•	•	•	•	•	•	•	•	•	•
photo essay/sequence	•			•	•	•	•	•			•	•
picture dictionary	•		•		•	•	•				•	•
poem/diamante/bio poem	•	•	•		•	•	•		•		•	•
rap/song (original)		•	•	•	•	•	•		•	•	•	•
rebus story	•		•		•	•	•	•			•	•
report (oral or written)		•	•		•	•	•				•	•
reverse crossword puzzle	•		•		•	•	•	•			•	
riddle/rhyme		•	•		•	•	•		•		•	•
role play	•	•		•	•					•	•	•
scavenger hunt	•		•	•	•	•	•			•	•	•
scrapbook	•		•	•	•	•	•				•	•
survey (with data graphed)	•		•		•	•	•				•	•
terrarium	•			•			•	•		•	•	•
time line	•		•		•	•	•				•	•
Venn diagram	•		•		•	•	•	•			•	•

Kingore, B. (2007). *Assessment,* 4th ed. Austin, TX: Professional Associates Publishing.

Figure 8.7B:
PRODUCT EXAMPLES FOR SCIENCE

Examples of potential products

- ACROSTIC–Using a concept or topic word such as *photosynthesis,* students brainstorm and write for each letter a scientific word, phrase, or sentence related to the topic that begins with that letter.
- AUDIO TAPE–Students record the sounds of a season or species for others to identify.
- BULLETIN BOARD–Students compare and contrast: 1. States of matter, or 2. Life forms in Antarctica with life in the Arctic Ocean.
- CENTER (STUDENT MADE)–Students collect and categorize items that magnets do or do not attract.
- CHART/POSTER–Students illustrate and label the physics principles demonstrated by amusement park attractions.
- CHORAL READING/READERS THEATER–In small groups, students perform one or more of the choral readings about insects in Joyful Noise: Poems for Two Voices[70] by Paul Fleischman and use that format to organize facts about other animals or plants.
- COLLECTION COLLAGE–Students use a digital camera to complete a collage of photographs of simple and complex machines found at home or school
- CRITIQUE–Students write a critique about how effectively the scientific method was applied during a specific experiment conducted in class.
- DEBATE–Students organize a class debate on the issues of DNA research or using animals for research studies.
- ENCYCLOPEDIA ENTRY–Using science-related affixes and roots, students write and illustrate a fictitious encyclopedia entry describing a newly discovered life form on another planet, including specific information about its anatomy, habitat, behavior, and life cycle.

- EXPERIMENT/DEMONSTRATION–Students demonstrate how to use and interpret the results from a piece of scientific equipment, such as a magnet or compound microscope.
- FLOW CHART–Students use a flow chart to explain and illustrate a cycle, such as the water cycle.
- GRAPH–Students graph the weather in their area for one month. They then compare it to a Farmer's Almanac 100 years earlier and record three inferences or conclusions.
- MOBILE–In small groups, students create mobiles that represent the relationship of our traditional solar system or galaxy to the latest discoveries in space.
- MODEL–Using common items as symbols, students construct a DNA chain and explain the reasoning behind the symbols they chose.
- POEM / DIAMANTE / BIO POEM–Students compose a diamante contrasting two opposing forces in nature.
- REVERSE CROSSWORD PUZZLE–Students write science terms in the grid and then challenge others to write the descriptors that result in those terms.
- RIDDLE/RHYME–Students create simple or more complex riddles using science concepts, such as: *I magnify things you can not see and focus them when you look through me.*
- SCAVENGER HUNT–Students conduct a scavenger hunt to identify and quantify the chemicals found in their kitchens.
- TERRARIUM–Students establish a terrarium and write out the sequence of procedures they used to complete it.
- TIME LINE–Students complete a time line mapping the progression of a major tropical storm and then compare their results with others in the class to interpret similarities.
- VENN DIAGRAM–Students: 1. Over-lap four circles to create a four-way Venn that compares the similarities and differences of four biomes, or 2. Use a Venn diagram to compare the attributes of two species or the same species living in two different biomes.

[70] Fleischman, 1992.

Figure 8.8: ELEMENTARY AND MIDDLE SCHOOL LITERATURE

1 Create an artifact bag for your book. In a paper sack, include six to ten items with a log book explaining how each symbolically represents a character, problem, key event, or solution from the story.	**2** Make an illustrated chart to compare five causes and their effects in the story. Rank them from most to least significant in the story and explain your rankings.	**3** Draw a story board with captions or a comic strip with speech balloons to sequence the major events and ideas in the story.
4 Write a telephone or e-mail dialogue between two of the characters. Have their conversations reveal their traits and the main ideas of the story.	**5** **Free Choice** Design your own book response. Meet with the teacher to present your plan.	**6** Construct a diorama of the most significant scenes. Use details to incorporate as much story content as possible. Include a display card to explain your diorama to others.
7 Imagine that the main characters are members of your school. Create a yearbook entry for each and include a picture, their school activities, what they would be voted, and a quotation.	**8** Create three analogies about the main characters in the story comparing each to another character, theme, or symbolic item. Illustrate and explain each analogy.	**9** Create a concept map which includes the sequence, problem, solution, and main idea of the story. Incorporate different symbols for the events and characters.

Kingore, B. (2007). *Assessment,* 4th ed. Austin, TX: Professional Associates Publishing.

Figure 8.9: ELEMENTARY WRITING

Make a list of ten things to which you would say, "Yes!"	Pretend you are the tallest person in the world. Write about what you can do and the problems you have.	Write three things you would do to make the world a better place.
Create your favorite pizza! Write the directions for someone to make it for you.	Write a letter to complain about a product or event. **OR** Write a letter to compliment someone.	Write about your favorite toy when you were younger.

Kingore, B. (2007). *Assessment,* 4th ed. Austin, TX: Professional Associates Publishing.

✂ -

Figure 8.10: PRIMARY MATHEMATICS

Graph the _____ (Post the subject here.) of ten classmates.	Show three ways to solve this problem. (Post the problem here.)	Create a paper chain of number sentences that result in the number: _____ (Post the number here.)
Write and illustrate a number story problem that uses _____ (Post the operation here.) and three people in it.	Use the tune to *Farmer in the Dell.* Create several verses to the song using math facts.	Write a letter to a classmate explaining how to complete this problem. (Post the problem here.)

Kingore, B. (2007). *Assessment,* 4th ed. Austin, TX: Professional Associates Publishing.

Products

Figure 8.11: SECONDARY HISTORY

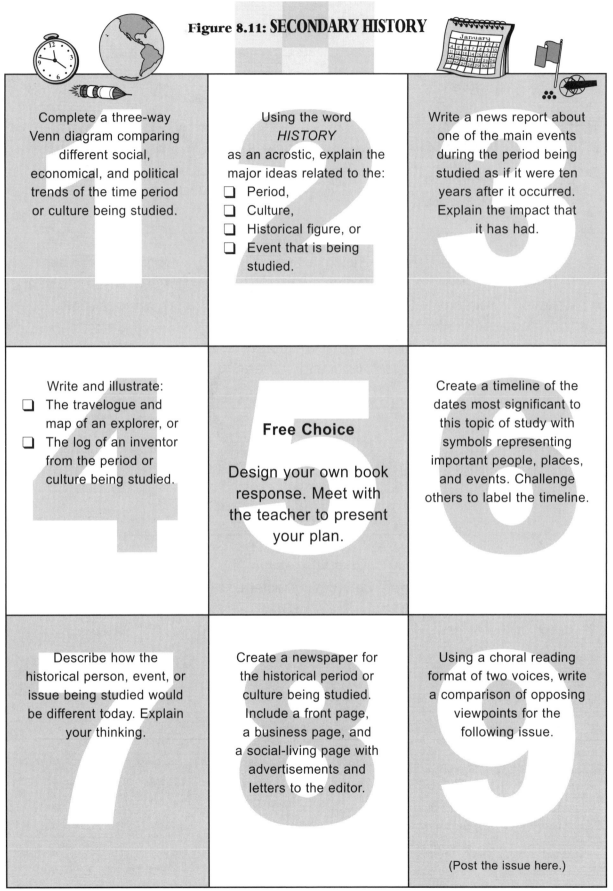

Complete a three-way Venn diagram comparing different social, economical, and political trends of the time period or culture being studied.	Using the word *HISTORY* as an acrostic, explain the major ideas related to the: ❑ Period, ❑ Culture, ❑ Historical figure, or ❑ Event that is being studied.	Write a news report about one of the main events during the period being studied as if it were ten years after it occurred. Explain the impact that it has had.
Write and illustrate: ❑ The travelogue and map of an explorer, or ❑ The log of an inventor from the period or culture being studied.	**Free Choice** Design your own book response. Meet with the teacher to present your plan.	Create a timeline of the dates most significant to this topic of study with symbols representing important people, places, and events. Challenge others to label the timeline.
Describe how the historical person, event, or issue being studied would be different today. Explain your thinking.	Create a newspaper for the historical period or culture being studied. Include a front page, a business page, and a social-living page with advertisements and letters to the editor.	Using a choral reading format of two voices, write a comparison of opposing viewpoints for the following issue. (Post the issue here.)

Kingore, B. (2007). *Assessment,* 4th ed. Austin, TX: Professional Associates Publishing.

CHAPTER 9

Integrating and Assessing Learning Standards

Standards are important resources for teachers
but have little meaning until teachers and administrators take
true ownership of them.
—*Judy Carr & Douglas Harris*

Learning standards are a national phenomenon. Virtually every state education department and national professional group advocates academic standards. These standards result from a reexamination of important achievement expectations and are based upon a significant body of nation-wide research and best practices instead of more random preferences. This research provides guidance to reshape curriculum and assessment into a coherent plan that incorporates standards and promotes student achievement.

Standards are articulated in the form of objectives and prescribed in terms of concepts, skills, or attitudes to promote student excellence. District-wide teams of teachers interpret these standards and translate them into classroom learning elements with achievement targets that guide students' development of proficiency. The intent is for standards to be seamlessly woven into instruction so they are natural rather than an isolated segment of learning or testing.

DEFINITIONS

Standards describe the desired results of students' educational experiences. They are statements identifying essential knowledge (what students should know) and skills (what students should be able to do). They are a consensus that clarifies expectations and quality. Throughout this chapter, *standards* and *learning standards* are used interchangeably for variety.

Benchmarks describe the steps along a K-12 continuum required to reach the standards. They are more specific, concrete statements to interpret standards into an instructional framework guiding classroom applications and assessments. Criteria are determined, often in the form of checklists or rubrics, to assess benchmarks.

Standards-based is a descriptor to suggest that curriculum components, including learning materials, processes, products, and assessments, have been aligned to relate to standards and to each other. The curriculum is specifically designed to focus on identified standards and ensure that all students have access to that knowledge and skill.

STANDARDS ASSESSMENT AND EVALUATION

Students' achievement of standards is evaluated at the classroom level and the results compared at school, district, state, and national levels. Rubrics and standardized tests are largely used to measure standards and provide samples of students' learning of the curriculum. The test is not the curriculum although some standardized test scores are perceived to have such high stakes that they seem to drive the curriculum.

District personnel analyze student achievement data from these standardized tests to determine what works and what is not an effective practice in order to initiate proactive steps to better students learning–at least as measured though standardized tests. Evaluating standards promotes changes in curriculum, instruction, assessment, and the data collection process.

In addition to evaluation through rubrics and standardized tests, standards are more informally and continually assessed in the classroom to focus attention on the quality of instruction and level of student achievement. This assessment of achievement employs multiple techniques to gather data and guide instruction. Such techniques include observation, checklists, conferences, and product assessment. Rubrics are used both to assess the steps toward reaching standards and to evaluate achievement levels.

Assessing learning standards requires that they are clearly understood by all participants and that all students have clear access to opportunities to learn. In standards-based classrooms, standards provide a common language to discuss and assess achievement; they clarify learning targets by specifying skills and outcomes.

Preassess students' mastery of standards and benchmarks within a segment of learning. The scored preassessment is stored as written documentation of achievement levels and skill needs. Each student can complete and attach to this product a list of learning standards and benchmarks showing areas of mastery as demonstrated by the preassessment. This process enables a productive instructional focus without redundant skill practice.

Are standards worthwhile? After teaching for several years and accumulating a great number of student examples, it seemed timely to review the mass and determine how much to continue saving. In so doing, I came across a writing experience students had completed over fifteen years before. Reviewing what had certainly been strong examples at that time, I realized how sophisticated our current writing standards have become. These seventh grade achievements are typical of our expectations in writing with fourth or fifth grade students today!

While some might interpret this example as pushing down the curriculum, I was reassured of the power of best practices and higher expectations. With standards, we know more about quality writing and how to guide students to that level. Standards can have a positive effect on achievement.

Kingore, B. (2007). *Assessment,* 4th ed. Austin, TX: Professional Associates Publishing.

IMPLEMENTING A STANDARDS-BASED CURRICULUM IN THE CLASSROOM

Teachers' have the pivotal responsibility for integrating and assessing students' achievement of the applicable standards for their grade levels and content areas. In a standards-based classroom, teachers incorporate standards in several different ways.

1. *Select learning tasks that are vehicles to implement the curriculum and standards.*
2. *Correlate standards across content areas.*
3. *Communicate standards clearly in student-friendly language.*
4. *Share the responsibility to document students' achievement of standards with them.*
5. *Correlate rubrics to state or district learning standards.*
6. *Communicate standards to parents.*
7. *Communicate standards on grading reports.*

1. *Select learning tasks that are vehicles to implement the curriculum and standards.*

In a standards-based classroom, activities are more than just *something students do*. Analyze learning experiences for potential instructional applications that will integrate standards within the curriculum. Then, select and plan learning assignments to develop or extend the standards and other learning objectives in the curriculum. Evaluate these learning tasks with rubrics.[71]

To accomplish this integration of standards and learning experiences, review the sequence of the curriculum topics or learning segments. Next, analyze intended outcomes and applicable standards before *reasoning in reverse* to select learning experiences with the potential to enable students to reach that objective. *I want students to learn these skills and concepts during this unit. The learning experiences to best achieve that outcome include...*

For each topic or segment of learning, use Figure 9.1 to list the related standards and learning experiences that document when specific skills and concepts are integrated throughout the unit. Then, when asked to map where a standard is addressed and taught in the curriculum, teachers have an efficient vehicle to communicate that information.

2. *Correlate standards across content areas.*

Seek as many ways as possible to integrate standards across content areas. Common wisdom such as *every teacher is a teacher of reading* and informal statements that reference *writing across the curriculum* are examples of the standards in one content area being reinforced in another subject. In some schools, it is productive to concretely analyze implementations of standards across the curriculum rather than leave such correlations to chance. Using the information in a content plan, such as Figure 9.1, teachers can build upon that information by correlating their content area segments of learning to the skills and concepts of another content area.

On Figure 9.2, list selected learning activities for a topic or segment of learning. Then, list applicable standards or benchmarks for two content areas. In each cell where standards intersect, record which activities apply. An example plotting writing skills in math is provided.

Learning Standards

---

[71] See Chapter 3 for examples of rubrics and processes for generating rubrics.

Kingore, B. (2007). *Assessment,* 4th ed. Austin, TX: Professional Associates Publishing.

Figure 9.1: CONTENT STANDARDS PLAN

CONTENT AREA _____ DATE _____

TOPIC/LEARNING SEGMENT _____

Standards:	Learning Experiences:

Kingore, B. (2007). *Assessment,* 4th ed. Austin, TX: Professional Associates Publishing.

✂ --

Figure 9.2 STANDARDS GRID

ACTIVITIES:

A: *Skill sheet applications*
B: *Cooperative problem solving*
C: *Creating story problems*
D: *Computer applications*
E: *Math in sports project*
F: _____
G: _____

STANDARDS FOR: *Writing*

STANDARDS FOR: *Mathematics*

	Writes to inform, express thoughts, influence, or entertain	Demonstrates a command of the conventions of spelling, capitalization, and punctuation	Recognizes and applies appropriate organization of ideas in written text	Writes in complete sentences using correct, varied, and effective sentence construction	Applies standard grammar and usage including subject-verb agreement and parts of speech	Employs appropriate and precise word choices	Uses prepositional phrases to elaborate written work	Uses conjunctions to connect ideas meaningfully
Uses place value to represent whole numbers (to 1,000,000,000) and decimals (to 0.001)	E	E	E	E	E	E	E	E
Uses equivalent fractions in problem-solving solutions	B C	B C	C	B C	C	C	C	C
Compares two fractional quantities using common denominators								
Relates decimals to fractions to the thousandths								
Adds, subtracts, multiplies, and divides with whole numbers, fractions and decimals	C E	C E	C E	C E	C E	C E	C E	C E
Identifies prime factors and common factors of whole numbers.								
Estimates to determine reasonable results.	B		B					

Kingore, B. (2005). *Assessment,* 3rd ed. Austin: Professional Associates Publishing.

3. Communicate standards clearly in student-friendly language.

As a class learning experience, involve students in determining the key words of each learning standard or benchmark and then restating that objective into kid-friendly language. This activity accents the relevancy of the standards to the learning objectives in the classroom and provides students some ownership in applying those standards to their learning. For example, a science standard, such as: *The student is expected to analyze, review, and critique scientific explanations, including hypothesis and theories, as to their strengths and weaknesses using scientific evidence and information,* can be simplified for students' daily reference to: *Analyzes the strengths and weaknesses of scientific explanations.* Guide students to determine the primary verb and subject; then, eliminate details that can be inferred.

Kingore, B. (2007). *Assessment,* 4th ed. Austin, TX: Professional Associates Publishing.

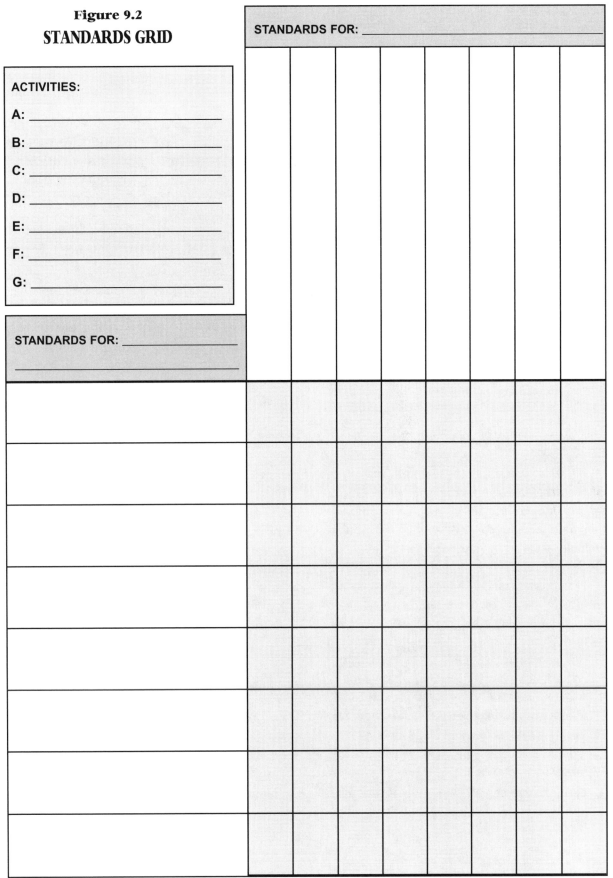

Figure 9.2
STANDARDS GRID

ACTIVITIES:

A: _____

B: _____

C: _____

D: _____

E: _____

F: _____

G: _____

STANDARDS FOR: _____

STANDARDS FOR: _____

Kingore, B. (2007). *Assessment,* 4th ed. Austin, TX: Professional Associates Publishing.

Learning Standards

In primary classrooms, teachers may conclude that this task is too difficult for young learners. In that case, determine which key words to post without children's interpretations. However, the children can still be involved in referring to and using the posted standards.

Middle School Science

❑ 1. Uses scientific inquiry methods.
❑ 2. Analyzes the strengths and weaknesses of scientific explanations.
❑ 3. Draws inferences based on data.
❑ 4. Uses lab equipment to collect data.
❑ 5. Knows the relationships between structure and function in living systems.
❑ 6. Is able to apply scientific

Post the students' interpretations on a simple graphic, such as the illustration above, for frequent reference during learning tasks. Laminate this standards graphic to be used in multiple ways as a reference tool throughout the school year.

- The posted standards communicate learning objectives to adults visiting the room.
- When teaching a skill or concept to a small group, check that skill on the posted standards graphic to emphasize its application.
- When students are working at a learning station or center, post the applicable standards graphic, check the skills or concepts to be practiced at that time, and require students to conclude their center experience by briefly noting in a learning log or on a sentence stem strip how they incorporated those skills or concepts in their work at the center.

4. Share the responsibility to document students' achievement of standards with them.

Teachers and students co-share the responsibility to document the students' achievement of learning standards. To increase students' active involvement in assessing their learning, use standards-based product captions, checklists, and sentence stems.

A. Standards Product Captions

Incorporate key words for learning standards on captions strips that students use to assess a product for their portfolio. In addition to reflection, these caption alternatives require each student to be responsible for analyzing and then checking the skills or concepts applied in that work. As adults assess products, these captions document a student's achievement level for those skills so that redundant experiences can be avoided.

Using a standards-based caption, such as Figure 9.3, fill in one or more skills specific to the assignment before duplicating the form for students to use. At other times, have students fill in the specific skills as they assess their work. This brief format is particularly applicable for elementary students or learners with special needs because it requires limited handwriting.

As an alternative format, use Figure 9.4 to list all of the standards for a content area before the form is duplicated. In this manner, the complete set of standards is always listed. A student completes the reflection, analyzes skills, and simply checks one or more of the standards-based skills demonstrated in that specific product.

Kingore, B. (2007). *Assessment,* 4th ed. Austin, TX: Professional Associates Publishing.

Figure 9.3: CAN DO SKILLS!

Can do!

NAME _Kate_ DATE _November 2_

This work shows that I can _make a good pattern with two attributes. I used color and shape._

I think _it looks neat._

I demonstrated these skills:
- ☑ _Pattern_
- ☑ _Sequence_
- ☑ _Left to right direction_
- ☑ _Geometric shapes_
- ☐ _Symmetry_
- ☐

Kingore, B. (2007). Assessment, 4th ed. Austin, TX: Professional Associates Publishing.

Figure 9.4: STANDARDS FOR _____

NAME _Stephan_ DATE _May 15_

This work shows that I can _effectively write a persuasive essay._

I think _my verb choices make this compelling. I choose my words carefully._

I demonstrated these standards:
- ☐ _Inform an audience_
- ☑ _Persuade an audience_
- ☐ _Express thoughts and entertain_
- ☐ _Sequence events or steps_
- ☑ _Develop/support/elaborate_
- ☑ _Complete sentences_
- ☐ _Plurals_
- ☑ _Subject-verb agreement_
- ☐ _Subject, object, and possessive forms_
- ☐ _Appropriate spelling_
- ☑ _Appropriate capitalization_
- ☑ _Appropriate punctuation_
- ☐ _Classification_
- ☐ _Precise adjectives_
- ☐ _Prepositional phrases_

Kingore, B. (2007). Assessment, 4th ed. Austin, TX: Professional Associates Publishing.

✂ -

Figure 9.3: CAN DO SKILLS!

Can do!

NAME _____ DATE _____

This work shows that I can _____

_____

_____

I think _____

_____

_____

I demonstrated these skills:

☐ _____   ☐ _____

☐ _____   ☐ _____

☐ _____   ☐ _____

Kingore, B. (2007). *Assessment,* 4th ed. Austin, TX: Professional Associates Publishing.

Learning Standards

Figure 9.4: STANDARDS FOR _____

NAME _____ DATE _____

This work shows that I can _____

_____

_____

I think _____

_____

_____

I demonstrated these standards:

☐ _____

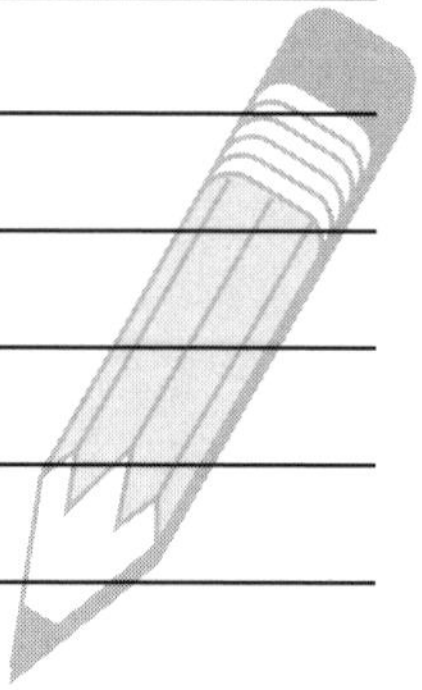

☐ _____

☐ _____

☐ _____

☐ _____

☐ _____

☐ _____

☐ _____

☐ _____

☐ _____

☐ _____

☐ _____

☐ _____

☐ _____

☐ _____

☐ _____

Kingore, B. (2007). *Assessment,* 4th ed. Austin, TX: Professional Associates Publishing.

B. Standards Checklists Folder

Duplicate the required learning standards for a content area on the outside of a file folder and provide one for each student. On the folder, students check a standard, record the graded product they completed that documents their level of achievement on that standard, and store the product in the file folder. The products are typically those graded with a shared rubric that is included with the checklist as substantiation.

The checklist is a useful reference when assessing products to document standards achievement. It is an efficient tool to organize the examples of all of the standards and is easily stored in the regular portfolio or in students' work folders.

Writing: Standards

Standards	Product	Grade
☐ Legible handwriting		
☐ Prepositional phrases		
☐ Complete complex sentences		
☐ Appropriate voice and style		
☐ Literary devices		
☐ Transitions; conjunctions		
☐ Cohesive organization		
☐ Logical support of ideas		
☐ Vivid, precise wording		
☐ Subject-verb agreement		

C. Standards Reflection

Provide sentence stems that prompt students to specifically reflect upon a learning standard application. Sentence strips, such as Figure 9.5, can be duplicated for students to complete and then attach to their work. These brief statements are a communication device to clarify learning accomplishments and document the applications of skills or concepts and are not limited to use on products selected for the portfolio. Teachers can request that students write a reflective sentence to staple on a product that is completed during independent work to be turned in for grading, during centers, or for the Standards Checklist Folder.

Figure 9.5: STANDARDS REFLECTION

NAME _Cindy_   DATE _October 13_

This work shows my ability with standard # _1 & 3_ because _I compared three similarities and three differences between the antagonists and protagonists in the two novels._

Kingore, B. (2007). *Assessment,* 4th ed. Austin, TX: Professional Associates Publishing.

Learning Standards

✂ -

Figure 9.5: STANDARDS REFLECTION

NAME _____   DATE _____

This work shows my ability with standard #_____ because _____

_____

_____

_____

Kingore, B. (2007). *Assessment,* 4th ed. Austin, TX: Professional Associates Publishing.

5. Correlate rubrics to state or district learning standards.

When standards are integrated into instruction, it follows logically to incorporate the skills of the standards as assessment levels on a rubric. While any rubric can be correlated to learning standards, one effective device is a holistic standards rubric prominently displayed as a poster in the classroom. This learning standards rubric concretely illustrates students' skill development over time though ascending skills or standards written on cards. Each card level is placed in the pocket chart of the poster when it is appropriate to express that level of challenge.[72]

The standards rubric takes the form of a poster in order to eliminate the need for paper copies and to post it where everyone in the room easily views it. Furthermore, anyone visiting the room can immediately identify current learning objectives.

The rubric is developmental because it begins with simpler levels of proficiencies and then increases achievement levels over time as skills develop. With primary children, simple icons and captions can be used to enhance the visual appeal and enable the poster rubric to be read and understood. More complex levels are appropriate for older students. Examples of ascending skills on rubric cards are shared in Figure 9.6 for typical first grade and fifth grade writing standards.

To translate any content area learning standards into a rubric format, initially refer to district standards to determine the desired levels and kinds of skills for the beginning of the school year. List those skills on one card to signal the grade-level proficiencies. (Card number four delineates that level on the shared first- and fifth-grade writing examples.) Next, determine the ascending levels of skills that build to the proficiencies on card four. Those skill levels are listed on cards one, two, and three.

Cards five through eight (or more) list the levels of skill proficiencies to be developed next. When students are proficient at level four, reorder the cards. Level one might remain the same to accent that a lack of effort will result in low achievement in the class. Card two is removed; shift the third and fourth cards down, and add card five as the new proficiency goal in the last position of the four-level rubric. Later, as skills accelerate, the card levels shift again and card six is placed in the rubric poster. Continue the process throughout the year by developing additional cards as skills reach new levels.

A standards rubric is effective for students' goal setting and self-assessment. Students can refer to the poster before starting a learning task to set the level they intend to achieve. After completion of the task, students again reference the rubric to self-assess and record on their work the level they achieved.

Learn✎ **Writing Standards Rubric**			
🙁	😐	🙂	😃
I did not follow directions. I did not work.	My writing is neat and legible. I wrote complete sentences and paragraphs that vary to match meaning and purpose. My writing is clearly developed using precise words and vivid images with no major errors.	My writing is legible. I clearly developed a main idea and details. My paragraphs are complete and vary to match meaning and purpose. My capitalization and punctuation enhance meaning. I used precise words and vivid images with no major errors.	My writing is legible with no major errors. My major ideas and details are clear and organized. I added, deleted, combined, and rearranged my writing to revise it. I use prepositional phrases. I used precise adjectives.
Novice	**Apprentice**	**Intermediate**	**Skilled**

[72] Construction procedures for a Standards rubric poster are detailed in Appendix E.

Kingore, B. (2007). *Assessment,* 4th ed. Austin, TX: Professional Associates Publishing.

Figure 9.6: WRITING SKILLS

Example of beginning first-grade writing skills			
I did not try. I did not work. **Card 1**	I drew a picture. I wrote some letters. **Card 2**	I neatly drew a picture. I wrote several letters. I wrote my name and the date. **Card 3**	My picture is neat and colorful. I can tell or write about it. I wrote my name, date, and other important words. **Card 4**
I wrote a sentence about my picture. I used capital and lowercase letters. I sounded out some words. **Card 5**	I wrote more than one sentence. I used capital letters, lowercase letters, and periods or question marks in my sentences. I sounded out some words. **Card 6**	My writing is neat and legible. My sentences are interesting. I used capitalization and punctuation correctly most times. I sounded out and spelled most of the words I used. **Card 7**	I wrote carefully and used good spacing. I wrote several interesting sentences. I used capitalization and punctuation correctly. I spelled my high-frequency words correctly. **Card 8**

Example of beginning fifth-grade writing skills			
I did not follow directions. I did not work. **Card 1**	My writing is neat and legible. I wrote complete sentences and paragraphs that vary to match meaning and purpose. My writing is clearly developed with no major errors. **Card 2**	My writing is legible. I clearly developed a main idea and details. My paragraphs are complete and vary to match meaning and purpose. My capitalization and punctuation enhance meaning. I used effective words with no major errors. **Card 3**	My writing is legible with no major errors. My major ideas and details are clear and organized. I revised my writing. I used prepositional phrases. I used precise verbs and adjectives. **Card 4**
My writing is legible with no major errors. I elaborated with details that increase interest and meaning. I added, deleted, combined, and rearranged my writing to revise it. My prepositional phrases and conjunctions elaborate ideas. I used vivid adjectives, verbs, and adverbs. **Card 5**	My writing is legible with no major errors. I use compound sentences with vivid words and images. My prepositional phrases and conjunctions elaborate ideas and increase interest. I used transitions. I edited grammar, usage, and spelling. **Card 6**	My writing is legible with no major errors. I use complex sentences with vivid words and images. My writing is related and interesting. My introduction and conclusion are strong. I used effective transitions. I edited grammar, usage, and spelling. **Card 7**	My writing is legible with no major errors; spelling is proficient. My composition has clearly related, well-developed ideas. My introduction and conclusion add clarity, depth, and interest. My writing is generally organized and smooth; transitions link ideas. I edited effectively. **Card 8**

Learning Standards

Kingore, B. (2007). *Assessment,* 4th ed. Austin, TX: Professional Associates Publishing.

6. Communicate standards to parents.

Parents demonstrate an increased level of concern about the quality of schools because of news stories and headlines. They express a legitimate interest in understanding how national and state learning standards affect their child's achievement. For example, at a recent parent session in Michigan, parents expressed frustration because they did not know what their children *should* be learning. They felt they had no way to gauge accomplishments or needs and wanted to know how to find out that information. The school district's wise response was to translate the district learning standards into parent terminology and provide copies to parents.

Once parents understand the importance of standards, they need an overview of the scope and sequence of selected standards-based learning elements to comprehend what their child is to learn next and how to support the school's effort. Communicating standards helps parents refocus their thinking about their child's learning from the negative *what is wrong* to constructive feedback that guides decision-making, such as *what are the learning needs* and *what do we do to support those needs.* Actively involved parents want to know: *Which skills and concepts do I watch for and discuss with my child?* Figure 9.7 is one example of a means to initiate an information exchange with parents about learning standards.

7. Communicate standards on grading reports.

Marzano (2000) stresses that a single letter grade or percentage score is an unsatisfactory means to report student achievement in any content area because it cannot present the level of detailed feedback necessary to guide effective learning. He challenges educators to explore standards-based alternatives. One example he poses is a reporting system based upon a list of content-area standards with a four-point scale. Report student achievement by marking the four-point scale for each standard and then calculating an overall achievement score for that subject, such as in Figure 9.8.

This approach will communicate more clearly, however, if a rubric were used instead of only a four-point score. The rubric in Figure 9.9, for example, clarifies the differences in the degrees on the scale to better substantiate student achievement. Educators will rightfully view the development of these standard rubrics as a major task. However, the ensuing professional conversations and clarifications about achievement are a substantially valuable result of the process.

Letter grades and percentage scores are so ingrained into our society that any departure is likely to be viewed with disdain by parents and community members in general. Hence, rather than replace report card grades, standard reports can be useful in interpreting or clarifying the grade designation to parents. If the traditional reporting card is continued, a list of standards can accompany it with student achievements marked for each standard.

Kingore, B. (2007). *Assessment,* 4th ed. Austin, TX: Professional Associates Publishing.

Figure 9.7:
A PARENT'S ROLE IN SUPPORTING LEARNING STANDARDS

Date _____

Dear Families,

Here are some ideas for how you can become more informed about learning standards and involved in your child's learning.

* Be aware of the school's learning expectations for your child.
* Request a copy of the standards for the grade level.
* Ask questions about a standard or practice you do not understand.
* Notice and discuss how a standards-based environment changes the school practices of the past.
* Focus on the learning rather than just attend to the grade. Discuss with your child:

> *What did you learn doing this?*
> *What is something you are pleased with about your work?*
> *What skills were you working on for this task? (In standards-based classrooms, learning objectives are openly discussed with students.)*

* Model reading and writing at home by personally engaging in authentic reading and writing tasks, such as reading books or newspapers, visiting a library with your child, and writing notes to your child.
* Seek ways to use math experiences at home, such as counting or measurement tasks, math-related games, and software.
* Be an advocate rather than an advisory.
* Acknowledge effective practices when you see them.

Please contact me at school if you have questions or would like to have further information about this important part of our learning environment.

Sincerely,

Kingore, B. (2007). *Assessment,* 4th ed. Austin, TX: Professional Associates Publishing.

Learning Standards

Figure 9.8: VOCAL MUSIC STANDARDS

	Standards Rating			
Standard 1–Music Appreciation				
1.1–Form opinions about music	1	2	3	4
1.2–Communication				
1.2a–Describe musical events	1	2	3	4
1.2b–Discuss music across the curriculum	1	2	3	4
Standard 2–Vocal Performance				
1.1–Sing diatonic melody	1	2	3	4
1.2–Perform rhythmic patterns	1	2	3	4
Standard 3–Notation	1	2	3	4
Standard 4–Composition	1	2	3	4

Figure 9.9: VOCAL MUSIC STANDARDS

	STANDARDS RATING			
	1	**2**	**3**	**4**
Standard 1–Music Appreciation				
1.1–Form opinions about music	Does not express opinions	Does not support opinions	Expresses and supports valid opinions	Supports opinions by comparing and contrasting musical styles
1.2–Communication 1.2a–Describe musical events	Unable to identify events such as form or climax of a piece	Identifies events and form with help	Describes the form and events in a piece	Uses musical terminology to compare genres and events
1.2b–Discuss music across the curriculum	Unable to discuss	Refers to a relationship	Identifies several relationships to art and history	Parallels the development of music with culture, history, and other subjects.
Standard 2–Vocal Performance 1.1–Sing diatonic melody	Uses a speaking voice	Sings less than 50% of the pitches correctly	Sings diatonic melody in tune	Uses an appropriate voice; sings in tune; excellent tone quality
1.2–Perform rhythmic patterns	Lacks rhythm	Performs pattern with help	Performs pattern correctly without help	Performs pattern fluently
Standard 3–Notation	Can not identify age-appropriate musical symbols	Identifies age-appropriate symbols with help	Names and writes age-appropriate musical symbols	Names and writes musical symbols fluently
Standard 4–Composition	Unable to compose	Composes with extensive help	Can compose and perform when given a musical framework	Writes and improvises original music

Kingore, B. (2007). *Assessment,* 4th ed. Austin, TX: Professional Associates Publishing.

• CHAPTER 10 •

Parent
Communication

What you're not up on, you're down on.

–Dutch Adage

Research supports a significant shift in the perspective of parent communication. Today, the objective is an information exchange with a collaborative attitude of mutual respect, cooperation, and shared responsibility rather than the traditional perspective of educators having information and parents needing to be informed. Parents and teachers develop a common vision of partnership. Parents participate in decisions about their child's education and teachers better understand the beliefs, values, opinions, lifestyles, and practices of families that influence interpretations.[73]

Communication between home and school is a significant component in the process of insuring that every student experiences continuous learning. Research documents that a substantial outreach to parents positively affects student achievement, attitudes toward learning, and self-esteem.[74]

Furthermore, children from low-income, culturally diverse, and racially diverse families experience greater success when schools enlist families as allies and build on their strengths.[75] Students, teachers, and parents benefit from exchanging knowledge.[76] Indeed, family involvement in a child's education is a more critical factor influencing achievement than family income or education.[77]

Many parents did not experience portfolios or authentic assessment procedures themselves. Educators want parents to understand that these assessment processes provide a greater depth and validity of information than report cards or standardized tests alone. The concrete evidence provided by selected products make portfolios a particularly effective means of productive communication among parents, a teacher, and a student. Teachers facilitate parents' understanding of how authentic assessment supports the work

[73] international Reading Association, 2002.

[74] High/Scope, 2005; International Reading Association, 2002; Jones, 2003.

[75] NAEYC & NAECS/SDE, 2003.

[76] High/Scope, 2005; International Reading Association, 2002.

[77] Marzano, 2000.

Kingore, B. (2007). *Assessment,* 4th ed. Austin, TX: Professional Associates Publishing.

students do and inspires students to have high expectations for themselves. Parent communication involves parents initiating communication with teachers, parents and students communicating at home and at school, and teachers initiating communication with parents.

PARENTS COMMUNICATE WITH TEACHERS

Parents know a great deal about their child. Particularly at the beginning of the school year, some parents have information they would like to share with teachers yet worry if teachers would welcome such input. Invite parents to communicate their observations and perspectives by providing a forum for this valuable exchange of information. The communication form in Figure 10.1 is an effective means to guide parents' responses when providing information to schools.

As an alternative application, invite parents to complete Figure 10.1 with their child. As parent and child discuss each question, the parent elicits and records the child's perspective to share with the school.

Parent communication with the teacher continues throughout the year through scheduled meetings as well as informal interactions and notes from home. Parent and teacher conferences continue as a significant component in this two-way, interactive communication.[78]

PARENTS COMMUNICATE WITH THEIR CHILDREN

Discussions at Home

Parents can learn much from their child's perceptions of learning experiences. Encourage parents to demonstrate their inter-

est by asking questions and talking with their children about their work at school and the products they bring home on a regular schedule. Active parent involvement can increase student's excitement about learning as it increases parental interest in the process.

As another effective parent communication device, invite parents to review and discuss their child's portfolio at home. The child takes the portfolio home overnight and then returns it the next day. This opportunity is especially valuable to parents working outside of the home who may be less available during school hours.

Portfolio procedures at the end of the year produce a particularly special opportunity for parent and child interactions at home. Invite parents to celebrate the bound portfolio book when it arrives at home at the completion of the school year. Chapter 11 elaborates information about this procedure.

Discussions at School

PARENTS VISIT THE SCHOOL

Parents better understand the learning environment and their child's role when they spend the day with their child at school. If not available for an entire day, parents can spend their lunch hour at school with their child.

PARENT NIGHTS AND PORTFOLIO EXHIBITIONS

Schools can plan special occasions for parents to share their child's portfolio. Organize a student-led portfolio exhibition at school so parents can share the child's portfolio in that learning environment. This alternative often works well during lunchtime or some evening events, such as parents nights or curriculum nights.

[78] See Chapter 5 for further discussion about conferences.

Kingore, B. (2007). *Assessment,* 4th ed. Austin, TX: Professional Associates Publishing.

Figure 10.1: FROM THE FAMILY TO SCHOOL, Page 1

The purpose of this communication form is to use your experienced observations to help us better know your child and how to best assist and advance learning at school. Continue writing on the back if you need more space. Please return this to school by: _____.

CHILD'S NAME _____   DATE _____

YOUR NAME _____   RELATIONSHIP _____

What do you want us to understand about your child?

Is there something special about your child that you want us to know?

How does your child feel about school?

What are your child's special interests or abilities?

In which group or organizations is your child involved?

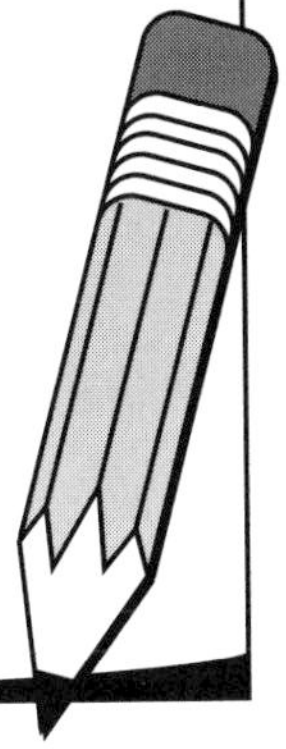

Kingore, B. (2007). *Assessment,* 4th ed. Austin, TX: Professional Associates Publishing.

Figure 10.1: FROM THE FAMILY TO SCHOOL, Page 2

What does your child like to do at home?

What responsibilities does your child have at home?

What can you tell us about your child's organization at home and how she or he cares for things?

In what ways do you feel we can best help your child at school?

Which four words can you think of to best describe your child?

Is there anything else that you would like to share about your child?

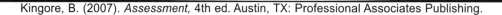

Kingore, B. (2007). *Assessment,* 4th ed. Austin, TX: Professional Associates Publishing.

STUDENT-INVOLVED CONFERENCES

Over time, parents and children benefit from the student more formally conferencing with parents to share items in the portfolio and discuss learning goals and achievements. Chapter 5 shares specific suggestions for student-involved conferences with parents.

Prepare invitations to parents that inform them of these special communication events. Three samples are included in Figures 10.6 through 10.8 that invite parents to share the portfolio with their child at home, to come to school for a portfolio exhibition, or to celebrate the bound portfolio book at the end of the year. Blank templates of several borders to use for invitations are included in Appendix C.

TEACHERS COMMUNICATE WITH PARENTS

To support learning goals at home, parents look to teachers for information and welcome ideas for nurturing their child's learning at home. In addition to the parent and teacher conferences discussed in Chapter 5, teachers initiate communication with parents through meetings, resources, and letters.

Parent Meeting

Plan a meeting with parents to discuss assessment. A more concrete and interactive meeting environment enables parents to better understand assessment procedures and the portfolio process. Consider which of the following suggestions to incorporate in the meeting to maximize the opportunity for a productive information exchange. Brainstorm additional ideas to enhance the experience.

❑ Explain authentic assessment and the educational benefits it provides.

❑ Briefly share an overview of assessment tools and plans, including specific information about the children's involvement and responsibilities. Invite parents to reflect and compare assessment procedures from when they were in school.

❑ Model the portfolio process that will be used so adults benefit from seeing concrete examples.

❑ On an overhead transparency, demonstrate a student's repeated tasks from the beginning, middle, and end of a previous year to clarify how products document learning growth and level of achievement.

❑ If portfolios were used last year, have a former student work with an adult to role-play a student-involved conference using a portfolio. Invite parents to question the student and teacher about the process if it is new to them.

❑ Discuss the multiple opportunities scheduled for parents to review students' portfolios and conference with teachers and/or their child about achievement and learning goals.

❑ Discuss the assessment process at the end of the year and what happens to the portfolio their child develops.

❑ Elicit parents' perspectives, questions, and reactions to the content of the meeting.

❑ Establish an open-ended invitation for continuing two-way communication between parents and teachers.

Assessment Resources

As parents express interest, respond with appropriate resources for parents to read more about authentic assessment. As a school community, compile a shelf of parental resources in the library to loan to parents as they request information. Additionally, share brief articles about authentic assessment. An introductory article is found at the end of this chapter and may be copied to share with the parents (Figure 10.9).

Letters to Families

Plan several letters to send home at different times throughout the year to broaden parents' understanding of portfolios and authentic assessments. Keeping parents informed about assessments helps them support the process.

Several letters are included as examples of potential content. They are not presented in a recommended sequence for copying and sending home. Instead, the intent is to provide examples that busy teachers review to more efficiently produce content for the letters they want to use. The border templates provided in Appendix C can be incorporated as stationery to add visual appeal to parent letters.

OVERVIEW OF LETTERS TO THE FAMILIES

*   ### Introducing the Portfolio Process
    Figure 10.2 is effectively used when beginning the portfolio process. The letter overviews the portfolio process and informs parents of the curriculum areas represented in the portfolio.

*   ### Product Selection
    Figure 10.3 accents the value of the analytical process as students select items for portfolios. Sharing examples of the criteria that students use to select an item helps parents understand that portfolios are more than just collections of students' best work.

*   ### Products Completed at Home
    Figure 10.4 is effectively used to encourage family participation after the portfolio process is established. Students' learning does not stop when the school day finishes. Many students, particularly young children, English language learners, or those with special learning needs, complete work at home that offers significant information about their interests and capabilities. This letter acknowledges the important role of the home environment in a child's learning and invites some items completed at home to be added to the school portfolio.[79] This letter also addresses the problem of work done at home that is completed by someone other than the student alone.

*   ### Student-Involved Parent Conference
    Figure 10.5 helps parents understand and prepare for their role in a conference that is led by their child. Providing samples of questions to ask during the interactive process helps parents maintain a positive experience with the child. When using this letter, consider also providing a copy of the Portfolio Response Letter (Figure 5.10) to guide parents' written response to their child.

*   ### Portfolio Discussions at Home
    Figure 10.6 informs parents when the portfolio is to be taken home for a parent and child discussion. The letter offers suggestions for using, protecting, and returning the portfolio.

*   ### Invitations
    Figures 10.7 and 10.8 inform parents of special portfolio occasions, such as a portfolio exhibition at school or the portfolio book at the end of the year.

---

[79] If desired, include captions such as those found in Chapter 4 for use at home.

Kingore, B. (2007). *Assessment,* 4th ed. Austin, TX: Professional Associates Publishing.

Figure 10.2: INTRODUCING THE PORTFOLIO PROCESS

DATE _____

Dear Families,

This year, your child will develop a portfolio of learning experiences throughout the school year. Just as professional writers and artists maintain a portfolio to showcase their accomplishments, student portfolios help us gain a better understanding of children's patterns of capabilities, interests, and progress. The actual work that students complete over time provides a richer and more authentic means than tests alone to assess how capable they are, what they are learning, and the depth of their thinking.

Collaboratively, your child and I will select many products for the portfolio in the following curriculum areas:

- _____
- _____
- _____
- _____

The portfolio will contain first drafts and refined pieces to document how your child thinks, works, and how much your child is learning. The students will manage their own portfolios to develop organization skills and extend their responsibility and ownership in their work.

The portfolio process involves collection, selection, and reflection. Students first collect their completed work for several days before they review it and select a product for their portfolio. Then, each student reflects about the selected product and attaches a caption to explain why that product was added to the portfolio. The products not selected for their portfolio are sent home. At the end of the year, this most exciting portfolio will be bound and sent home for your family to keep.

During the year, there will be several sharing and conferencing opportunities for you to examine the work in progress. Through this portfolio, you will discover your child's perspective of learning and enjoy the concrete examples that demonstrate the growth your child experiences this year.

Sincerely,

Parent Communication

Kingore, B. (2007). *Assessment,* 4th ed. Austin, TX: Professional Associates Publishing.

Figure 10.3: PRODUCT SELECTION

DATE _____

Dear Families,

Each student has designed a portfolio, and we have started to select the contents from our learning experiences. You may remember that the portfolio process involves collection, selection and reflection. Students continue to collect their completed work at school for several days before the students and/or I review it to select a product for their portfolio. Then, each student reflects on the selected product and attaches a caption to explain why that product was added to the portfolio. Items not selected for the portfolio are taken home for your immediate review.

Through product selection for their portfolios, students increase their capacity for self-reflection and making judgments. As students determine which products to include, they learn to think about important evaluation criteria, such as:

- What does this product document about learning?
- What examples should be kept in the portfolio to best represent growth throughout the year?
- Which products best document current achievements of learning standards?
- Which pieces demonstrate something significant that you think, feel, or care about your work?
- Which products show growth in important skills or concepts you have worked on?
- Which products demonstrate progress made in a specific subject area?
- What makes a piece satisfying to you?

Judging the merits of one's own work is a life skill that your child is practicing and refining through the portfolio process. Please contact me at school if you have questions or would like to have further information about this important part of our learning environment.

Sincerely,

Kingore, B. (2007). *Assessment,* 4th ed. Austin, TX: Professional Associates Publishing.

Figure 10.4: PRODUCTS COMPLETED AT HOME

DATE _____

Dear Families,

Some of you have asked what you can do at home to help us identify your child's special learning interests and potentials. Each reporting period, encourage your child to bring one example from home to include in the portfolio that shows some work your child initiated at home or a product that is especially well done. Hopefully, these products will be completed not as homework but because your child is enjoying learning. You may send a photograph of the product if it is a three-dimensional item such as a model, construction, or sculpture. Other examples may include:

- Writings,
- Collections,
- A child-developed science experiment,
- Tape recordings or photographs of drama or musical productions,
- Drawings, paintings, or original photographs,
- Original math problems or graphs,
- Self-initiated projects, and
- Photocopies of awards.

It is very important to your child's self-esteem that you send products that were completed by your child alone. We want children to feel proud of their work because they tried hard to do their best. When others complete work for children, it is harder for children to feel proud and confident. They learn, instead, to depend on others to do for them and that they can never do well enough alone. That is not the life message parents want a child to learn. From time to time, praise your child's efforts and encourage your child to select a product that he or she worked on alone and has done well to include in the portfolio at school.

Please always be sure your child's name and the date are written on the back of the product. Complete with your child a brief note to attach to the product to help us better understand what your child thinks about that product.

Thank you for all you do at home to encourage your child to value learning. Please contact me at school if I can help you or answer questions.

Sincerely,

Kingore, B. (2007). *Assessment,* 4th ed. Austin, TX: Professional Associates Publishing.

Parent Communication

Figure 10.5: STUDENT-INVOLVED CONFERENCE

DATE _____

Dear Families,

Your child is prepared to share school learning experiences with you in student-involved conferences. Each child has selected some products to discuss, but ask about additional products as you wish. As you review the work together, please remember that your child has worked very hard to complete this. It shows how much has been learned and accomplished since the beginning of this school year.

Consider the following suggestions to ensure a positive experience with your child.

1. Try to listen carefully and encourage your child to talk more than you. Careful listening helps you understand your child's accomplishments and perspective about those achievements.

2. Let your child lead the portfolio sharing. Ask: *What do you want to show me first?*

3. Continue asking questions that let your child explain the products and learning process to you. Ask open-ended questions such as:
   a. *What is your favorite part of this product?*
   b. *What is something that makes you feel especially proud of what you have learned?*
   c. *What is something that was hard to do?*
   d. *How did you get your idea for this work?*
   e. *What is something important you have learned about your work?*

4. Notice and respond to as many positive points as possible. Continue to comment on the strengths and improvements you observe in your child's work. Encouragement helps your child know you are proud of what has been learned. Your positive feedback helps your child feel more eager to share with you again at a later time. Too many negative comments cause some children to want to hide their work instead of sharing it with others.

5. When you and your child finish reviewing the portfolio, consider writing a note to your child about the experience. This is a special opportunity to write some words of recognition. Many children highly value these notes and save them in the portfolio.

If you have questions or concerns about anything you see or hear, please contact me at school so we can discuss them together. Thank you for participating in your child's education.

Sincerely,

Kingore, B. (2007). *Assessment,* 4th ed. Austin, TX: Professional Associates Publishing.

Figure 10.6: PORTFOLIO SHARING WITH PARENTS

DATE _____

Dear Families,

On _____, your child is bringing home his or her portfolio to share with you. Please plan to set aside fifteen minutes to review the portfolio together so it may be returned to school the next day. This is a special opportunity for you to learn about your child's accomplishments and model to your child that school and learning are very important to your family.

Products attached with a teacher product choice caption are teacher-selected items every student is asked to include. Many of them serve as examples to document learning achievements since the beginning of the school year. You can compare earlier and later work samples to see how your child has developed as a learner.

This portfolio sharing time is an excellent opportunity to encourage organization and responsibility. Help your child handle the products carefully. Plan a special place to put the portfolio so it will be easily seen and remembered. Please be sure to return the portfolio the next school day.

Sincerely,

Kingore, B. (2007). *Assessment,* 4th ed. Austin, TX: Professional Associates Publishing.

Figure 10.7: PORTFOLIO EXHIBITION

DATE _____

Dear Families,

 You are invited to a portfolio exhibition at school. Please come to our class on:

_____

Your child has prepared a portfolio of valued accomplishments and would like to spend about 15 minutes showing you how much is being learned.

 Sincerely,

Kingore, B. (2007). *Assessment,* 4th ed. Austin, TX: Professional Associates Publishing.

Figure 10.8: THE PORTFOLIO BOOK

DATE _____

Dear Families,

 Your child is bringing you a treasured book on _____. It is the portfolio book we have worked on all year to provide an organized record of accomplishments and growth. This work is very important to the children and they feel so proud of themselves for all they have learned. We hope you will celebrate this special book with your child and grant it a special place in your hearts and on your bookshelf.

 This book now belongs to your family to keep and enjoy over the years. Look forward to a portfolio book every year to herald your child's learning.

 Sincerely,

Kingore, B. (2007). *Assessment,* 4th ed. Austin, TX: Professional Associates Publishing.

Introducing Parents to Student-Managed Portfolios:

A collaborative effort toward authentic assessment

The products that children produce throughout the school year help parents and educators gain a better understanding of children's capabilities, interests, and progress. The actual work that children complete over time provides a richer and more authentic way than tests alone to assess what they are learning and the depth of their thinking.

Thus, in many schools across the nation, educators and students collaborate to collect and store a selection of each student's products in curriculum areas such as writing, math, reading, social studies, science, and/or art. This collection is called a portfolio and may contain first drafts as well as refined pieces to better show how a child thinks, works, and how much the child is learning.

DEFINITION

A portfolio is a systematic collection of work that is typical for a student. The student and teacher assemble products to document readiness, achievement levels, and learning growth over time.

Currently, parents and schools view standardized test results as indicators of children's abilities and achievements. However, standardized tests typically only measure right answers rather than high-level thinking skills and responses, such as strategies, problem solving, flexibility in thinking, organization, and decision-making. Instead of debating whether standardized tests or portfolios are better indicators, professional educators are working to effectively use both to provide a more complete picture of the multiple facets of a child's abilities and potential.

Portfolios are largely managed by the children to develop their organization skills and extend their responsibility and ownership in their work. Children are encouraged to produce quality work, value their own progress, and select products for their portfolio that document what they are learning.

PRODUCT SELECTION

Not every product a child completes is placed in the portfolio. Children typically keep their work at school for several days and then review it to select a product for their portfolio. Each product placed in the portfolio has the child's name and date on it so growth over time can be determined. Each product also has a caption or brief note attached to explain in the child's own words why this product was selected. The products not selected for the portfolio are sent home so parents consistently have examples of the student's work.

Children also produce things at home that show their interests and talents. Throughout the year, parents can encourage children to take to school a few examples of what they have done well at home to include in their portfolio.

It is very important to a child's self-esteem, however, that parents send products that children have completed by themselves. We want children to feel proud of their work because they have tried hard to do their best. When others complete work for children, it is harder for children to feel proud and confident. They learn, instead, to depend on others to do for them because they can never do well enough alone. That is not the life message parents want a child to learn.

Kingore, B. (2007). *Assessment,* 4th ed. Austin, TX: Professional Associates Publishing.

Parent Communication

PORTFOLIO USE

Teachers use the portfolio process to teach students to critique their work and reflect on its merits. When children are reviewing their work to select a product to go in their portfolios, teachers prompt students' analysis and decision-making skills by asking them to think about questions such as the following.

- *What makes a high-quality product?*
- *What examples do you want to keep in your portfolio to represent what you are learning throughout the year?*
- *Which products document your achievements of learning standards?*
- *How does this product show something important that you think?*
- *How does this product show something important that you have learned?*
- *How does this product demonstrate the progress you've made in a specific topic or subject area?*

During the year, the portfolio may be used in several productive and informative ways. A teacher can discuss a child's portfolio with the child to help clarify the child's growth, celebrate current achievement, and establish future learning goals. A child might discuss the portfolio with a peer or family member to celebrate a success and share ideas for future products. Furthermore, during a parent and teacher or a student-involved conference, the portfolio is a useful tool to concretely document the learning achievements and potential of the child.

At the year's end, in many portfolio projects, the teacher collaboratively reviews the portfolio with the student to select a few representative products to place in a School Career Portfolio. This portfolio showcases the student's growth, quality work, and highest achievements; it typically is added to each school year to provide a window to the child's thinking and achievements over several school years. Some schools bind this School Career Portfolio and present it to the student after several years or as a part of graduation.

Each year, the portfolio products not placed in the School Career Portfolio can be bound together and taken home at the end of the school year for parents and children to keep. Parents and children alike treasure this organized book of products. As one parent commented: *Now I can throw away a whole drawer full of papers. The whole year is in this one book!*

When many adults were in school themselves, they may not have experienced product portfolios as a key component in their educational assessment. Be willing to learn about portfolios because this process has a tremendous potential to add importance to the work children do and inspire them toward higher expectations for themselves. Portfolios can also help parents increase their awareness of the abilities and potential of their children. Parents are encouraged to read, ask questions, and talk to children about the portfolio process. It is an exciting experience.

SELECTED RESOURCES

Kingore, B. (2001). Parent assessment: Developing a portfolio to document your child's talents. In *The Kingore Observation Inventory (KOI),* 2nd ed. Austin: Professional Associates Publishing. 63-64.

MacDonald, S. (2005). *The portfolio and its use: A roadmap for assessment,* 2nd ed. Little Rock, AR: Southern Early Childhood Association.

Ratcliff, N. (2001). Using authentic assessments to document the emerging literacy skills of young children. *Childhood Education, 78,* 66-68.

• CHAPTER 11 •
The End of the Year

A hard beginning maketh a good ending.
—John Heywood

Educators often wonder what to do with portfolios at the end of the year. For optimum value, the portfolio process should continue over several years. However, work with many schools reveals that passing the entire portfolio on to next year's teacher is not productive. Portfolios that grow an inch each year get large rather quickly. Subsequently, these portfolios are often stuck away in a closet. Teachers report that they do not need to review that much from the past to prepare them to effectively work with their new class.

Therefore, the recommended process at the end of the year is to select only a few products for next year's teacher to help guide instructional planning. The remaining portfolio items are sent home as a portfolio book. At the end of the year, the natural closure of the students' assessment process and learning experiences involves either selecting products for the School Career Portfolio or encouraging high school students to evaluate items for a Professional Portfolio. Then assemble the remaining products into individual students' books.

THE SCHOOL CAREER PORTFOLIO

One value of a portfolio is its documentation of a student's learning development and achievements over time. School Career Portfolios maximize the potential of this value without excessive volumes of products. At the end of each school year, select a few representative products from the yearly portfolio to go into the School Career Portfolio, and send it to next year's teacher. The remaining products in the yearly portfolio are bound together in a book that goes home as a keepsake. This publishing process is elaborated later in this chapter.

The School Career Portfolio is typically a file folder to which products are added each year. It is usually stored with the cumulative file or with the current homeroom teacher and can be bound and presented to each student at graduation or at the end of the portfolio process. As another option, use a computer disk or CD-ROM to store the School Career Portfolio.

Kingore, B. (2007). *Assessment,* 4th ed. Austin, TX: Professional Associates Publishing.

To avoid excessive work for any one person, arrange for the scanning of the selected products to be completed by each student as a learning experience during computer lab times.

A table of contents is initiated to list the title, date, and location of each product within the School Career Portfolio. The student continues to add new products and update the contents page until the end of each school year.

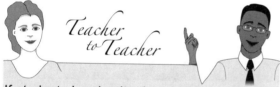

If students hand-write the contents page, over time it presents a clear view of their handwriting development.

Products in the School Career Portfolio

Primary Grades

Three or four products are chosen to document growth and achievement. The teacher is primarily responsible for the choices and includes one piece from the beginning, middle and end of the year. Frequently, one additional special piece or *best piece* is also included.

Intermediate, Middle School, and High School

Four to six pieces are chosen to document growth, learning standards, thinking process, and highest academic accomplishments. The student and teacher collaboratively select the products. Validate growth and achievement by insuring that products are chosen from throughout the school year and have captions attached explaining the learning standards integrated within the work. Demonstrate growth in thinking process skills through the student's metacognitive reflection about a learning process or task, such as a completed written piece with its first draft attached. Accompany the student's choice for highest academic accomplishment or *best piece* with the student's written reflection discussing the work and why it is considered the highest accomplishment for the year.

Uses for the School Career Portfolio

•   **Document the student's learning achievements**
    When continued over several years, the school career portfolio documents the student's changes as a learner and enhances self-worth as the student discovers how much has been achieved.

•   **Guide instruction**
    This portfolio guides a teacher's instructional decisions about the long-term development and learning needs of each student. The teacher is able to review the concrete product examples in the portfolio instead of only the numbers, letters, grades, and percentages typical of reporting files.

•   **Represent students**
    At the beginning of the school year, students can choose one piece from their portfolios to share with their new class as an introduction of themselves and their achievements.

•   **Celebrate total school experience**
    At graduation or the end of the portfolio process, the School Career Portfolio can be bound and presented to the student as a wonderful closure and valued keepsake.

Kingore, B. (2007). *Assessment,* 4th ed. Austin, TX: Professional Associates Publishing.

When the School Career Portfolio is completed, students create a special title page for it that includes a title, symbol, and explanation of how this portfolio represents the student.

I decided to use just my name for a title and a map for my symbol because I see my portfolio as a map of my school days. It plots my learning travels. This represents most of my life and the learning experiences that have brought me to where I am right now. I already know I am going to enjoy looking back at this portfolio later.

Joel, High School Senior

THE PROFESSIONAL PORTFOLIO

In high school, especially during the junior and senior years, students begin restructuring their portfolios to develop a Professional Portfolio. Products from the yearly portfolio and the School Career Portfolio can be evaluated for inclusion in the Professional Portfolio. The purpose of this portfolio is to demonstrate how a student's different experiences, achievements, and capabilities translate into the specific abilities required in the future. This portfolio simultaneously prepares students for the process of job placement and/or college admission interviews, as it results in products to feature at either interview.

Rather than follow a generic formula for what to include, each Professional Portfolio should be as unique as the individual who develops it. The items in the portfolio should specifically relate to the capabilities, interests, and aspirations of the student. The products should specifically address the abilities and skills required where the student intends to work or apply to college rather than attempt to present a global view of talents that might fit any situation.

Reflective Questions to Guide Selection

What am I consistently good at that I want to demonstrate in my portfolio?

What products best reflect my preparation for my career choice?

What products might an employer or college want to view in order to evaluate my talents and potential?

Which pieces are most satisfying to me? How are they effective or important?

What am I doing to continue the development of my talents and accomplish my goals?

For maximum impact, the Professional Portfolio should be concise, neat, and clearly organized. Keeping the portfolio concise means it is more likely to be willingly viewed by busy interviewers. It also requires that the student is thoughtful about which items to select instead of mindlessly including too much. A neat portfolio is important to convey an image of pride and care in preparation. Clear organization is vital because the portfolio

Kingore, B. (2007). *Assessment,* 4th ed. Austin, TX: Professional Associates Publishing.

The End of the Year

is intended to effectively communicate with others. Develop a table of contents to guide the reader. Use subdivisions as the main categories by which the student wants to represent herself or himself to others. Subheadings can further delineate specific talents.

Think an inch. Purchase a one or two inch binder for use as a Professional Portfolio. Develop a table of contents, and use tabs to clearly mark the subdivisions within the portfolio. Make every item easy to find. Use three-ring plastic sleeves to hold special products so those items do not have to be hole punched.

PUBLISHING THE YEARLY PORTFOLIO IN THE ELEMENTARY AND SECONDARY GRADES

Products not selected for the School Career Portfolio are bound and sent home as a keepsake. Parents and students love having these books as a record of learning experiences and growth. To begin the publishing process, encourage students to analyze the parts of trade books and build as many of those features into their portfolio books as is appropriate. The more these portfolio books are made to look like published books the better. They should look as important as they are. The following are examples of ideas incorporated into portfolio books by some classes.

Components of Published Portfolio Books

Book Cover
If they have not already done so, students design a front and back cover for their portfolio

book. As an alternative, they cut apart their portfolio container folder or envelope on the fold line to create the front and back cover of their book.

Title Page
Students write a title page complete with an inventive publishing company incorporating the school's name and the copyright year for their book. The teacher is often named as the Executive Editor. Title examples include: *My Treasury from Mrs. Wilhelm's Second Grade* and *The Life and Times of Kent Matthew in Seventh Grade*.

Contents
Students use copies of a simple table of contents form, such as Figures 11.1 and 11.2, or develop their own organizational formats. If the portfolio contents are organized chronologically, students write the names of the months, list their products in order, and complete the table for their portfolio book. If the contents are organized by areas of the curriculum, the table of contents should reflect that organization.

Figure 11.1: CONTENTS	
September	**PAGE**
• Autobiography	1
• Self-portrait	3
• Repeated Task: Hardest Division Problem	4
• Author Study: E. L. Konigsburg	5
• U. S. Map	6
•	
•	
October	
• Folk Tales Project	7
• Writing Directions: Action Figures	12
• Still Life Drawing	14
• Math in Soccer	15
• Weather Experiment	18
•	
•	
November	
• Novel Study: Number the Stars	20
• Comparative Essay	26
• Time Line of Manifest Destiny	28
• Animal Watercolor	29
• Division Mastery Test	30
•	
•	

Figure 11.1: CONTENTS

	PAGE

Kingore, B. (2007). *Assessment,* 4th ed. Austin, TX: Professional Associates Publishing.

Figure 11.2: CONTENTS

	PAGE

- _____ _____
- _____ _____
- _____ _____

- _____ _____
- _____ _____
- _____ _____

- _____ _____
- _____ _____
- _____ _____

- _____ _____
- _____ _____
- _____ _____

- _____ _____
- _____ _____
- _____ _____

- _____ _____
- _____ _____
- _____ _____

Kingore, B. (2007). *Assessment,* 4th ed. Austin, TX: Professional Associates Publishing.

Kingore, B. (2007). Assessment, 4th ed. Austin, TX: Professional Associates Publishing.

Once students create a table of contents for their portfolio, they begin to use these contents pages in other books with renewed interest and ability.

About the Author

Just as information about the author is included on the book jacket of many published books, each student writes an About the Author paragraph or page. One example of a form is shared as Figure 11.3. Including a personal or school photograph on the page is an attractive idea. The photograph is an added delight when students later look back at these special books. Some students who like to talk about themselves in multiple roles

may also include an About the Illustrator page.

Dedication Page

Students might also include a dedication page in their portfolio books. It is interesting to see to whom students dedicate their books. They sometimes dedicate their book to their teacher, a wonderful validation of the caring and hard work teachers expend to help students achieve success in learning.

Products

The main feature of the portfolio is the set of products assembled throughout the year. These products are arranged according to the selected organizational option discussed in Chapter 2.

Highlights of the Year

Highlights of the Year is another page students love to have in their books. Students list on this page the events during the school year that they most enjoyed or want to remember. It is fascinating to read what each student chooses as Highlights of the Year. The students' selections are seldom the educational aims on which teachers spend the most time.

Letter of Recommendation[80]

Letters of recommendation are an important component when working with secondary students on their professional portfolios, but these letters can be a welcomed addition to a portfolio book for any age of student. Students may ask a friend, family member, or significant adult to write a letter of recommendation for them. It is interesting over time to look back on these encouraging statements.

Friends and Classmates

One or two pages for the autographs of friends and learning colleagues are a great interactive addition to these books if the school does not

[80] When including letters of recommendation, teachers suggest students use individuals other than the teacher. Writing a large quantity of recommendation letters for students at the end of the year is not a prudent task for busy teachers.

Kingore, B. (2007). *Assessment,* 4th ed. Austin, TX: Professional Associates Publishing.

Figure 11.3: ABOUT THE AUTHOR

NAME _____   DATE _____

PHOTOGRAPH OR SYMBOL	FAVORITES
	MUSICIAN: _____
	ALBUM: _____
	ARTIST: _____
	MOVIE: _____
	ACTOR: _____
	SPORT: _____
	ATHLETE: _____
	HOBBY: _____
	FOOD: _____

Three words that others would use to describe me:

Two books I love and how each has influenced me:

Something I have done that makes me proud:

Something I want to do in the future:

produce a yearbook. Just as high school students have a yearbook signing time, classes have portfolio book signings during which classmates write graffiti-style messages to one another.

Reflections through the Years

Consider placing one or two pages at the end of the portfolio book that provides a space to add notes over time. In later years, as students revisit this particular portfolio book, they can record the date and write themselves a note about how they now feel about the contents or the process. As one third-grader expressed: *It will be fun to look back at this when I'm old and in middle school!*

Binding

Finally, the yearly portfolio books are bound in some way, such as using plastic bindings, three-hole punching the pages and placing them in a notebook, or three-hole punching and using metal rings or yarn to hold the pages together. It is exciting to see the pride students demonstrate in these finished portfolio books!

Arrange for a parent volunteer or aide to complete the process of binding the portfolios. There is too much for you to do toward the end of the year to expend your energy and time in binding books. If you are a perfectionist and need the books finished perfectly, choose a parent who is also a perfectionist and model for that parent how to accomplish exactly what you want.

If many classes in your building have portfolios, avoid frustration by coordinating the use of the publishing or binding materials and equipment so everyone is not trying to complete the process at the same time.

Celebrating the Published Portfolio Books

The portfolio is a year-long process and a significant part of the learning environment. Use the bound portfolio books to reach closure on this process. Consider organizing a portfolio celebration with the students before the books are taken home. If appropriate, plan refreshments together for the celebration.

When the bound portfolio books are handed back to the students, they have excited smiles and look around to see how other books turned out. Since it is obvious they are eager to share their books, group the students in pairs or trios and encourage them to share their book with their classmates. Most groups will talk incessantly and be genuinely impressed with each other's work. The portfolio books boost self-esteem and confidence as well as validate their efforts and encourage their continuous learning. Consider providing time for students to autograph each other's books.

When finalizing the publications, send a letter to the parents announcing when each book will arrive at home and that it represents significant learning accomplishments from the entire year.[81] Consider elaborating this letter with several comments from your students about their books. Their enthusiastic comments are infectious to others' enthusiasm and help establish a positive attitude toward sharing what has been learned as the books are celebrated together at home.

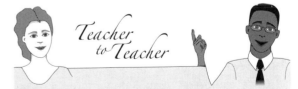

Videotape your class as they share their bound books and talk about them together. It will be a great motivator for introducing next year's class to your portfolio process.

---

[81] A sample letter is included in Chapter 10 (Figure 10.6)

Kingore, B. (2007). *Assessment,* 4th ed. Austin, TX: Professional Associates Publishing.

PUBLISHING THE YEARLY PORTFOLIO IN EARLY CHILDHOOD

Early childhood learners have fewer products in their portfolios because much of their learning is process oriented without a product. At the end of the year, their portfolio books will be thin. However, teachers still report that the parents are thrilled to get the bound books. The young children are also thrilled because they love their work to look important. The following is a typical list of the contents of their bound books.

Consider laminating the front and back covers of the bound portfolios to protect them for years to come. There is no need to laminate each page of the book. Laminating every page adds expense and extensive preparation time to the process yet may not result in longer-lasting books.

Components of Published Portfolio Books for Young Children

Book Cover

Many different choices for the cover are possible, but a favorite idea is to use pictures the child has completed at the beginning and the end of the year for the front and back covers of the bound portfolio. For example, the front cover might be a picture of the student or the student's family drawn at the beginning of year and dated; the back cover might be a picture of the same subject drawn at the end of year and dated. As another option, Figures 11.4 and 11.5 are examples of book cover templates for children to use. As a repeated task, children write their names and draw a picture on the front cover at the beginning of the year and then complete the back cover at the end of the year.

Contents

Some children can use the blank, chronological table of contents in Figure 11.1. However, teachers may prefer to simply duplicate for each child's portfolio a list of topics studied during the year with the dates each topic was completed so parents have a chronological overview of how the products relate to the learning experiences.

About the Author

Use Figure 11.6 to record the child's ideas and include a current photograph from home or school. Adding their thumbprint is fun for students because they know from everyone's fingerprint is different. The sentence prompts can be completed by the children writing in their temporary (invented) spelling or by Big Buddies, aides, or parent volunteers who act as scribes for the children.

If colored inkpads are not available, let the children color the thumbprint area of their thumb with a marker, and then press it on the paper.

Poem

Include a poem that addresses the philosophy of the class. Dorothy Law Nolte's *Children Learn What They Live* is an effective example to consider. Parents benefit from this gentle reminder of developmentally appropriate practices and expectations for young children.

Products

Place the products selected during the year by the child and the teacher in chronological order here to substantiate the child's growth throughout the year.

Friends and Classmates

Young learners love collecting signatures from other kids. Provide one or two pages

Figure 11.4: PORTFOLIO FRONT COVER

A BOOK ABOUT

_____

I drew this picture.

DATE _____

Kingore, B. (2007). Assessment, 4th ed. Austin, TX: Professional Associates Publishing.

Figure 11.5: PORTFOLIO BACK COVER

I drew this picture.

DATE _____

The End

Figure 11.6: ABOUT THE AUTHOR

My Thumbprint:

NAME _____

DATE _____

My Picture:

My favorite thing at school:

My favorite book: _____

        By: _____

Something I like to do and why:

Something I do not like to do and why:

I want to be:

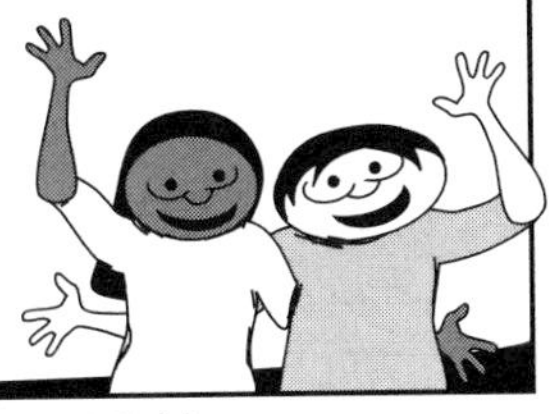

that children can use to collect the auto-graphs of friends and classmates.

Binding[82]

Bind these portfolio books by using plastic comb bindings, three-hole punching and placing pages in a notebook, or three-hole punching and using metal rings or yarn to hold the pages together. Young children are proud of these special books.

Several primary teachers use Figure 11.6 with small groups of students as a teacher-directed language arts activity at the beginning of the year. This initial task is a preassessment to inform teachers of the many aspects of children's readiness, such as oral language development and emergent literacy skills. The form is then used again at the end of the school year. This application produces two important portfolio products and is an interesting way to assess children's changing view of their abilities and preferences at school.

Celebrating Published Portfolio Books with Young Children

Plan a celebration sharing the finished books with the children before the books are taken home. If appropriate, plan a class activity to make refreshments together for your portfolio book party.

As a kindergarten teacher observed: *My children are so surprised at their books. They look at each page as if they had never seen it before!* Pair the children and let them read and share their books with each other.

Use a large piece of chart paper and record the children's comments and reactions as a language experience. Their responses document the pleasure and self-esteem enhancement the portfolio books bring to each author.

When preparing the books to take home, send a letter to the parents announcing when each book is to arrive at home and what it represents.[83] As a language arts task, add to the letter several comments from the children about their books to infect their parents with children's enthusiasm for their accomplishments.

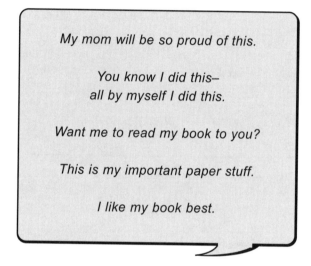

Referring to her drawing of her family at the beginning and end of the year, one child told her teacher:

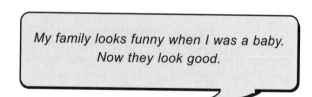

---

[82] Refer to the implementation tip for binding discussed in this chapter at the end of the *Publishing the Yearly Portfolio in the Elementary and Secondary Grades* section.
[83] Figure 10.6 is a sample letter.

Kingore, B. (2007). *Assessment,* 4th ed. Austin, TX: Professional Associates Publishing.

· APPENDIX A ·
Implementing Portfolios

Whether as members of an assessment committee as an individual, use the following suggestions to guide decisions regarding a sequence for portfolio implementation. Taking time to plan implementation will increase success and may save hours of frustration later. Prioritize by developing a portfolio definition and determining the portfolio objectives. Then, plan how to best organize the process so it begins smoothly and operates effectively. Next, focus on the kinds and levels of communication needed among educators, parents, and students. With those decisions made, plan how to effectively model the process to students to prompt their enthusiasm about developing their own portfolios. Consider how to integrate the process into the regular classroom routine to avoid portfolios becoming something extra to do.

1. Prioritize

- Develop a definition of portfolios that clearly communicates the objectives.
- List what to do and what to accomplish through implementing portfolios; prioritize that list.
- Avoid attempting too much at once. Rather than stressing to do it all now, begin small and let the process develop and grow with time and experience.
- Plan portfolios that reflect the personal goals, styles, strengths, and needs of the students and curricular requirements.

2. Organize

If not confident with organization and management procedures, revisit this listing after reading Chapter 2.

- Determine the portfolio containers, collection folders, filing system, storage location, and management procedures.
- Decide the number of products that may be selected, the time, day, and process for the selection.
- Determine when students' work will go home and communicate that schedule to parents.
- Prepare needed forms and collect needed materials.
- Plan the first item for students to file in their portfolio so the process begins smoothly and quickly. For example, determine a specific repeated task for students to complete and file the first week of the portfolio process.

3. Communicate

COMMUNICATE WITH OTHER TEACHERS AND ADMINISTRATORS.

- Share articles, books, and information about portfolios.
- Network with other interested educators to nurture ideas as well as share successes and concerns or problems. Plan to meet regularly rather than leave it to chance. Educators are all too busy for communication to occur if interaction times are not scheduled.
- Discuss together how to use portfolios to validate the variety of modalities, styles, and intelligences represented by the students.
- Brainstorm: *Are there easier ways to do this?*
- Discuss together how to best use portfolios to benefit students and document capabilities, achievement, and grades.

Kingore, B. (2007). *Assessment,* 4th ed. Austin, TX: Professional Associates Publishing.

- Begin an ongoing *Need to Know* list. Write the questions that occur to guide networking with and learning from other professionals using portfolios.

COMMUNICATE WITH FAMILIES.

- Share brief articles about portfolios and authentic assessment.
- Regularly send informative letters to families. Consider developing one letter a month as a beginning goal to share information about students' progress and the use of portfolios.
- Hold meetings with parents to model portfolios, have students share their portfolios, discuss the process, and note the growth and pride the students demonstrate. Emphasize to families: *Through your child's portfolio, you will be better informed about your child's capabilities, achievements, and potential because of the concrete examples.*

COMMUNICATE WITH STUDENTS.

- Show students what a portfolio is in this class, the reasons for developing it, and what benefits it provides. Discuss how older students in some states use portfolios for job interviews and college entrances. Explain how adults use portfolios for job advancement or to obtain a new job.
- Discuss ownership, choice, and pride. Tell students: *Your portfolio will become the finest book you have ever developed. It represents you when you are not available to represent yourself. You will be making choices from the work you produce to represent the most important things you learn and the things most significant to you. Years in the future, you can look back through this portfolio to remember and celebrate your learning.*

4. Model

Modeling a portfolio can inspire students' interest and enthusiasm in developing their own portfolios. People always show personal pleasure when they present and discuss the items in their portfolio. Thus, modeling is a powerful asset because pride of accomplishment shines through. Students see for themselves what portfolios can become.

If you and your students have not experienced portfolios before, conduct a product show and tell as well as have an adult model a professional portfolio.

- Hold a product show and tell by asking students to bring in any piece of work they produced in school before this year. Each student then explains any of the following factors that are appropriate.
  - CIRCUMSTANCES: *How or why did you produce this product?*
  - TIME: *When was it done? How much time and effort was involved?*
  - RATIONALE: *Why did you originally decide to save this piece? Why did you decide to share it today?*
  - REFLECTION: *What does it mean to you now?*

- Ask an adult to model her or his professional portfolio for the class. Artists, models, photographers, and authors (professional or amateur) typically have a selection of products and materials that represent their greatest professional accomplishments. Ask one or more to show a portfolio, share why it is personally important, and discuss why some pieces were selected rather than others. List the criteria these adults deemed important in their portfolio selections. Later, discuss these criteria as a class and determine criteria significant to students in their personal selections for portfolios.

Kingore, B. (2007). *Assessment,* 4th ed. Austin, TX: Professional Associates Publishing.

If you have previously implemented portfolios in your classes but this year's students have not experienced portfolios, consider presenting a portfolio panel.

PORTFOLIO PANEL

- Invite students from last year's class to present and discuss their portfolios with this year's students. This panel can highlight the process and how they feel about portfolios. Discuss how individual and different the portfolios are because they reflect personal strengths and choices.

- Encourage this year's class to ask questions. Then together, develop a list of possible criteria to guide the selection of portfolio items.

If this year's students have developed portfolios before, model the continuation of portfolios by using their previous selections to share products with peers.

- Have each student select one item from last year's portfolio or from their School Career Portfolio to share in this class as an introduction to themselves and their achievements.

- Discuss what is satisfying to them about their portfolios. Elicit their suggestions for making portfolios even more significant this year.

5. Integrate

Portfolios reflect the instructional decisions and authentic learning experiences in a class. Integrate portfolios into the regular routine in the class rather than as something extra to do.

- Establish a specific time each week or every other week when portfolio selection occurs.

- Consider organizing a bulletin board to showcase portfolio selections. One example of a portfolio selection bulletin board is illustrated in Chapter 2.

- Integrate portfolios as a part of authentic learning experiences. Analyze where the different aspects of the portfolio process best integrate into instruction. For example, students' product selections and reflections about their learning provide an effective closure to a topic of study.

- Integrate portfolios into students' daily learning. Frequently discuss criteria for quality work and elicit students' perspectives and reactions to what they are learning.

- Integrate portfolios with assessment goals and curricular objectives. Plan how to most effectively use portfolios to document students' learning accomplishments.

- Integrate portfolios with instructional decisions that benefit students. How do portfolios showcase the kind of instructional experiences that enable students to experience continuous learning? How do portfolios support a wide array of learning tasks beyond simple fill-in-the-blank responses?

- Relate portfolios to students' capabilities and potential. Integrate multiple modalities, multiple intelligences, and students' interests in the product opportunities.

6. Implement

- Teach the process to students. Over time, help them practice and refine their collection, selection, and reflection procedures.

- Reflect often on the effectiveness of the process. Discuss with students what they think is working well and what needs to be changed. Elicit their opinions regarding the products or projects that should be continued with next year's class and why certain products are not effective learning experiences.

- Revise procedures as needed or when changes prove more efficient.

- Plan next steps. What can be incorporated next so the process develops and expands?

Kingore, B. (2007). *Assessment,* 4th ed. Austin, TX: Professional Associates Publishing.

· APPENDIX B ·
Pictorial Rubric Poster

MATERIALS:
- **Two (or more) pieces of poster board**
- **A title and criteria icons**
- **Crayons, markers, or colored paper**
- **Glue**
- **Velcro™**

Especially when working with young children, rather than provide a paper copy of a pictorial rubric for each child, teachers can enlarge the pictures to create a rubric poster for the wall. On colored paper, print the enlarged versions of the Pictorial Rubric Generator icons,[84] or develop unique icons that address the specific needs of the students or task. When creating additional criteria icons, invite students to draw images to represent the ascending levels of the criteria. This saves teacher preparation time, increases students' ownership in the assessment process, and effectively communicates the different criteria levels to the students.

Procedure:
1. Cut the first piece of poster board according to the dotted lines on the diagram. These cuts result in five pieces to be used as the five-inch-tall criteria strips.
2. On one side of each strip, glue a criterion icon and the three corresponding pictured levels.
3. On the back of each strip, attach a piece of Velcro™ at each end. Ensure that the

Velcro™ is in the same place on each strip so the strips are interchangeable on the poster.
4. Four strips fit on the finished rubric poster at one time. Create several different criteria strips to be able to quickly exchange them and adjust for different tasks throughout the day without requiring multiple rubrics.
5. The second piece of poster board is the foundation of the rubric. Create a title and attach it to the top four inches of the poster.
6. Attach the Velcro™ pieces that hold the criteria strips in place.
7. On each criterion strip, with the Velcro™ pieces in place (leaving the fricative sides of each piece of Velcro™ exposed), press each strip onto the poster backing so the Velcro™ pieces adhere to each other.

The velcro pieces hold each criterion strip in place on the poster and allow the criteria to be easily changed in order to match any learning experience. Being careful to place the Velcro™ strips in the same place on each criteria strip and on the poster ensures that the criteria strips align in any sequence.

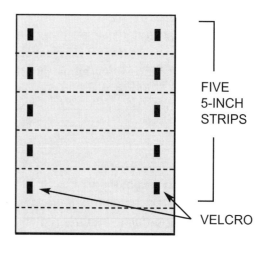

FIVE 5-INCH STRIPS

VELCRO

---

[84] Full-sized versions of the icon are included on the *Assessment Interactive CD-ROM*, Kingore, 2007. See Chapter 3 for more information about the Pictorial Rubric Generator.

Kingore, B. (2007). *Assessment,* 4th ed. Austin, TX: Professional Associates Publishing.

· APPENDIX C ·
Borders

encouraged to use the pages in this appendix for several applications, such as:

- Communications with parents,
- Invitations to school and classroom events,
- Announcements,
- Learning experiences,
- Project descriptions,
- Assignment task cards,
- Cover sheets, and
- Many additional portfolio applications.

Border pages are fun to use and add visual appeal to communications and projects. Some teachers report that they do not have a computer in their classroom and that they have difficulty accessing graphic packages. Therefore, teachers and students are

Additional border designs are used in Chapter 10 on the example letters to parents. Use these freely as well.

Kingore, B. (2007). *Assessment,* 4th ed. Austin, TX: Professional Associates Publishing.

Kingore, B. (2007). *Assessment,* 4th ed. Austin, TX: Professional Associates Publishing.

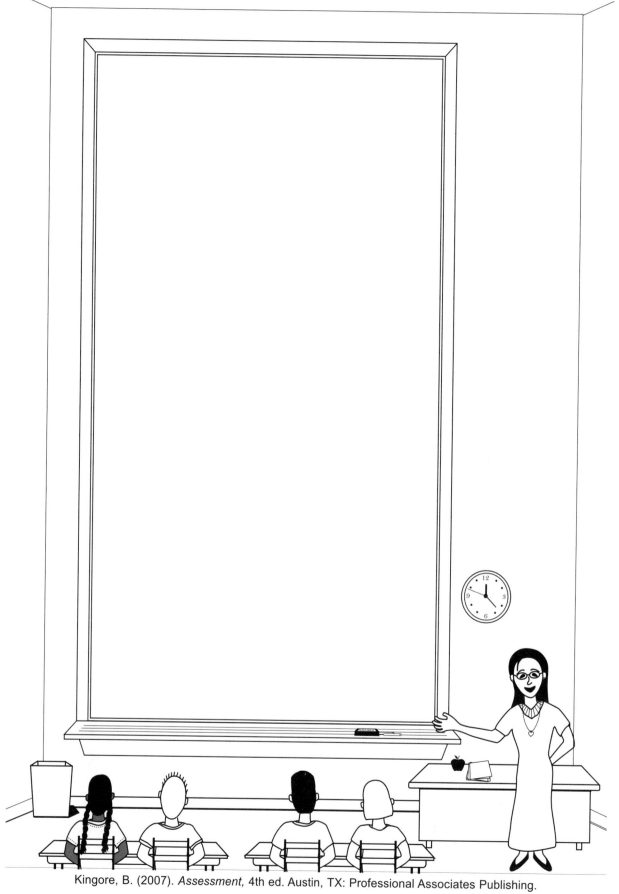

· APPENDIX D ·
Assessing Multiple Intelligences

Researchers are reexamining the definition of intelligence. One theory, offered by Harvard University professor Howard Gardner (1996, Spring), proposes different kinds of intelligence that are all equal in value and importance. Gardner's theory originally consisted of seven intelligences, but in 1995, he added an eighth intelligence–naturalist. The following is a brief overview of these eight intelligences.

- **Linguistic**
  Is sensitivity to spoken or written language
- **Logical-Mathematical**
  Reasons with logical or numerical patterns
- **Naturalist**
  Recognizes species of plants or animals
- **Spatial**
  Visualizes, forms a mental image, and perceives configurations
- **Musical**
  Produces and appreciates rhythm and musical expression
- **Bodily-Kinesthetic**
  Problem solves with body movement
- **Interpersonal**
  Understands other people and works effectively with them; other-driven
- **Intrapersonal**
  Is sensitive to one's own feelings, thoughts, and desires; self-driven

Gardner defines intelligence as the ability to solve problems or create things valued in a culture. Everyone possibly has all of these intelligences, but each person typically has high areas in one or more.

It is important to understand each student's pattern of intelligences. From Gardner's (1995) perspective, it is more important to identify and build upon areas of strength than it is to fret too much about areas of weakness. As minority populations continue to increase, schools need to recognize and appreciate diversity in learning since different cultures value different abilities. Encourage students to use strengths to succeed that are not traditionally accented in classrooms. Observe and analyze the intelligences that children favor while learning or applying what they learned. Use that insight to provide learning experiences that incorporate those patterns of strength to help all students view themselves as capable.

Only to the degree that instruction offers opportunities for the highest levels of performance on a wide range of student-selected contents and products can the portfolio process support the search for multiple talents and diverse abilities.

Intermediate, middle school, and high school teachers find that students increase self-understanding when they analyze their own patterns of intelligences. Students are typically fascinated with learning more about how they best succeed and why some learning tasks are harder for them. Simple tools, such as My Pattern of Intelligences on the next page, can help students informally determine their multiple intelligences. These tools were piloted with hundreds of educators in workshops and multiple upper-elementary through high school students in classrooms across the country. Most people reported that their personal pattern of intelligences included three or four of the eight multiple intelligences. Students can apply that insight to the Product Grids in Chapter 8.

Kingore, B. (2007). *Assessment,* 4th ed. Austin, TX: Professional Associates Publishing.

MY PATTERN OF INTELLIGENCES

NAME _____ DATE _____

Analyze your multiple intelligences by rating how an intelligence is typical of you on a scale from 1 to 10 (with 10 being extremely high). What pattern do you see about your ways to be smart?

Linguistic
Writing, word plays, reading, speeches, oral presentations, effectively uses words to teach others

1   5   10

Logical/Mathematical
Problem solving, math, logic problems, tangrams, analyzes, likes to create new math problems

1   5   10

Naturalist
Science, nature, exploring outdoors, categorizing, interested in birds and animals

1   5   10

Spatial
Graphic organizers, drawing, visualizing, maps, implements graphics when teaching others

1   5   10

Bodily/Kinesthetic
Manipulating physical objects, body movement, role-play, prefers to be in motion

1   5   10

Musical
Rhythmical, raps, sings or play instruments, prefers to have music playing while learning, creates songs

1   5   10

Interpersonal
Collaboration, solving human conflicts, group skills, prefers to talk with others to solve problems

1   5   10

Intrapersonal
Self-sufficient, self-understanding, journals, diaries, prefers to think alone to solve problems

1   5   10

The areas in which you scored the highest suggest your pattern of intelligences. These may be the strengths that most help you to learn, succeed in solving problems, and complete classroom assignments. What do you think are your strengths in the intelligences you scored highest?

INTELLIGENCE   STRENGTH

• _____   _____

• _____   _____

• _____   _____

Kingore, B. (2007). *Assessment,* 4th ed. Austin, TX: Professional Associates Publishing.

• APPENDIX E •
Standards Rubric Poster

A standards rubric poster clearly displays ascending levels of standards that lead to grade-level proficiency. It is developmental and changes as students' skills increase.

MATERIALS:

- **Two pieces of poster board**
- **A title bar, faces or icons, and captions**
- **Text for four or more cards**
- **Markers or colored paper**
- **Glue**

Cut one poster board according to the dotted lines on the diagram. These cuts result in one strip for the pocket of the poster and six cards. The cards display the skill proficiencies; ascending skills or standards are written on each of the cards to place in the poster when it is appropriate to express that level of challenge. (Using the front and back of each card produces 12 cards.) Customize the skills to reflect the readiness levels of the class as well as the relevant standards.

The second poster board is the foundation of the poster. Create a title to communicate the purpose of the rubric, and glue faces or other icons onto the poster. Glue corresponding captions onto each pocket strip to clearly communicate the proficiency levels to the students. Develop captions that focus on either the effort demonstrated when learning or the achievement levels. Attach them to the pocket strip, and then, create a pocket for the caption cards by stapling it onto the bottom of the poster as well as between each card.[85]

Write skill-level descriptors that best communicate instructional priorities. Use language that communicates clearly to the students.

Use markers to draw faces, other icons, or grading scores, and then, color each caption to match. These matching colors help clarify the evaluation levels to young learners. Even young children know that *I did not work* is not the desired behavior because the unhappy face and that caption use the same color. (Creating the icons and captions on four differently colored pieces of paper saves time.) Finally, personalize the poster with additional color and designs. Include students in the creation of the rubric to increase the students' ownership in the assessment process.

4-INCH POCKET

6-INCH-WIDE RUBRIC CARDS

14 INCHES   14 INCHES

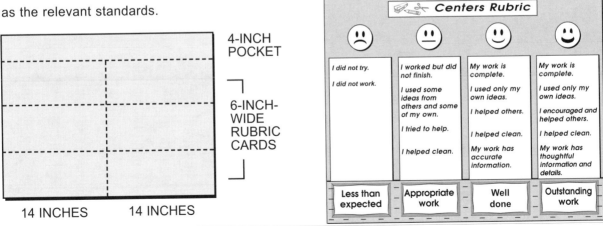

[85] Face pieces, customizable captions, title icons, and formatted cards are included on the *Assessment Interactive CD-ROM,* Kingore, 2007.

Kingore, B. (2007). *Assessment,* 4th ed. Austin, TX: Professional Associates Publishing.

References

Amabile,T. M. (1983). *The social psychology of creativity*. New York: Springer-Verlag.

Anderson, L. & Krathwohl, D. (Eds.). (2001). *A taxonomy for learning, teaching, and assessing: A revision of Bloom's taxonomy of educational objectives.* New York: Addison-Wesley Longman.

Association for Supervision and Curriculum Development (ASCD). (2006a). *Multiple measures of assessment:* Policy paper. Alexandria, VA: Author.

Association for Supervision and Curriculum Development (ASCD). (2006b). *Building academic vocabulary: Research-based, comprehensive strategies.* Research Report. Alexandria, VA: Author.

Betts, G. & Kercher, J. (1999). *Autonomous learner model: Optimizing ability.* Greeley, CO: ALPS Publishing.

Black, P., Harrison, C., Lee, C., Marshall, B., & Wiliam, D. (2004). Working inside the black box: Assessment for learning in the classroom. *Phi Delta Kappan, 86*(1), 8-21.

Caine, R., Caine, G., Klimek, K., & McClintic, C. (2004). *12 Brain/mind learning principles in action.* Thousand Oaks, CA: SAGE Publications.

Carr, J. & Harris, D. (2001). *Succeeding with standards: Linking curriculum, assessment, and action planning.* Alexandria, VA: Association for Supervision and Curriculum Development.

Castellano, J. & Diaz, E. (2002). *Reaching new horizons: Gifted and talented education for culturally and linguistically diverse students.* Boston: Allyn and Bacon.

Cook, N. (2005). Using time-saving technology to facilitate differentiated instruction. *Understanding Our Gifted, 17*(4), 16-19.

Cooper, J. & Kiger, N. (2005). *Literacy assessment-helping teachers plan instruction.* Boston: Houghton Mifflin

Costa, A. L., & Kallick, B. (1992). Reassessing assessment. In A. L. Costa, J. A. Bellanca, & R. Fogarty (Eds.), *If minds matter: A foreword to the future, Volume 11* (pp. 275-280). Palatine, IL: IRI/Skylight.

Csikszentmihalyi, M. (1997). *Creative flow and the psychology of discovery and invention.* New York: Harper Collins.

De Bono, E. (1993). *Teach your child how to think.* New York: Penguin Books.

Erickson, H. (2007). *Concept-based curriculum and instruction for the thinking classroom.* Thousand Oaks, CA: Corwin Press.

Farr, R. & Tone, B. (1998). *Portfolio and performance assessment.* Ft. Worth: Harcourt Brace College Publishers.

Fleischman, P. (1992). *Joyful noise. Poems for two voices.* New York: HarperCollins.

Freedman, R. (1989). *Lincoln: A photobiography.* New York: Scott Foresman.

Gardner, H. (1993). *Multiple intelligences: Theory in practice.* New York: Basic Books.

Gardner, H. (1996, Spring). Your child's intelligence(s). *Scholastic Parent & Child,* 32-37.

Grigorenko, E., & Sterberg, R. (1997). Styles of thinking, abilities, and academic performance. *Exceptional Children, 63,* 295-312.

Henkes, K. (1996). *Chrysanthemum.* New York: HarperTrophy.

Herman, J., Baker, W., & Linn, R. (2004). *Accountability systems in support of student learning: Moving to the next generation.* CRESST LINE. Los Angeles: University of California, National Center for Research on Evaluation, Standards, and Student Testing.

High/Scope Educational Research Foundation. (2005). *Lifetime effects: The High/Scope Perry Preschool study through age 40.* Ypsilanti, MI: High/Scope.

Hoberman, M. (2004). *You read to me, I'll read to you: Very short fairy tales to read together.* New York: Little, Brown.

International Baccalaureate Organization. (2007). *Making the PYP happen: A curriculum framework for international primary education.* Guide. Cardiff, Wales: Peterson House.

International Reading Association (IRA). (1999).*High-stakes assessment in reading.* Position statement. Newark, DE: Author.

International Reading Association (IRA). (2002). *Family-school partnerships: Essential elements of literacy instruction in the United States.* Position statement. Newark, DE: Author.

Jones, J. (2003). *Early literacy assessment systems: Essential elements.* Princeton, NJ: Educational Testing Service.

Kingore, B. (2001). *The Kingore observation inventory (KOI),* 2nd ed. Austin, TX: Professional Associates Publishing.

Kingore, B. (2004). *Differentiation: Simplified, realistic, and effective.* Austin, TX: Professional Associates Publishing.

Kingore, B. (2007a). *Assessment interactive CD-ROM,* 2nd ed. Austin, TX: Professional Associates Publishing.

Kingore, B. (2007b). *Reaching all learners: Making differentiation work.* Austin, TX: Professional Associates Publishing.

Kingore, B. (2008). *Portfolios and authentic assessments for young children.* Thousand Oaks, CA: Corwin Press. (In press)

Leahy, S., Lyon,C., Thompson, M., Wiliam, D. (2005). Classroom assessment: Minute by minute, day by day. *Educational Leadership 63*(3), 19-24.

MacDonald, S. (2005). *The portfolio and its use: A roadmap for assessment,* 2nd ed. Little Rock, AR: Southern Early Childhood Association.

Marzano, R. (2000). *Transforming classroom grading.* Alexandria, VA: Association for Supervision and Curriculum Development.

Marzano, R. (2004). *Building background knowledge for academic achievement: Research on what works in schools.* Alexandria, VA: Association for Supervision and Curriculum Development.

Marzano, R., Pickering, D., & Pollock, J. (2001). *Classroom instruction that works: Research-based strategies for increasing student achievement.* Alexandria, VA: Association for Supervision and Curriculum Development.

McNeil, N., Grandau, L., Knuth, E., Alibali, M., Stephens, A., Hattikudur, S., & Krill, D. (2006). Middle-school students' understanding of the equal sign: The books they read can't help. *Cognition and Instruction, 24*(3), 367–385.

McTighe, J. & O'Connor,K. (2005). Seven practices for effective learning. *Educational Leadership, 63* (3), 10-17.

Ministry of Education. (1991). *Supporting learning: Understanding and assessing the progress of children in the primary program: A resource for parents and teachers.* British Columbia, Canada.

National Association for the Education of Young Children (NAEYC). (1997). *Developmentally appropriate practice in early childhood programs serving children from birth through age 8.* Position statement. Washington, D.C.: Author.

National Association for the Education of Young Children & National Association of Early Childhood Specialists in State Departments of Education (NAEYC & NAECS/SDE). (2003). *Early childhood curriculum, assessment, and program evaluation: Building an effective, accountable system in programs for children birth through age 8.* Position statement. Washington, D.C.: National Association for the Education of Young Children

.

National Council of Teachers of Mathematics (NCTM). (2006). *High-stakes tests.* Position statement. Reston, VA: Author.

National Council of Teachers of Mathematics & National Association for the Education of Young Children (NCTM & NAEYC). (2002). *Early childhood mathematics: Promoting good beginnings.* Position statement. Washington, D.C.: National Association for the Education of Young Children.

National Reading Panel (NRP). (2000). *Teaching children to read: An evidence-based assessment of the scientific research literature on reading and its implications for reading instruction.* Jessup, MD: National Institute for Literacy at ED Pubs.

Neuschwander, C. (1997). Sir Cumference and the first round table. (1999). Sir Cumference and the dragon of pi. (2002). Sir Cumference and the great knight of angleland. (2003). Sir Cumference and the sword in the cone. (2006). Sir Cumference and the Isle of Immeter. Watertown, MA: Charlesbridge.

Ogle, D. (1986). KWL: A teaching model that develops active reading of expository text. *The Reading Teacher, 36*, 564-570.

Payne, R. (2003). *A framework for understanding poverty*, 3rd ed. Highlands, TX: aha! Process, Inc.

Potter, E. (1999). What should I put in my portfolio? Supporting young children's goals and evaluations. *Childhood Education, 75*, 210–214.

Ratcliff, N. (2001). Using authentic assessment to document the emerging literacy skills of young children. *Childhood Education, 78*, 66-68.

Ross, P. (1993). *National excellence: A case for developing America's talent.* Washington, DC: US Department of Education.

Scott-Little, C., Kagan, S., & Frelow, V. (2003). Creating the conditions for success with early learning standards: Results from a national study of state-level standards for children's learning prior to kindergarten. *Early Childhood Research and Practice, 5*, 2. Retrieved February 28, 2007 from http://ecrp.uiuc.edu/v5n2/index.html.

Shepard, L. (1997). *Measuring achievement: What does it mean to test for robust understanding?* Princeton, NJ: Educational Testing Service.

Shepard, L., Kagan, S. & Wurtz, E. (1998). *Principles and recommendations for early childhood assessment.* Washington, DC: National Education Goals Panel.

Sousa, D. (2001). *How the brain learns*, 2nd ed. Thousand Oaks, CA: Corwin Press.

Stenmark, J. K., Bush, W. S., & Allen, C. (2001). *Classroom assessment for school mathematics, K-12*. Reston, VA: NCTM.

Stiggins, R. (2005). *Using student-involved classroom assessment to close achievement gaps*, 4th ed. Columbus, OH: Merrill Prentice Hall.

Sylwester, R. (2003). *A biological brain in a cultural classroom*, 2nd ed. Thousand Oaks, CA: Corwin Press.

Tomlinson, C. (2003). *Fulfilling the promise of the differentiated classroom*. Alexandria, VA: Association for Supervision and Curriculum Development.

Tomlinson, C., Kaplan, S., Renzulli, J., Purcell, J., Leppien J., & Burns, D. (2002). *The parallel curriculum: A design to develop high potential and challenge high-ability learners*. Thousand Oaks, CA: Corwin Press.

Vygotsky, L. (1962). *Thought and language*. Cambridge: MIT Press.

Wiggins, G. (1998). *Educative assessment: Designing assessments to inform and improve student performance*. San Francisco: Jossey-Bass.

Wiggins, G. & McTighe, J. (2005). *Understanding by design*, 2nd ed. Alexandria, VA: Association for Supervision and Curriculum Development.

Willis, J. (2006). *Research-based strategies to ignite student learning: Insights from a neurologist and classroom teacher*. Alexandria, VA: Association for Supervision and Curriculum Development.

Woodward, H. (2000). Portfolios: Narratives for learning. *Journal of In-Service Education, 26* (2), 329-349.

Index

Assessment Interactive CD-ROM

Bertie Kingore & Jeffery Kingore
ID CODE: BK-06

Grades: K - 12

This fully interactive and customizable CD-ROM provides the forms from the *Assessment* book, almost all of which are **completely customizable**. If computers are available in the classroom, students can also complete the assessments on the computer to save and print! Included are:

• Tier I, II, and III of the Rubric Generator.
  – An expanded pictorial rubric generator to use to build rubrics as posters or handouts for young learners or ELL students,
  – An expanded rubric generator with two tiers to choose from dozens of customizable criteria or to develop your own, creating an endless number of rubrics on the computer in minutes, and
• Over 140 completely customizable self-evaluations, assessments, interviews, conference forms, goal-setting forms, product grids, learning options posters, borders, and parent letters!

PO Box 28056 • Austin, Texas 78755-8056
Toll free phone/fax: 866-335-1460
www.kingore.com